PSYCHOTHERAPY
PROCESS
RESEARCH

OTHER RECENT VOLUMES IN THE
SAGE FOCUS EDITIONS

PSYCHOTHERAPY PROCESS RESEARCH

Paradigmatic and Narrative Approaches

Shaké G. Toukmanian
David L. Rennie
editors

SAGE PUBLICATIONS
International Educational and Professional Publisher
Newbury Park   London   New Delhi

For information address:

SAGE Publications, Inc.
2455 Teller Road
Newbury Park, California 91320

SAGE Publications Ltd.
6 Bonhill Street
London EC2A 4PU
United Kingdom

SAGE Publications India Pvt. Ltd.
M-32 Market
Greater Kailash I
New Delhi 110 048 India

Printed in the United States of America

Library of Congress Cataloging-in-Publication Data

Main entry under title:
Psychotherapy process research: paradigmatic and narrative approaches
/ Shaké G. Toukmanian, David L. Rennie, editors.
   p. cm.—(Sage focus editions)
   Includes bibliographical references and index.
   ISBN 0-8039-4354-7.—ISBN 0-8039-4355-5 (pbk.)
   1. Psychotherapy—Research. 2. Psychotherapy—Research—Methodology.
I. Toukmanian, Shaké G. II. Rennie, David L.
RC337.P767 1992
616.89'14'072—dc20   92-12391

92 93 94 95 10 9 8 7 6 5 4 3 2 1

Sage Production Editor: Diane S. Foster

Contents

Preface

Inquiry into the processes involved in psychotherapy became systematized more than three decades ago through the efforts of Carl Rogers. In his famous formulation of the necessary and sufficient conditions for positive therapeutic change, he forged an uneasy alliance between his phenomenological and existential view of the person and the logico-empirical approach to explanation. For two decades, this formulation and the approach to explanation underpinning it set the tone for therapy process research. There have been some recent developments, however, by investigators identified primarily with the person-centered and experiential therapeutic traditions. Some of these developments challenge Rogers's theory of change while subscribing to the logico-empirical research tradition that his program inspired. Other developments challenge the received view of method, expressing a focus on the client's intentionality. Although it hardly can be seen as a deliberate attempt to redress the imbalance in perspective created by Rogers's adoption of the logico-empirical method, this last development nevertheless gives expression to his theory of the person that he had difficulty instantiating as a researcher.

This volume leads off with chapters representing the "new paradigm" approach to therapy process research advocated by Rice and Greenberg. In this initiative, the Rogerian view that there is a global relationship between the therapist's attitudes and the client's processes of change is abandoned. It is replaced with the view that therapeutic change is localized in change "episodes" or "events" involving particular performances by the client in response to particular performances by the therapist. Types of change episodes are discovered inductively and then are modeled through a logico-empirical approach to theory construction. Rice traces the history of her research career beginning at the Counseling and Psychotherapy Research Center at the University of Chicago and carrying through to her current interest in the resolution of problematic reactions as a type of change episode. Greenberg uses a specific example to illustrate his model of the resolution of "conflict splits," as seen from the perspective of Gestalt therapy, as a second type of change episode. And Wiseman describes the use of the replay of videotape to the client to elicit hitherto unreported subjective experience as a way of validating, from the client's perspective, Rice's model of the resolution of problematic reactions.

Other investigators are currently interpreting the therapy process in terms of constructs derived from cognitive science. This work is counterbalancing the search for micro theories of change in that explanation at the level of cognition may prove to be generically applicable to a wide variety of change episodes at the level of performance. In this vein, Toukmanian describes her research program involving the development and validation of a model of the client's perceptual processing in therapy. Next, Martin provides an overview of the development of his "cognitive-mediational" model of the therapy process in which he addresses the cognitive and affective processing of both the client and the therapist.

Another development is the systematic analysis of verbal reports on the subjective experience of therapy. Along these lines, Lietaer describes some of the returns from a large content analysis of clients' and therapists' reports on their session-to-session experience of a full course of therapy. Elliott and Shapiro depict how the grounded theory approach to qualitative analysis of subjective reports increasingly is being incorporated into Elliott's Comprehensive Process Analysis, which examines the same critical event in therapy from the perspective of the client, the therapist, and the third-party observer. As a representation of a multi-methodological approach to the analysis of verbal reports, Angus describes a program in which she is applying both qualitative and quantitative research strategies to the study of metaphor in therapy. Finally, Rennie describes the exlusive use of qualitative research in the form of the grounded theory method in his study of the client's subjective experience of an entire hour of therapy.

In the final chapter, we address the main themes represented in these contributions. We see five dimensions underlying them and psychotherapy process research in general. Each dimension entails issues problematic for the researcher. More fundamentally, these issues are seen to reflect the deeper question of what constitutes an appropriate approach to explanation in human science. The research programs under consideration variously reflect what Bruner describes as either "paradigmatic" explanation or "narrative" explanation. The former involves objectivism, the search for lawful relationships between causes and effects, and quantification as the preferred mode of representing those relationships. The latter entails subjectivism, the search for reasons for particular events, and the method of qualitative analysis of meaning embodied in verbal reports. We examine each of these approaches to explanation in terms of its logic of justification and discuss the feasibility of integrating them as a way of coming to grips with the complexity of the psychotherapeutic process.

—Shaké G. Toukmanian
David L. Rennie

1

From Naturalistic Observation of Psychotherapy Process to Micro Theories of Change

LAURA N. RICE

The focus of this chapter is on tracing the development of my research on psychotherapy process from the mid-1950s to this time. The purpose of this historical approach is to track rather specifically the assumptions on which my process research was based in the different "eras" and the changes in methodology that were adopted as a result of my inspection of the kinds of productive or unproductive yield that emerged. The examination of some of the research from each stage will be followed by some conclusions that shaped my approaches in the next stage. Many of these conclusions still seem to me important for the future productivity of psychotherapy research.

When selecting a graduate program for my doctoral work in psychology, the University of Chicago was my first choice for two reasons. One reason was that it offered an excellent program in theoretical psychology with a strong research focus. The second reason was the presence on the faculty of Carl Rogers. His views on human functioning and therapeutic change attracted me, and Rogers and some of his colleagues and students at the Counseling Center were already engaged in an interesting research program. Their work appealed to two parts of me that had previously seemed conflicting, the part that wanted to be a therapist, actively participating in facilitating human growth, and the part that wanted to be a scientist, observing, understanding, and engaging in rigorous research.

In 1951, when I entered the University of Chicago, Rogers's book *Client-Centered Therapy: Its Current Practice, Implications and Theory*, containing some of his most important theoretical ideas, had just been published. Some of these ideas were based on the intensive study of 30 fully recorded and transcribed therapy cases. Some therapy process research studies had already been published (Haigh, 1949; Raskin, 1949; Seeman, 1949). Inasmuch as there was at that time no rigid theoretical system guiding therapist interventions or specifying what kinds of client participation would lead to change, the attitude in listening to tapes together was highly naturalistic and discovery oriented, with the expectation that we could learn a great deal from listening to tapes and discussing them. This was an era in which, almost without exception, therapists from other orientations objected strongly to the recording of sessions and relied only on the therapist's case notes.

The emphasis at this stage was on listening to tapes of sessions, either one's own or those of colleagues, and trying to recognize and understand the kinds of client changes that seemed to be taking place in successful psychotherapy and identifying some of the important ingredients in the therapist's contribution. Categories were tentatively derived from the observations rather than being imposed on them. Although content was not disregarded, the emphasis was primarily on the *style* of functioning rather than on content categories.

Quantitative Naturalistic Research

In the late 1950s and early 1960s, Butler, Wagstaff, and I undertook a National Institute of Mental Health-supported research program conducted at the Counseling and Psychotherapy Research Center at the University of Chicago. In this short-term "availability" program, clients were offered one-hour therapy sessions twice a week for 10 weeks, followed by a tentative termination, at which time a battery of posttherapy measures were administered. The agreement was that the client would then have 10 weeks without therapy (unless some special crisis arose) and then could continue with the same therapist for another 10 weeks, at which time there was another tentative termination. It was understood that this "availability" pattern could continue as long as the client required. All sessions were tape-recorded. The underlying philosophy of this process study was similar to that established by the Rogerian group described above, that is, that one would start with intensive naturalistic observation leading to a level of understanding from which process theory would be derived. This was in contrast to the more usual approach of structuring observations by means of theory-derived category systems.

During this era, in the very young field of psychotherapy research, investigators were in the difficult position of trying to use standard hypothetico-deductive methods to study phenomena of tremendous complexity, often attempting to use a theoretical base for which there was little hard evidence.

The approach proposed by Butler, Wagstaff, and myself as a solution for some of these difficulties was *quantitative naturalistic research* (Butler, Rice, & Wagstaff, 1962, 1963) in which a factor analytic methodology was used to locate meaningful clusters of process categories, not as a means of testing theoretical hypotheses but as a means of generating fruitful hypotheses concerning the underlying structure that eventually could be subjected to rigorous testing:

> A naturalistic investigation is concluded when analysis of the data results in a demonstration that the system is unproductive or productive, as the case may be. If the system is productive the end result would be a sharpened and refined set of hypotheses leading to a better classification system with which to approach the domain. Or it may result in a set of hypotheses so refined as to indicate what is to be controlled and varied in an experimental attack upon the domain of inquiry. (Butler et al., 1963, p. 10)

Some guiding principles were used in constructing the category systems: (a) the client and therapist categories should involve the type of process engaged in rather than the particular content; (b) as a method of discovery, each category within a process system should contain behaviors that are similar *as* behaviors rather than containing different behaviors that are assumed to be conceptually related; (c) each classification system should contain mutually exclusive categories, with no remainder class; (d) the categories for each system should be nominal, not ordinal, and thus not ordered in terms of previous assumptions; (e) the process systems should exhibit reasonable reliability, though they should not be trivialized to obtain higher reliability; and (f) several different process category systems should be constructed for clients and for therapists to ensure that several dimensions of functioning are included for each. One further very basic decision followed from the assumption that the client's process styles would be influenced by the therapist's style of participation. Thus, in constructing systems, we first tried to identify dimensions of client process and only then focused on the therapist processes that seemed likely to facilitate these client processes. This was the reverse of the more usual approach of focusing first on therapist behavior but was consistent with our belief that productive client process was the key to understanding psychotherapy.

Client Process Systems

To construct these client systems, Wagstaff and I listened intensively to tapes supplied by 10 therapists at the center. Each therapist supplied one interview that he or she considered very good and one that seemed poor (though not necessarily from the same client).

Somewhat to our surprise, the client stylistic aspect that felt most different in the "good" hours was the vocal quality of the client. The client's voice often had a quality of turning inward, exploring inside, which we jokingly began to call "eyeballs inward." There seemed to be plenty of energy but it was turned inward rather than directed outward toward the therapist. At other times in the good hours, the vocal pattern was disrupted by emotional expression such as sobbing or fighting down emotion. In the poor hours, there seemed to be either a strong focus outward, talking *at* the therapist, or a thin quality with little energy and a pitch level somewhat above the person's own vocal platform.

These four categories were later specified for the raters much more precisely in terms of the vocal features characteristic of each one. The four categories for this system were Focused, Emotional, Externalizing, and Limited. These category labels were *not* given to the raters.

The second category system, which we called Expressive Stance, was a verbal category that involved the level at which the client was dealing with whatever subject matter was under discussion. In this system, there were four categories: (1) Objective Analysis, (2) Subjective Reaction, (3) Static Feeling Description, and (4) Differentiated Exploration of Feeling.

The second interviews from 64 clients from the "availability project" who had completed the first 10-week treatment block, involving 20 sessions, or had terminated before the fifth session were factor analyzed by Rice and Wagstaff (1967), using the approach described in Butler, Rice, and Wagstaff (1962, 1963). In contrast to the more usual analysis, which starts with a matrix of intercorrelations, this analysis involved a matrix of entries that represented on a scale between zero and unity the degree to which pairs of interviews shared the same behavior. With communality estimates added, each matrix was factored using the principal-axis method, and Varimax rotation was carried out.

Because of the report of Cartwright, Kirtner, and Fiske (1963) indicating a low relationship between therapist and client views of outcome, we decided to compare five outcome groups: (a) successful from both client and therapist perspectives, (b) successful from therapist's but not client's perspective, (c) successful from client's but not therapist's perspective, (d) unsuccessful from both perspectives, and (e) attrition. The results from the analysis of second interviews will be reported briefly here.

Factor I, which was characterized by Externalizing voice and Objective Analysis, seemed to be a component of all interviews, distinguishing significantly only between success and attrition. Factor II, which was characterized by Focused voice and a mix of Subjective Reaction and Objective Analysis, discriminated significantly between the unequivocal success group and all other groups except the mixed group (group b above). Factor III, which was characterized by Limited vocal quality and an Expressive Stance of Objective Analysis, discriminated significantly between the unsuccessful group (d) and all other groups except the attrition group (e).

The clearest conclusion from this analysis was that client vocal quality (CVQ) was the best predictor of outcome, with Focused voice clearly related to success, Limited voice clearly related to failure, and Externalizing not making any clear differentiations between groups. The results also provided some confirmation for the Subjective Reaction category as a positive indicator and for the preponderance of Objective Analysis as a negative indicator. Category 4, Differentiated Exploration of Feeling, did not occur often enough in second interviews to be represented on any of the factors. In the analysis of 11th interviews, however, Factor IV, involving Focused voice and a combination of Subjective Reaction and Differentiated Exploration of Feeling, discriminated significantly between the unequivocal success group and all other groups.

Therapist Process Systems

Following the same procedure as that described above for client process systems, Wagstaff and I also constructed three therapist process systems designed to be relevant to the client processes in therapy. The first aspect was Freshness of Words and Combinations, which contained two subclasses: (a) Fresh, Connotative Language and (b) Ordinary Language. The second aspect was Therapist Vocal Quality, with three classes: Expressive, Usual, and Distorted. For this third subclass, the most distinguishing feature was the regular emphasis pattern, seemingly for effect rather than for spontaneous meaning. The third aspect was Functional Level, containing three subclasses. The first was called Inner Exploring, because the focus is on exploration of the client's immediate inner experience. The second was called Observing, because the therapist joins the client in his or her focus on observing and analyzing him- or herself. The third was Outside Focus, in which the therapist's responses are within the client's frame of reference but the focus is on something outside the client.

A factor analysis similar to that described for client process was carried out on a preliminary sample of 24 completed cases, yielding three interview types (Rice, 1965). Type I interviews were characterized by therapist responses expressed in Ordinary Language. The vocal quality tended to be Usual, while the Functional Level of responses was primarily a reflection of client self-observation, with only a few at the level of Inner Exploring and none with an Outside Focus. Type II interviews were fairly similar to Type I in the use of language and Functional Level, but distinctly different in vocal quality, with more than half their responses involving the Distorted vocal quality.

Type III interviews differed from Type I in all of the aspects, with the therapists using more Fresh, Connotative Language; with two thirds of the responses involving Expressive vocal quality; and more than half of the responses on the Functional Level of Inner Exploring.

Rank-order correlations were obtained between the factor loadings for the second and next-to-last sessions and five posttherapy change measures. Type I therapist style in second interviews was only related significantly to one of the posttherapy change measures. For next-to-last interviews, no significant relationships were found between Type I therapist style and any of the posttherapy measures. For Type II therapist style in the second and next-to-last sessions, significant *negative* correlations were found with two of the outcome measures and were close to significance with the other three.

Contrary to our expectations, Type III therapist style in second interviews was not significantly related to any of the outcome measures. In next-to-last interviews, however, it was significantly positively related to three of the outcome measures and close to significance with the other two. Based on these findings, Type III seemed to be a correlate but not a predictor of therapeutic change.

Conclusions From this Era

Client Vocal Quality was clearly the best predictor for clients, and there was some indication of its importance for therapists, although the therapist system needed some revisions. There has since been considerable evidence from later studies (Rice & Koke, 1981) that the client's Focused voice may be a reliable indictor of clients' moment-to-moment deployment of attentional energy, involving a turning inward and tracking of their own inner experience, a process that is central in client-centered therapy. This has influenced the way I function as a therapist, leading me to hear moments when a client's voice shifts into Focused, even briefly, and to center my reflection on whatever is being expressed at that point.

The finding that the appearance of the Type III therapist process in second interviews did not predict posttherapy measures of outcome, but that in next-to-last interviews it correlated significantly with a number of positive posttherapy change measures, raised a thorny question. Did the good therapist process influence client style and thus lead to better outcome, or was the good therapist process simply a correlate of client style rather than a determinant of change? Another possibility was that the more "garden variety" Type I therapist style felt more comfortable for clients early in therapy while a more expressive style would be valuable later.

My most primary conclusion from these studies was that we needed to find better ways of tracking the therapy process and its effects over time, moving from the relevant client pretherapy characteristics, through the different stages of the therapeutic process, to the posttherapy changes in clients' symptoms and levels of functioning.

Further Analyses of the Origins and
Consequences of Client and Therapist Process

In the late 1960s and early 1970s at York University, my work on process research had four general areas of focus. The first focus was on analyzing some of the data from the Chicago project in ways that would provide a better identification and understanding of the "resources" that clients bring to therapy, which enable them to participate in the process in ways that lead to positive changes in their lives. The second focus was on reanalyzing some of the Chicago project data to derive more understanding of the whole issue of the degree to which the therapist process influences client process. Third, I also planned to try out other process systems in the field to see whether they might supplement the systems we had constructed. The fourth plan was to take a fresh look at the theory and practice of client-centered therapy based on my own experience as a therapist, as an intern supervisor, and in teaching courses in theories of psychotherapy and counseling.

Client Resources

The Client Vocal Quality (CVQ) system had clearly proved to be the most important component in defining the client factors derived from the factor analytic studies described above. Focused voice was a significantly positive predictor of outcome as early as the first and second interviews. Thus it seemed that the internal mode of functioning, of which Focused voice was the external sign, might well be one of the most valuable "resources" brought by clients to client-centered therapy.

As a therapist, it had seemed to me that, from the very beginning, some clients were able to engage in a process of turning inward and getting in touch with their own complex inner experience, exploring it and symbolizing it in words. It therefore seemed important from a research standpoint to be able to assess these "resources" independently of the actual therapeutic interaction. (In most studies with different orientations, measures of client pathology had *not* proved to be good predictors of therapy outcome.)

By this time, Gaylin (1966) had reanalyzed the Rorschach scores of the clients in the Chicago project, using adaptations of scores derived mainly from the Beck system (1944). He began with a theoretical distinction between "function" scores, which seemed to be associated with qualities observed in creative individuals, and "structure" scores, which he considered to be "highly dependent on normative-adjustment criteria." He isolated seven function scores and four structure scores.

In a later study (Rice & Gaylin, 1973), involving 52 clients from the Chicago project, we tentatively viewed these function scores as "immediately available resources for engaging in a creative perceptual process." Thus our prediction was that this style of functioning would enable clients to turn inward in a process of creative exploration in therapy. We predicted that these pretherapy function scores would be positively related to the amount of Focused voice in early therapy interviews, while the structure scores would be unrelated to Focused voice.

Because the Rorschach subscores were complexly interrelated and because the three vocal qualities were somewhat intercorrelated, we decided to compare relatively pure groups of 11 clients for each of the vocal patterns, using a stepwise multiple discriminant analysis. In this analysis, the first three variables, Non-F% (determinants other than form), R (total number of responses), and Z (organizational complexity) discriminated significantly between all pairs of vocal groups. The high Focused voice group showed high energy output, indicated by high R, with an average of 50 responses. Their substantial number of determinants other than form, such as movement, color, and shading, suggested a high level of internal complexity. Their relatively high level of Z suggested that they were able to organize this complexity in meaningful and original ways. These findings suggested that the high Focused clients were able to bring to the therapeutic exploration important, immediately available resources such as energy coupled with the availability of inner input that could be explored in complex and creative ways.

The high Externalizing group were sharply different. Their mean number of responses was 27, and comparatively few of their responses involved movement, color, or shading. This tended to confirm our impression of little availability of inner awareness and a preoccupation with the formal at the expense of the affective. The low number of responses was puzzling in view of the high energy component of Externalizing voice. We concluded, however, that this discrepancy could be explained by the fact that the energy in Externalizing voice seems to be used instrumentally, directed toward the outside rather than toward getting in touch with inner awareness. In the Rorschach task, only the inner awareness was assessed. The low-energy quality of the Limited vocal quality was confirmed by the low average number of 20 responses. It is interesting, in spite of this low output, that they showed a high proportion of nonform determinants, suggesting that they might have more ability to get in touch with their inner affective sphere than did the Externalizing clients, resembling more closely the Focused clients. Their organizational ability (Z) was the lowest of the three vocal groups. We speculated that perhaps both the vocal quality and the Rorschach performance reflected a withholding of affect that was potentially available, possibly in quantities too difficult to handle.

Although this study left a number of questions unanswered, it yielded two interesting products. In the first place, it tended to confirm some of our impressions concerning the internal processes underlying the different vocal qualities assessed by the CVQ. Second, it identified a set of pretherapy resources that could be used in the next study in which an attempt was made to track the entire time line from pre- to posttherapy.

Therapist Influence

In an attempt to get some answers to the complex questions concerning therapist influence on client process, as well as further questions concerning the complex interplay between client resources, therapist style, and therapy outcome, a further analysis of the data from the Chicago project was undertaken. As Kiesler (1971) had pointed out, psychotherapy researchers had seldom focused within the same study on the whole complex sequence of pretherapy prognosis, in-therapy process, and therapy outcome.

A study was designed to tackle three related questions (Rice, 1973). The first question concerned the degree to which each participant is influential in shaping the quality of the in-therapy process. One difficulty in previous process studies had been that, even in the first interview, the contribution of each participant was already influenced by the participation of the other. This problem was addressed in the current study in two ways. In the first place, the measure of initial client resources used was Gaylin's (1966) measure of Rorschach function scores discussed above. The seven function scores were converted to standard scores and summed. The 48 clients in this study were divided into three subgroups: low-resource, moderate-resource, and high-resource clients. Thus this classification was independent of therapist participation. In the second place, the measure of therapist style, which was a revised version of the Type III behavior described in the previous section, was based on style measures derived from his or her interviews with the three or more *other* clients seen in the Chicago study, thus yielding a measure that was independent of the client in the particular dyad. Thus it was possible to address the second question of whether or not the therapist's style would have a differential effect on the in-therapy process of clients with low, middle, or high resources.

A 2 by 3 analysis of variance (fixed effects model) was performed for each of the three time periods, with client resources and therapist style the two independent variables and client process scores for the first, second, or tenth (middle) session as the dependent variable. As expected, the client resources measure was significantly correlated with client process in the first and second interviews, but the therapist participation style was not. By the tenth interview, however, both the client resources and the therapist style main effects were highly significant beyond the .01 level. Clearly, by the middle of therapy, the client level of favorable process was strongly related both to the resources brought by the clients and to the participation styles brought by the therapists.

Finally, the correlations of therapist style, client resources, and client process in the first, second, and tenth interviews with outcome measures from the client's, therapist's, and diagnostician's perspective were computed. Although neither of the two pretherapy measures, client resources and therapist style, was a significant predictor of therapy outcome, client process in the tenth interview was significantly correlated with favorable outcome as assessed by clients, therapists, and diagnosticians. By the middle of therapy, the two participants seemed to have achieved a kind of interaction that enabled clients to focus inward and to explore their subjective reactions and inner experience with a high degree of energy.

An interesting methodological point emerging from this study was that neither of the two pretherapy measures predicted the outcome of therapy. If the study had not included the intervening client and therapist in-therapy process measures, one might have concluded that neither therapist style nor client resources assessed by the Rorschach would be a useful predictor of therapy outcome in further studies. Both measures *did* predict the tenth interview process, however, and this in turn proved to be significantly related to the three outcome measures. My conclusion was that making an accurate prognosis is like solving a set of equations in which one has to insert something new at each point and that, perhaps by the middle (tenth) session, one can make an accurate prediction concerning outcome.

Trying out Different Process Systems

As my process research continued, it became apparent that one could make more meaningful descriptions of client or therapist engagement at particular points by using a number of different process measures, thus enabling one to describe the nature of this engagement at various points by means of a cluster of process scores from different dimensions. My conclusion from inspecting different systems in the field and trying them out on some of the material from this project was that the Experiencing Scale (Klein, Mathieu, Gendlin, & Kiesler, 1970) would be an important supplement to the client measures described above, and it was incorporated into later studies. It also seemed clear that a relationship measure such as that of Barrett-Lennard (1962) could improve our predictive "equations."

**A New Look at the Theory and
Practice of Client-Centered Therapy**

One further development in the early 1970s centered on issues in understanding both the theory and the practice of client-centered therapy. The central importance of the therapist conditions of empathy, unconditional positive regard, and congruence (Rogers, 1957) in leading to client change still seemed very clear as I listened to tapes of the therapists in the Chicago project. Evidence on the importance of these conditions had been somewhat ambiguous in the therapy research literature as a whole (Howard & Orlinsky, 1972), and it seemed clear that more complex studies had to be designed. But my own subjective conclusion was that these conditions were important for all clients and absolutely crucial for some.

A number of former students and faculty at the Counseling and Psychotherapy Research Center at Chicago were becoming increasingly interested in taking a new look at therapy process and trying to understand, in a more detailed fashion, the particular and significant ways client and therapist interactions seemed to lead to change. We were somewhat disturbed by the fact that the Rogerian necessary and sufficient conditions (Rogers, 1957, 1959) were concerned mainly with the qualities of the therapist participation, with the only conditions stated for the client being that he or she perceived these qualities of the therapist, at least to some extent, and that he or she was vulnerable and anxious, in a state of incongruence. We felt strongly that the style of the client's participation needed to be examined in more depth. This was further motivated by our awareness of current developments in theoretical psychology as well as the potential importance of developments in cognitive information processing in understanding human functioning. David Wexler and I decided to edit a book focused on some of the "innovations" in client-centered therapy. The chapters by Anderson (1974), Wexler (1974), Zimring (1974), and Pearson (1974) clearly were very much influenced by developments in cognitive psychology.

In my own chapter (Rice, 1974), I focused on the importance of enduring constructions or "schemas" in guiding healthy or disturbed functioning. The basic assumption discussed in that chapter is that, for any person, some classes of experience have not been adequately processed and, for some people, there are a number of important classes of experience that have not been adequately processed. This in turn will lead to maladaptive and unsatisfying experiences in various classes of situations. Furthermore, these classes of inadequately processed experience are idiosyncratic and will be very different for different clients. The implication for the conduct of therapy was that the targets of therapy should be the schemas relevant to the recurring classes of situations in which the client finds him- or herself functioning in unsatisfying and maladaptive ways. I concluded that an important issue for therapy practice was to find a method by which a client could be facilitated in reprocessing an important experience from such a problem class in an undistorted fashion, which could, in turn, lead to the reorganization of the inadequate and distorting schemas.

In thinking about this theoretically, and in trying to facilitate this kind of exploration in some of my own clients, it became apparent that this approach was especially effective when clients reported a reaction of their own that they felt to be in conflict with their own expectations and thus were motivated to explore it. This observation, in turn, led to my developing ways of bringing the situation alive and facilitating the client's reexperiencing the situation to some extent, and recognizing the nature of their own idiosyncratic construal of the self-relevant impact of the stimulus situation. Especially important was the identification of client indicators, suggesting times when such facilitation might be especially successful. This also seemed to fit with my increasing awareness, from the process research reported previously, that some clients could engage in crucial inner exploration quite easily but that for many others it is much more difficult to engage in productive process. Furthermore, even for those who were able to turn inward spontaneously, it seemed important to identify moments when a certain kind of exploration was needed and to identify therapist processes that would facilitate it.

Conclusions and Recommendations

Psychotherapy process research had had a surge of popularity in the late 1950s and 1960s but since then, until recently, had been in a decline. One reason for this seemed to be the conviction that the first priority should be to conduct comparative outcome studies. A substantial number of such studies had been done by the early 1970s, some of them very well designed, but the results had been rather unsatisfying. In general, the different approaches seemed to yield results that were approximately equal (Bergin & Lambert, 1978). One could conclude that this indicated a general factor in all methods. My conviction, however, was that each approach had its own strengths and contained operations that fit particularly well for certain clients at certain times. It seemed to me that, until we could study systematically some of these productive and unproductive interactions, we would not be able to improve success rates substantially, nor would we begin to understand the mechanisms of therapeutic change.

In view of these observations, I made the following three recommendations at the 1977 conference of the Society for Psychotherapy Research. The first point was that our typical designs in therapy research, even complex multifactor designs that included both treatment and organismic variables, were just not appropriate for studying sequences of therapeutic transactions in which each participant influences the other. We needed to use more flexible and innovative designs, possibly using single case studies involving experimental therapeutic interventions or possibly using some of the newer stochastic methods that addressed the sequential dependencies involved in a series of client-therapist transactions occurring over time.

Second, we needed to put more emphasis on when and in what context a particular kind of process appears. An aggregate approach made some sense when conducting prognostic studies but, for understanding interactions, we needed to recognize that a given kind of behavior may have very different meanings in different contexts. Also, we needed to develop process systems sensitive to behaviors that may not be unambiguously "good" or "poor" process but that may be highly significant when understood as parts of patterns that we can describe and replicate.

A third conclusion was a confirmation of the decisions made in constructing our original process systems, that is, that process systems should be *descriptive,* grouping together behaviors that are similar as behaviors rather than systems that include very dissimilar behaviors that seem to define some construct. An example of the latter approach would be establishing a class called *defensiveness* and including in it such diverse behaviors as silence, abrupt change of topic, and "yes-butting."

Identifying and Studying Change Events

The most compelling conclusion that I derived from the work described in the previous section was the importance of identifying and studying intensively different classes of change events. Although the kind of tracking over time of the mutual impact of client and therapist, described above, and its relationship to outcome were important, I believed that we could learn much more if we could add to the "equations" the successful completion of particular kinds of events during the course of therapy.

During the early 1970s, Leslie Greenberg and I considered and tried out ways of addressing some of these issues. First, we attempted to capture regularities in client-therapist sequences using Markov chain analyses but, as we explored stochastic procedures for analyzing interactions, we became aware of their inadequacy in capturing the phenomena we observed in the data. Essentially, these sequential analyses, though linking steps in a chain, were still not sufficiently sensitive to the contexts in which they occurred. One major problem was the implicit assumption in these methods that a given client or therapist process has the same meaning at different times and in different contexts.

I continued to examine and experiment with the evocative unfolding of "problematic reactions," identifying times in therapy sessions when clients seemed to be puzzled by some reaction of their own and seemed motivated to explore it. As a therapist, I also experimented with ways of engaging in the evocative unfolding of the incident, leading to the client's awareness of relevant feelings and stimulus construals that had not been fully processed at the time of the incident. I also tried to begin to describe, in terms of process measures, the kinds of client engagement that seemed to be present at different times in the unfolding process, using the process systems described in the previous section as well as new ones such as Toukmanian's (1986) perceptual processing measure that seemed relevant to this particular class of events.

In a preliminary test of the potency of this event, 12 volunteer clients were seen by three experienced client-centered therapists for two sessions.

The clients had been given a general description of problematic reaction points (PRP) and had been asked to bring a PRP to each session. In one session, the therapist used systematic evocative unfolding and in the other session the same therapist used a nonspecific client-centered approach. The order of the different treatments was counterbalanced. Clients' ratings on a five-point productivity scale administered after each session were compared for the two kinds of interviews. Clients' productivity ratings for the sessions involving the evocative unfolding were significantly higher than for the nonspecific sessions, although therapist empathy as assessed on the Barrett-Lennard Relationship Inventory (1962) was approximately equal for the two kinds of sessions. Research on this task is described by Rice and Saperia (1984) and by Wiseman (this volume). An interesting methodological point emerged in Wiseman's detailed studies of PRPs. It became apparent that modifications of the sequential designs, which we had rejected earlier, could be used productively in the analysis of particular classes of events (Wiseman, 1986; Wiseman & Rice, 1989).

Meanwhile, Greenberg had become interested in isolating and studying a class of events derived from the Gestalt approach, which he called "conflict splits." In his ongoing participation in a Gestalt training group, he had become sharply aware of some of the specific intervention sequences used by Gestalt therapists that were applied at particular points. These decision points (markers in our terms) had not been clearly delineated or researched by Gestalt theorists, but there seemed to be some potentially interesting guiding principles. Greenberg and I were both strongly influenced during this period by Pascual-Leone's neo-Piagetian approach to the analysis of different kinds of developmental tasks (Pascual-Leone, 1976a, 1976b; Piaget, 1970). Greenberg became increasingly interested in "task analysis" as an approach to understanding client and therapist processes in psychotherapy and incorporated some of the methodology of Newell and Simon (1972) in developing a task analytic method for constructing models of the clients' paths to resolution in different classes of change tasks. He developed a model of the resolution of "conflict splits" and conducted some tests of the potency of this event. The task analytic methodology and research on conflict splits are described by Greenberg (1984a, 1984b).

The thinking and research in which Greenberg and I engaged during this period led to our proposing a new paradigm for therapy process research (Rice & Greenberg, 1984). This new view of the route to identifying and understanding mechanisms of change led us to make a number of recommendations for research in the field of therapy process research.

Our most central point was that, rather than assuming that a given kind of process has the same significance at any time in therapy, and thus sampling randomly from interviews, we recommended the segmentation of therapy into episodes in which a particular kind of clinically meaningful event seemed to be taking place. Once such a class of change events had been identified, a valuable strategy for understanding its essential structure would be the rational-empirical approach to task analysis (Greenberg, 1984b). This approach is described in some detail by Greenberg (this volume).

Each class of change events should be studied by identifying the sequence of process patterns that unfold over time. In other words, in describing segments, it is not simply the *amount* of a particular client process but the *pattern* of the client process during that segment that should be studied. Successful analysis of events depends on making detailed descriptions of the processes engaged in over time. Thus patterns defined by *clusters* of different process measures are essential for the identification of each stage. Furthermore, the process categories should be at the descriptive level rather than containing an inferential mix of behaviors presumed beforehand to be conceptually related.

We recommended that the focus of this task analytic approach should be on the *client* steps that are necessary for the resolution of the event being studied. It is only after these steps have been identified that one can study the necessary therapist processes, viewing them as an important source of influence on the client's process. Thus appropriate therapist responses can be selected from a more informed position.

In our proposed new paradigm for psychotherapy research, the investigator does not begin with the formulation and testing of hypotheses. Hypothesis testing should be the final step in a rigorous program of discovery and understanding.

Plans for the Future

One important feature of the new approach described above is that it forges a firmer link between research and clinical practice. The models of the exploratory processes in which clients need to engage during the different stages of particular change tasks, and the ways in which the therapist process can facilitate the completion of these stages, can provide a theory-grounded resource for clinicians to consider in the presence of relevant markers. Also, thoughtful clinicians can make theoretical contributions by recognizing productive incidents in their own practice, studying them in detail, and sharing them with other clinicians and researchers.

It also seems clear that the understanding of these change events, isolated and studied by means of this rational-empirical approach, can be sharpened and extended by obtaining the client's perspective by means of Interpersonal Process Recall (e.g., Elliott, this volume; Wiseman, this volume).

The research plan that Greenberg and I have developed for the future is to construct a "process-experiential" therapy that will combine a number of different change tasks, instigated at appropriate markers of client readiness, within the climate of an empathic, prizing relationship. It would include two events developed by Greenberg within the Gestalt approach and two developed by Rice within the client-centered approach. The focus of the proposed research program will be on tracking the process of change during the whole course of therapy, from initial client resources to final outcome. A postsession measure would be completed by the therapist after each session, and the client would complete a more detailed postsession evaluation as well as an intersession report before the next session. Standard pre-post therapy measures also would be completed by clients at four-week intervals. The effects of this integrated treatment would be compared with a treatment involving the Rogerian conditions to test whether this integrated approach is more effective than a single well-administered approach.

The emphasis of the study would not be primarily on comparative outcome, however, but on tracking the process and its effects over time. How do the different kinds of marker-driven sessions compare with each other and with regular client-centered sessions? Are they leading to the kinds of in-session, postsession, and intersession yields that we have predicted from the nature of the tasks?

In addition, we could begin to address some more qualitative, speculative questions. For instance, are some kinds of markers more prevalent for some clients than for others, and do these clients have some particular pretherapy or early-session characteristics? Do clients with primarily Externalizing vocal quality have more successful resolutions in events such as conflict splits that involve more active expression than they do in those events such as problematic reactions that seem to involve primarily experiential search? Are there perhaps events in which clients with primarily Limited vocal quality seem to participate better than in other events or in client-centered therapy in general? We will be attempting to construct increasingly complex and illuminating "equations" linking client resources, therapist interventions, client engagement in particular kinds of processes, and outcome over time.

The investigative journey described in this chapter began with the Rogerian approach of intensive listening to tapes of therapy sessions as a basis for identifying and speculating about the important ingredients in successful therapy. It seems appropriate that this journey is continuing with an approach that depends heavily on intensive observations, leading to the construction of increasingly well-grounded and detailed micro theories concerning the different routes to therapeutic changes.

References

Anderson, W. (1974). Personal growth and client-centered therapy: An information-processing view. In D. A. Wexler & L. N. Rice (Eds.), *Innovations in client-centered therapy* (pp. 21-48). New York: John Wiley.

Barrett-Lennard, G. T. (1962). Dimensions of therapist response as causal factors in therapeutic change. *Psychological Monographs, 76* (Whole No. 562).

Beck, S. J. (1944). *Rorschach's test.* New York: Grune & Stratton.

Bergin, A. E., & Lambert, M. J. (1978). The evaluation of therapeutic outcomes. In S. L. Garfield & A. E. Bergin (Eds.), *Handbook of psychotherapy and behavior change* (2nd ed., pp. 139-190). New York: John Wiley.

Butler, J. M., Rice, L. N., & Wagstaff, A. K. (1962). On the naturalistic definition of variables: An analogue of clinical analysis. In H. H. Strupp & L. Luborsky (Eds.), *Research in psychotherapy* (Vol. 2). Washington, DC: American Psychological Association.

Butler, J. M., Rice, L. N., & Wagstaff, A. K. (1963). *Quantitative naturalistic research.* Englewood Cliffs, NJ: Prentice-Hall.

Cartwright, D. S., Kirtner, W. L., & Fiske, D. W. (1963). Method factors in changes associated with psychotherapy. *Journal of Abnormal and Social Psychology, 66,* 165-174.

Gaylin, N. L. (1966). Psychotherapy and psychological health: A Rorschach function and structure analysis. *Journal of Consulting Psychology, 30,* 494-500.

Greenberg, L. S. (1984a). A task analysis of intrapersonal conflict resolution. In L. N. Rice & L. S. Greenberg (Eds.), *Patterns of change: Intensive analysis of psychotherapy process* (pp. 76-123). New York: Guilford.

Greenberg, L. S. (1984b). Task analysis: The general approach. In L. N. Rice & L. S. Greenberg (Eds.), *Patterns of change: Intensive analysis of psychotherapy process* (pp. 124-148). New York: Guilford.

20   Micro Theories of Change

Haigh, G. (1949). Defensive behavior in client-centered therapy. *Journal of Consulting Psychology, 13,* 181-189.

Howard, K. I., & Orlinsky, D. E. (1972). Psychotherapeutic processes. *Annual Review of Psychology, 23,* 615-668.

Kiesler, D. J. (1971). Experimental designs in psychotherapy research. In A. E. Bergin & S. L. Garfield (Eds.), *Handbook of psychotherapy and behavior change* (pp. 23-62). New York: John Wiley.

Klein, M. H., Mathieu, P. L., Gendlin, E. T., & Kiesler, D. J. (1970). *The Experiencing Scale: A research and training manual.* Madison: University of Wisconsin.

Newell, A., & Simon, H. (1972). *Human problem solving.* New York: Prentice-Hall.

Orlinsky, D. E., & Howard, K. I. (1978). The relation of process to outcome in psychotherapy. In S. L. Garfield & A. E. Bergin (Eds.), *Handbook of psychotherapy and behavior change* (2nd ed., pp. 283-330). New York: John Wiley.

Pascual-Leone, J. (1976a). Metasubjective problems of constructive cognition: Forms of knowing and their psychological mechanism. *Canadian Psychological Review, 17,* 110-122.

Pascual-Leone, J. (1976b). A view of cognition from a formalist's perspective. In K. Riegel & J. Meacham (Eds.), *The developing individual in a changing world.* The Hague, the Netherlands: Mouton.

Pearson, P. H. (1974). Conceptualizing and measuring openness to experience in the context of psychotherapy. In D. A. Wexler & L. N. Rice (Eds.), *Innovations in client-centered therapy* (pp. 139-170). New York: John Wiley.

Piaget, J. (1970). *Structuralism.* New York: Basic Books.

Raskin, N. J. (1949). An analysis of six parallel studies of therapeutic process. *Journal of Consulting Psychology, 13,* 206-220.

Rice, L. N. (1965). Therapist's style of participation and case outcome. *Journal of Consulting Psychology, 29,* 155-160.

Rice, L. N. (1973). Client behavior as a function of therapist style and client resources. *Journal of Counseling Psychology, 20,* 306-311.

Rice, L. N. (1974). The evocative function of the therapist. In D. A. Wexler & L. N. Rice (Eds.), *Innovations in client-centered therapy* (pp. 289-312). New York: John Wiley.

Rice, L. N., & Gaylin, N. L. (1973). Personality processes reflected in client vocal style and Rorschach performance. *Journal of Consulting and Clinical Psychology, 40,* 133-138.

Rice, L. N., & Greenberg, L. S. (Eds.). (1984). *Patterns of change: Intensive analysis of psychotherapy process.* New York: Guilford.

Rice, L. N., & Koke, C. J. (1981). Vocal style and the process of psychotherapy. In J. K. Darby (Ed.), *Speech evaluation in psychiatry* (pp. 151-170). New York: Grune & Stratton.

Rice, L. N., & Saperia, E. P. (1984). Task analysis of the resolution of problematic reactions. In L. N. Rice & L. S. Greenberg (Eds.), *Patterns of change: Intensive analysis of psychotherapy process* (pp. 29-66). New York: Guilford.

Rice, L. N., & Wagstaff, A. K. (1967). Client vocal quality and expressive style as indexes of productive psychotherapy. *Journal of Consulting Psychology, 31,* 557-563.

Rogers, C. R. (1951). *Client-centered therapy: Its current practice, implications and theory.* Boston: Houghton-Mifflin.

Rogers, C. R. (1957). The necessary and sufficient conditions of therapeutic personality change. *Journal of Consulting Psychology, 21,* 95-103.

Rogers, C. R. (1959). A theory of therapy, personality and interpersonal relationships as developed in the client-centered framework. In S. Koch (Ed.). *Psychology: A study of science: Formulations of the person and the social context* (pp. 184-256). New York: McGraw-Hill.

Seeman, J. (1949). A study of the process of nondirective therapy. *Journal of Consulting Psychology, 13,* 157-168.

Toukmanian, S. G. (1986). A measure of client perceptual processing. In L. S. Greenberg & W. M. Pinsof (Eds.), *The therapeutic process: A research handbook* (pp. 107-130). New York: Guilford.

Wexler, D. A. (1974). A cognitive theory of experiencing, self-actualization, and therapeutic process. In D. A. Wexler & L. N. Rice (Eds.), *Innovations in client-centered therapy* (pp. 49-116). New York: John Wiley.

Wiseman, H. (1986). Single-case studies of the resolution of problematic reactions in short-term client-centered therapy: A task-focused approach. *Dissertation Abstracts International, 47, 4669B.*

Wiseman, H., & Rice, L. N. (1989). Sequential analyses of therapist-client interaction during change events: A task-focused approach. *Journal of Consulting and Clinical Psychology, 57,* 281-286.

Zimring, F. M. (1974). Theory and practice of client-centered therapy: A cognitive view. In D. A. Wexler & L. N. Rice (Eds.), *Innovations in client-centered therapy* (pp. 139-170). New York: John Wiley.

2

Task Analysis

Identifying Components
of Intrapersonal Conflict Resolution

LESLIE S. GREENBERG

A model of the process of intrapsychic conflict resolution in Gestalt two-chair dialogue, in which the two opposing aspects of the conflict move through different steps toward resolution, has been progressively refined and tested in a number of studies across a number of clients and therapists (Greenberg, 1980a, 1983, 1984). This model was developed by means of a task analysis of resolution performances. In this chapter, the task analytic method for studying change events is described. This will be followed by the presentation of a study aimed at identifying components of the resolution process. This study emanates from a task analytically oriented program of research on the resolution of conflict by means of two-chair dialogue.

Task Analysis

In our view, "task analysis" offers a promising alternative to the experimental and correlational paradigms in which psychotherapy research has been trapped (Greenberg, 1979, 1984; Rice & Greenberg,

1984). Researchers in a number of areas (Ericsson & Simon, 1984; Fischer & Pipp, 1984; Pascual-Leone, 1980, 1989) for some time have been using task analytic methods to make detailed performance analyses of human problem solving. For example, Newell and Simon (1972), in their study of human problem solving and chess playing, used task analyses to make detailed observational records of single individuals as they proceeded to solve reasoning problems. From these records, they inferred the way the problem was construed, the hypotheses tried, the ways in which the task instructions impeded or facilitated solution, and finally the kinds of mental capacities required to generate the performance.

Task analysis is a research strategy that involves the detailed study of individuals actually engaged in performing tasks, rather than relating dependent and independent variables as in experimental approaches. The focus in task analysis is on understanding the process of task solution and the underlying mechanisms involved and building explanatory models of the process of resolution. In performing a task analysis, one selects for study a task that is "interesting" because of the nature of the demands it makes on the human processing system and also, in many cases, because the task is one that is itself important in successful human functioning. The long-range goal of the analysis is to construct a model of a human system and the psychological processes that would be capable of producing the particular performance under study.

In addition to its focus on understanding complex ongoing processes, several other characteristics of the task analytic strategy fit particularly well with the subject matter of psychotherapy research. Perhaps the most basic difference from either the experimental or the correlational paradigm is that a substantial part of the research effort is discovery oriented and is invested in observational, inductive postdictive strategies. One makes extensive, rigorous observations of single individuals performing tasks and from these identifies the different strategies being used and the characteristics of successful performances and/or error strategies (Simon, 1979). A task analytic approach leads the investigator to view persons not as purely reactive but as actively engaged in construing the demands and possibilities of situations in relation to their own goals and then organizing their behavior accordingly. The strategy an individual adopts for performing a given task will depend on this construal process, and the actual performance will, of course, depend on the strategy adopted.

The task analytic approach has faced squarely the complexities of studying human beings engaged in interesting tasks. Some of the intuitions and methods of task analysis can be adapted productively to spell out an investigative strategy for the study of psychotherapy. A task analytic approach adapted from the work of Pascual-Leone (1980, 1989) was developed to study therapeutic events, and a version of these steps, which have been presented and discussed more fully elsewhere (Greenberg, 1991; Rice & Greenberg, 1984), is presented below.

1. Explication of the Implicit Map of Experts

We begin with an expert clinician who has an explicit general model of human functioning, that is, a personality theory and a related general theory of therapy. The clinician also has a more implicit cognitive map concerning some of the important events of psychotherapy. This rich but often implicit cognitive map is usually based not only on the general theory but on reflections of the clinician's own clinical experience, and sometimes on the comments of especially perceptive and articulate clients. Often the clinician is the investigator, in which case we have a clinician-scientist; in other cases, the investigation works with a master clinician to explicate his or her own map.

In either case, the investigator approaches the study of therapeutic transactions not as a naive observer but as someone with differentiated ideas about human performance in certain kinds of task situations. The clinician's cognitive map thus provides a framework for beginning to look at performances, thus maximizing the chance of locating interesting and therapeutically significant phenomena. The first step of task analysis therefore involves explicating the clinician's implicit map to guide the investigation of change.

2. Selection and Decription of a Task

Informed by a general model of functioning and by intensive reflections on clinical experiences, the investigator selects an interesting task and makes a detailed description of the task and the task situation. The most basic assumption that underlies our research program is that psychotherapy can be broken down into a series of client tasks, the resolution of which advances the course of therapy and leads to change. In addition to the view of therapy as being constituted by client tasks such as trying to resolve conflicts, problematic reactions (Rice & Greenberg, 1984), or unfinished business (Perls, 1969), we also view therapy as consisting of events in which therapists intervene in specific ways to try to help clients resolve these problems. Although each session of psychotherapy is a complex personal and unique interpersonal experience, a skilled clinician clearly has some implicit or explicit guidelines concerning recurring kinds of "when-then" behavioral events that occur in therapy. For instance, for some clinicians, an example might be "when a client shows some awareness of a discrepancy between what he says and what he does, then the therapist confronts him with it explicitly." Different "when-then" events can be regarded as characterizing different therapeutic approaches. In any particular approach, some client performance pattern (verbal or nonverbal) comes to be recognized by the therapist as signaling that there is some issue that needs to be resolved and that the client is ready to focus on it. Particular client performance patterns indicate the beginning of affective tasks (the "when" referred to above). These are called "markers" (Rice & Greenberg, 1984) because they indicate some state of internal functioning that becomes a therapeutic target. I contend that experienced therapists often make a kind of momentary "process diagnosis," in the sense of recognizing certain functional markers, and hypothesizing that, if a given client marker is followed by the appropriate therapist operation, the client will be able to work toward affective resolutions. Thus the marker, the therapist operation, the resultant client process, and a final resolution performance make up a discriminable event in therapy, which has an identifiable beginning and end. Furthermore, these events do appear to have sufficient structural similarity to warrant detailed study (Greenberg, 1979; Rice & Greenberg, 1984).

Thus an event that seems to be recurrent within and across clients, and that seems to be potent in producing change, is selected for study. The investigator thereby begins a process that will lead to the specification of active ingredients in the therapeutic approach. Having selected an event, precise behavioral definitions of the distinctive features of the marker and the distinctive features of the appropriate therapist operation are constructed.

The description of the marker provides a process diagnosis of a type of cognitive/affective problem the client is trying to resolve while the therapist operation provides an intervention manual for dealing with this type of problem. This manual constitutes the definition of the task environment. While the marker initially defines the client task, the therapist operation is viewed as a set of task instructions that influences the client's construal of the task and the successive reconstruals as the task unfolds.

For a class of markers designated as "splits," in which the client is struggling to resolve a conflict between two opposing aspects of the self, Greenberg (1979) hypothesized that the therapist operation, which he called the two-chair experiment, would facilitate task resolution. This behaviorally specified operation encourages the client in a present-centered dialectical process to express the internal dialogue underlying the split. The therapist gives instruction to keep the two tendencies of the split separate and to heighten this separation to increase the person's awareness of different aspects of his or her experience. Integration is promoted through a process of increased attention to differentiated aspects of the conflict and particularly to negative cognitions on the one hand and to feelings and needs on the other (Greenberg, 1980a, 1984; Perls, Hefferline, & Goodman, 1951).

3. Verification of the Significance of Task Resolution

The task to be studied is selected because it seems to be potent in producing a change. A clinical hunch, however, often is derived from a few memorable clients or events. Therefore, after the event has been selected and described structurally in terms of discriminable features, it becomes important to verify the fact that successful engagement in the task leads to change. In other words, it is important to make sure that events of this class contain some of the active ingredients of change and are worth studying intensively. This verification of the potency of the event could be obtained by means of a number of different experimental methods using single case and/or group designs. Pre-post or postsession client report forms, filled out routinely for each session, can be used to determine whether the client felt that task resolution had occurred in particular sessions in which the therapist's operation had been programmed experimentally. In addition, measures of process changes during the hours when such events did or did not occur could provide a rigorous observer's perspective as to the relative potency of the event. A number of studies documenting this step of the approach have been conducted. These have demonstrated the effects of two-chair work at a split by comparing it with empathic reflection at a split (Greenberg & Dompierre, 1981) and by comparing it with problem solving for resolving decisional conflict (Clarke & Greenberg, 1986).

4. The Rational Analysis: Constructing Performance Diagrams

In the description below, we will assume, for simplicity, that the investigator is the expert clinician. Having selected and defined a task and shown its therapeutic significance, the investigator now begins the intensive analysis of the client's task performance. This is a highly creative step, involving two phases. In the first phase, the investigator draws on his or her general model of human functioning, his or her implicit map formed from accumulated clinical experience, and often some intensive scrutiny of a few tape-recorded interviews to generate possible resolution performance paths; he or she then *diagrams* these. The investigator thus conducts a kind of "thought experiment" (Husserl, 1973) in which possible resolution performances are varied freely in imagination to extract the essential nature of the performances and the fundamental strategy underlying the performance. Using this approach to study conflict resolution (Greenberg, 1984), multistep performance diagrams have been constructed to make explicit the steps of possible paths to split resolution using different strategies. Steps such as criticizing the self, affective reactions to the criticism, and stating wants and needs represent the type of different possible states along the path of a two-chair dialogue performance.

The purpose of the multistep performance diagram is to provide a *framework* for understanding the actual performance of the client. Thus, when observing the client's actual performance in the next step of the task analysis, it is possible to be guided by this diagrammatic framework in comparing the actual performance with the possible performances described in this step. This greatly helps to determine which of the possible strategies and states actually took place and in what sequence the states occurred. As one recycles through Steps 4 through 6 of a task analysis, the nature of the thought experiment changes. At first, one is spelling out possiblities, not trying to predict what the person *will* do. As one understands more and more about the essential nature of the task performance, the results of one's thought experiments are in part predictions concerning the paths that lead to resolution that then can be tested using randomization and nonparametric tests.

In the second phase of this rational analysis, the investigator considers how to recognize and measure these different classes of performances and how these performances could be expressed in terms of observables that could be rated by a naive observer. The investigator thus would translate the strategies obtained from the thought experiment into performances that could be measured by standard process rating systems and would perhaps construct new ones to pick up some dimensions that are not covered by the available systems. Thus one might use established systems such as the Experiencing Scale (Klein, Mathieu, Gendlin, & Kiesler, 1970), the Client Voice Quality system (Rice, Koke, Greenberg, & Wagstaff, 1979), the Levels of Client Perceptual Processing (Toukmanian, 1986) as well as some more content-oriented classification system such as the Structural Analysis of Social Behavior (Benjamin, 1974) to measure performances associated with the resolution of the task being studied. This step is essentially a disciplined form of creative clinical thinking stated in some kind of precise process language.

5. Empirical Analysis: Description of the Actual Performances

Having developed a diagram of possible performances, the observer now makes a detailed sequential description of the actual performance of one or more single individuals engaged in the particular therapeutic task under study. Although error strategies become interesting at later points in the investigation, the first few performances studied should be those involving successful resolution. These sequential descriptions should use performance categories that are minimally inferential and yet serve to reduce the complexities involved to manageable proportions. The more thoroughly the task is understood, the more fine-grained the analysis can profitably become.

It is crucially important that either the descriptions of possible task performances in Step 4 above and the description of actual performance here in Step 5 be stated in the *same* process language or at least that the language of Step 5 be unequivocally translatable into the language of Step 4. There are some process systems available at this level in the area of psychotherapy research but others should be constructed and/or considered (Greenberg & Pinsof, 1986). Also, because temporal patterns are notoriously easy to impose on sequential data in which none exist, we need some simple rules (statistical tests) for verifying that certain performance patterns are in fact appearing repeatedly across different instances of the same task. For example, statistically significant differences for different stages of split resolution tasks were repeatedly found (Greenberg, 1979, 1984) in both depth of experiencing and associated voice quality. This demonstrated the operation, in these events, of specific psychological processes associated with successful conflict resolution.

6. Comparison of Actual Performance with Possible Performances: Model Building

Comparison of actual and possible performances has two kinds of yield. First, it confirms or disconfirms the assumptions of the thought experiment concerning the strategies and performance steps that lead to successful resolution. In other words, if these are verified, one can begin to place some confidence in one's cognitive map. Second, from detailed inspection of the actual performances within the framework of the thought experiment, one is in a position to begin constructing a moment-by-moment description of the human system engaged in the affective resolution of a task.

The investigator therefore compares the actual performance with the possible performances (Steps 5 and 4) and, from this comparison, begins to construct a specific model, consistent with the general model of the kind of performances that could have generated the observed performance. In building a specific model, the investigator is able progressively to correct, expand, and make more explicit his or her understanding of the processes involved in generating resolution performances. It is at this stage that the clinician-scientist attempts to conceptualize the mechanisms that enable the process of therapeutic change. The construction of a detailed, specific model of the components of resolution involving successive repetitions of Steps 1 to 6 is the long-range goal of the model building effort. In the early stages, the bulk of the effort is directed to the postdictive, inductive steps. In the later stages, the model becomes sufficiently accurate and refined that it can be subjected to testing.

Although the specific model of the process of client change is the central goal, the researcher also attempts to understand the ways in which the therapist, as a crucial party to task resolution, can retard or facilitate the process in which the client is able to achieve resolution. The analysis of resolution performances into component psychological processes provides insight into which elements require change and how they change. This knowledge in turn suggests or invites the invention of specific intervention strategies to facilitate these change processes.

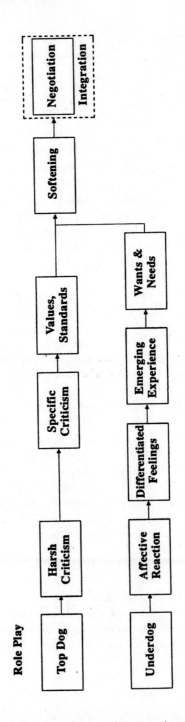

Figure 2.1. Refined Performance Model of Conflict Resolution.

The final model of intrapsychic conflict resolution developed from a number of intensive analyses of resolution performances in the manner described in Steps 1 to 6 above is shown in Figure 2.1. This model suggests that a harsh self-critical state, on its way to a more affiliative softening state, moves through steps in which the criticisms become more specific and then, although still somewhat controlling, become less harsh and speak more from an inner sense of values. In the model, this later state is called the expression of "standards and values" by the other chair. The model also suggests that the experiencing self, after being initially reactive to the critic, moves through a state of experiencing previously unacknowledged feelings followed by the expression to the other chair of a want based on these feelings.

7. Verification

Although the major research effort in this investigative strategy is concentrated in the inductive postdictive steps (repeated cycling from Steps 4 through 6), verification steps are essential and some already have been included. In the first place, verification that the events selected for intensive analysis are related to client perceived change is handled in Step 3. Second, the last few cycles of Steps 4 through 6 are in effect demonstrating that a series of additional clients do indeed follow the predicted paths to change.

Step 7, however, constitutes the major predictive hypothesis testing phase of this approach. In this step, making use of the newly constructed specific model, hypotheses concerning client performance on the task are advanced. Resolution and nonresolution performances are compared to verify that the specified components discriminate between the successful and unsuccessful performances. The hypothesized and observed performances are compared, using statistical tests. If the observed patterns and components are found to be those that have been predicted and also are found to discriminate between resolution and nonresolution performances, credibility is added to the specific model. A verification study illustrating this step is presented in the next section.

8. Relating Outcome to Process

As a final step in a research program of this nature, more traditional studies of outcome effects are done, in which the relationship between successful client performances and long-term outcome are studied and the links between therapeutic methods, which lead to these client performances, and outcome are demonstrated. The advantage of planning this step at this stage of a research program is that a hypothesized causal link between specified client processes and outcome provides increased control of client performance variance. This approach therefore holds promise of improved prediction and control as well as improved explanation of therapeutic change.

Having built a descriptive model through the procedures described above, Greenberg and Webster (1982) completed a study relating the process of conflict resolution across sessions to final outcome. This study showed that, in the context of a good working alliance (Bordin, 1979), characterized by client perceptions of the therapist as empathic (Barrett-Lennard, 1962) and the therapeutic task as relevant (Horvath & Greenberg, 1986), the therapy outcomes were predicted by conflict resolution performances that followed a particular path. This path was characterized by an initial expression by one part of the personality of both criticism and lack of acceptance of another part of the personality. This was followed by a deepening of experiencing and an assertion of *wants* in the previously unaccepted part. The final essential component on the path to resolution was a softening in attitude toward the self by the previously harsh critic. The combined presence of these components predicted outcome at termination and at follow-up.

A Verfication Study

In this section, a verification study emanating from a task analytic research program is reported. In the Greenberg and Webster (1982) study relating process to outcome, a softening in attitude of the previously harsh critic appeared to be the critical component of competence, without which resolution did not occur. The two preceding components of the model, however, shown in Figure 2.1—namely, expression of values and standards in the critic and feelings and wants in the experiencing chair (combined into one component called "felt wants")—appeared to be essential for the occurrence of the softening in attitude. It seemed that the "dual" process of deeply experiencing felt wants in the experiencing chair and becoming aware of and clearly expressing differentiated values and standards in the other chair were the soil from which softening emerged. Therefore a study (McDonald,

1985) was mounted to see whether these two components were necessary conditions for softening and whether these components themselves discriminated between resolution and nonresolution two-chair dialogue sessions. More specifically, the study was designed to test (a) whether or not the resolution and nonresolution sessions differed significantly in the frequency of occurrence of the values and standards performance patterns in the other chair and the felt wants patterns in the experiencing chair; (b) whether or not all softening performances in resolution sessions were preceded by both standards and values and felt wants; and (c) whether or not two-chair dialogue sessions, judged by clients and therapists as leading to resolution, contained more softening client performance patterns than nonresolution sessions. In addition, we were interested in finding out from clients, by means of an Interpersonal Process Recall (see Elliott, 1986) review of the resolution dialogues, where in the resolution dialogue they perceived the most significant change point. These client perception data were then used to test further the validity of the model.

Method

Event Selection

For this study, 18 two-chair dialogues, 9 resolution and 9 nonresolution performances, were obtained from 18 clients. The clients came from a population of 111 clients who had requested counseling at a university counseling facility to resolve decisional conflict in response to advertisements of a counseling program for this purpose. A total of 64 subjects were screened initially for evidence of lack of severe disturbance, using Malan's (1976) criteria for brief analytic therapy, to ensure that the clients selected were able to engage in a relationship and were not highly suicidal, depressed, or anxious. Ultimately, 36 of those accepted for the project were assigned randomly to an eight-session, time-limited Gestalt therapy that used two-chair dialogue to work on decisional conflict, and 14 were assigned to a two-session brief treatment. In each treatment session, measures were administered to determine the degree of session resolution.

Two-chair dialogue resolution performances were chosen on the following criteria: (a) both clients and therapists had to indicate a postsession score of 5 or above on the 7-point Conflict Resolution

Box Scale (Greenberg & Dompierre, 1981), and (b) clients had to report a shift of 5 or more points between their pre- and postsession scores on the Target Complaints Discomfort Box Scale (Battle et al., 1966). Nine sessions from nine clients were identified as resolution sessions according to these criteria. The fifth session of nine other clients involved in the eight-session treatment who did not show these gains in the fifth session were selected randomly as a control sample. In addition to the above criteria, all subjects had to be available to complete an Interpersonal Process Recall (IPR) of the session within two days of the session. The sample in this study therefore represented the first nine resolution events collected in the project that had been subjected to the IPR procedure, plus a control sample that had been subjected to the IPR procedure.

The clients in this study were seen by four therapists who had two to nine years of experience with Gestalt methods. All the therapists had been trained in the use of the Gestalt two-chair dialogue (Greenberg, 1979, 1980b, 1984) and were familiar with Gestalt ideas regarding conflict resolution being achieved by integration and a softening of the attitude toward the self. Five of the resolution and two of the nonresolution events came from one therapist, four other resolution events plus one nonresolution event came from another therapist, and the remaining six nonresolution events came from the two other therapists.

Description of Treatment

A *conflict split* was defined as the occurrence of the following four features in the client's in-session presentation of a conflict: There is a tendency or partial aspect of the self (e.g., "I really don't want to do this"); a statement of a second tendency or partial aspect of the self (e.g., "I feel I have to"); an indication of intrapersonal contradiction indicating that the two parts are being set against each other (e.g., "but"); and a verbal or nonverbal indication that the person is involved in a conflict and is struggling, striving, or self-coercive (e.g., "I have to"). An example of a conflict split that emerged from a decisional conflict in this study follows: "I feel so lonely. I want to reach out to people, but I just don't seem to be able to. When I'm with friends, I start getting this closed-in feeling and I end up pushing them away."

The Gestalt two-chair treatment consisted of a series of suggestions and observations made by the therapist to separate clearly the two aspects or partial tendencies of the client's self and to facilitate direct communication between them. The five principles that guided the treatment interventions included maintaining clear separation and contact between the partial aspects of the self, directing clients to assume responsibility for the true nature of their experience, directing clients' attention to particular aspects of their current functioning, highlighting aspects of experience by increasing the level of arousal, and making concrete and specific that which was intellectual or abstract (Greenberg, 1979).

One side of the conflict designated as the "Experiencing Chair," also referred to in the data as Chair 2, represents the experiencing of the person that is initially held in check by the other chair. The other side of the conflict designated as the "Other Chair," also referred to in the data as Chair 1, represents other parts of the personality such as introjects, attributions, and projections. This side also can be thought of as the "inner critic," although this criticizing function changes as the dialogue progresses toward resolution.

Measuring Instruments

The Experiencing Scale (Klein et al., 1970) was used to measure the in-process, statement-by-statement level of client experiencing in both chairs. This scale is a 7-point annotated and anchored rating device created for the purpose of assessing the quality of client involvement or "experiencing" in psychotherapy. Klein et al. (1970) have defined *experiencing* as

> the quality of an individual's experiencing of himself, the extent to which his ongoing, bodily, felt flow of experiencing is the basic datum of his awareness and communications about himself, and the extent to which this inner datum is integral to action and thought. (p. 1)

Because of its sensitivity to changes in clients' involvement, the Experiencing Scale is a particularly valuable rating device for microscopic process studies such as this one. The lower levels of the scale are characterized by impersonal or superficial references to self. Moving up the scale, there is a progression from simple, limited, or externalized references to self to an elaborate description of feelings. At the highest levels of experiencing, exploration of feelings and new awareness lead to problem solving and greater self-understanding.

The Client Vocal Quality (CVQ) Classification System (Rice et al., 1979) was used in this study to track the quality of voice in the two-chair dialogue as a measure of involvement and processing level in the moment. The CVQ distinguishes four voice patterns (focused, external, limited, and emotional), each identified in terms of (a) perceived energy, (b) primary stress, (c) regularity of stress, (d) pace, (e) timbre, and (f) contours. Vocal quality has been shown to be a good predictor of success and failure in therapy (Rice & Wagstaff, 1967) and a sensitive index of productive and nonproductive processing styles (Rice & Gaylin, 1973).

The Structural Analysis of Social Behavior (SASB) Model (Benjamin, 1979), a content scale comprising three two-dimensional grids, was used to measure the changing quality of social interaction between the two chairs. The first grid depicts social behaviors for which the focus is on the other person (in this study, the other partial aspect of self). The second grid displays social behaviors for which the focus is on the self. The third grid, portraying what happens when behaviors represented on the first grid are turned inward, was not necessary in this study because, in effect, the introjects of other to self were acted out directly between the chairs. On each grid, the horizontal axis runs from disaffiliation to affiliation and the vertical axis from dependence to independence. Each chart point within each quadrant of the grid is then composed of a proportionate amount of the behaviors described by each of the axes. The first digit of a rated three-digit SASB code refers to the grid, the second number to the quadrant, and the third number to one of eight possible topic tracks. A 217 SASB rating, for instance, indicates a client statement focused on self (Grid 2), with positive affiliation and independence (Quadrant 1), on the topic of intimacy-distance (Track 7). The abbreviated description of this 217 behavior is "assert on own."

Because of its detailed structure, the use of the SASB provides a highly specific rating of conflictual interaction. Dialogue can be examined, utterance by utterance, with each statement characterized by one of the 72 chart points.

The Levels of Client Perceptual Processing (LCPP; Toukmanian, 1986) was used to explore further the process of resolution and to see whether it could add to the descriptive specificity of the components. The LCPP is a seven-category system that measures the type of information processing in which the client is engaged in therapy on a moment-to-moment basis. Categories of undifferentiated statement, elaboration and differentiation with an external, analytic, or internal focus as well as categories of reevaluation and integration allow one to rate the different modes with which clients perceive and process information in formulating their experiences in therapy.

The Conflict Resolution Scale (Greenberg & Dompierre, 1981), a self-report measure of the extent to which conflict has been resolved, was used as one of the outcome criteria for identifying resolution events. Both client and therapist were required to report a minimum of 5 on this 7-point scale for the dialogue to be considered a resolution event. The 7-point scale ranged from not at all resolved (1) through somewhat resolved (4) to totally resolved (7). This scale has been shown to correlate with other outcome measures and to discriminate between more and less effective resolution sessions using two-chair dialogue and empathic reflection (Greenberg & Dompierre, 1981).

The Target Complaints Discomfort Box Scale (Battle et al., 1966), a 13-point self-report measure of the amount of discomfort clients experience in relation to their current complaints, was used as a pre- and postsession measure of client progress toward resolution on the particular issue presented in the session. A shift of 5 or more points between pre- and postsession scores was one of the criteria necessary for a session to qualify as a conflict resolution.

Unit of Analysis

Conflict events within the session were identified by two raters who viewed the videotape and, by working back from the end of the session, established a unit that began with the client statement of a split, which was subsequently worked on with two-chair dialogue, and ended at the end of the session. Within two days of a client's resolution session, clients met with a recall consultant, who reviewed with them the videotape of the conflict resolution event. According to procedures set forth in Elliott's (1979) research manual, the recall consultant asked clients to select from four to seven "significant moments" in their process of change and then to rate the significance of these moments on a 9-point scale. The "most significant change point" was then selected. This was the moment in the client's experience that was rated as having the highest significance for the resolution of his or her conflict. For the nonresolution performances, clients reviewed conflict events from the fifth session and selected from four to seven significant moments of change. Given that the clients did not report highly significant moments of change in the control dialogues, it

Process patterns of client statements in other chair

	Resolution Performances									Non-Resolution Performances								
1	2	3	4	5	6	7	8	9	A	B	C	D	E	F	G	H	I
138	138	136	138	137	138	135	137	138	137	137	136	144	136	138	135	135	135
X2	F3	F2	F2	F2	X2	X2	F2	F3	X2	X2	X2	X2	X2	X2	X2	X2	X2
138	138	138	138	137	135	135	137	138	137	138	135	143	135	138	135	135	136
X2	X2	F3	F2	F2	X2	X2	F3	X2	X2	X2	X2	X3	X2	X2	X2	X3	L2
136	138	136	138	137	135	135	137	136	136	138	135	148	138	135	135	138	138
X3	F3	F2	X2	F3	X2	F2	X2	X3	X2	X2	X2	X3	X2	F3	X2	X2	F3
136	216	136	137	137	135	138	138	138	136	137	135	135	138	135	135	138	138
X3	X3	F3	X2	X2	X2	F3	X3	X3	X2	X2	X3	X2	X2	X3	X2	X2	L2
138	215	144	136	131	216	138	138	138	136	131	138	144	138	136	138	138	136
X2	X4	X2	F2	F2	X3	F2	F3	X3	X2	X2	F3	X3	X2	X2	X4	X3	X3
138	233	217	137	216	216	135	227	138	136	138	138	144	144	135	138	214	135
X3	X3	X4	F3	F4	X5	X2	X3	X3	X2	X2	X2	X2	X2	X2	E2	X3	X3
215	226	217	137	131	216	135	215	144	136	136	138	135	136	135	138	215	136
F4	X3	F5	X3	F4	X5	X2	F4	F2	X2	L4	X2	X2	X7	X2	X2	F3	X3
138	233	113	135	131	215	135	143	216	138	136	138	138	135	136	137	215	136
F3	X4	X4	F4	F4	F5	X3	F4	F5	X2	L3	X2	X2	X2	F3	F3	X2	L2
144	233	113	215	131	216	135	143	214	138	138	138	144	135	138	138	136	148
F5	E4	F5	X4	X4	X5	F3	F5	X4	X2	L3	X2	X2	X2	X3	X3	X3	X2
215	216	215	145	131	216	135	138	216	136	136	138	138	136	136	135	135	148
F5	E4	F5	F4	F4	X5	E3	X4	X4	X2	X3	X2	X2	X2	X2	X3	X3	X2
115	215	215	215	215	147	215	215	215	136	138	138	138	135	144	137	135	135
F5	F5	F6	F5	F5	X5	F5	F5	F5	X2	X3	X2	X3	X2	X2	X2	X3	X2
215	143	215	112	215	147	216	214	245	136	214	138	138	136	136	137	135	136
F5	F5	F6	F5	F5	X5	X5	X5	F5	X2	X3	X2	X3	X2	X2	X3	X3	X2
215	215	215	112	216	147	215	245	216	136	137	138	144	136	216	136	138	138
F5	F5	F6	F5	F5	F5	F5	F5	F6	X2	X3	X2	X3	X2	X2	X3	X3	X2
215	112	215	143	143	147	112	215	216	136	214	138	144	138	138	136	136	148
F5	F5	F5	F5	F5	X5	F5	F5	F6	X2	X3	X2	X2	X2	X2	X3	X3	X2
143	112	215	143	END	147	215	216	END	136	137	138	138	136	144	135	214	148
F5	F5	F5	F5		X5	F5	F5		X2	X3	X2	X3	X2	X2	X2	X3	Y2

cont'd......

Figure 2.2. Process Patterns of Client Statements in Resolution Performances

was decided to select a "control change point" by taking the mean time of the most significant moments of the resolution performances. This was found to be 47 minutes into the interview. This then served as a comparable point to the most significant change point in the resolution dialogues.

Across each of the 18 performances, a pattern search for the hypothesized resolution components was performed around the identified change

Process patterns of client statements in experiencing chair

	Resolution Performances									Non-Resolution Performances								
	1	2	3	4	5	6	7	8	9	A	B	C	D	E	F	G	H	I
	217 F4	135 X3	212 F5	243 F4	214 X3	215 X4	135 X4	217 X4	215 F4	215 X3	217 X3	233 X2	214 X3	215 X3	214 X3	216 X3	224 X2	227 X3
	217 F4	136 X3	214 F5	243 F4	217 X3	215 X4	135 X4	243 F4	216 X4	215 X3	215 X4	215 X2	215 X4	215 X4	215 X3	216 X3	231 F3	227 L3
	217 X4	135 E3	113 F5	243 X4	217 F4	215 X4	217 F4	215 F4	216 F4	215 X4	233 X3	215 X2	215 X3	217 X3	135 X3	216 X4	224 X2	227 L3
	217 X4	230 E3	243 F5	243 X4	216 F4	217 F4	217 X4	243 F4	216 F5	233 X3	135 F3	233 X3	215 E3	237 X3	227 X3	236 X3	224 F2	227 L3
	217 F4	233 E4	243 F5	243 X4	217 X4	217 X4	144 X4	217 F5	217 F5	233 X3	214 X3	233 X3	215 E4	217 X3	237 X2	216 F4	215 X3	227 X3

Note: ☐ "Values and Standards" pattern   SASB 137 or 138, focused voice. exp. level 3.

▽ "Felt Wants" pattern   SASB 217 or 243, focused voice. exp. level 4 or above.

○ "Softening" pattern   SASB 215 focused voice. exp. level 5.

Figure 2.2. Continued

point. Once resolution and control sessions were selected in the above manner, the conflict performance events within the sessions were identified by the following procedure. In both sets of sessions, the beginning of the dialogue was isolated. In the resolution session, the dialogue was traced backward from the end of the tape to whichever came first, either a clear statement of conflict split followed by two-chair dialogue or until the beginning of the event characterized by the statement of a conflict split and the introduction of two-chair dialogue (see Figure 2.2). Initially, a search for the two resolution components in the other chair (i.e., values and standards and softening) was conducted in the five dialogue statements preceding and the five dialogue statements following the client-indicated "most significant change point," while the initial search for the resolution component in the experiencing chair (i.e., felt wants) was carried out in the five dialogue statements preceding this point. If the components were not found, the context was to be expanded by five statements in each chair.

An ideal study investigating hypothesized patterned components would include a pattern search across the client's entire therapy performance on the particular conflict split. Due to the time and cost factors in transcribing and rating client performances, however, the unit of analysis in this study was selected as specified above. This decision rule resulted finally in 20 dialogue statements for each performance, 10 in the other chair preceding the most significant moment and 5 following it plus 5 in the experiencing chair preceding the most significant moment. The decision to limit the pattern search to dialogue statements around the client-identified change point was based on the model of resolution, which suggests that (a) a softening of the internal critic is central to change for the client and that (b) the co-occurrence of the hypothesized patterned components of "oppositional values and standards" from one side of the conflict and the "felt wants" from the other side seem to trigger the client's experience of "softening."

Identifying the Components

The Experiencing Scale (Klein et al., 1970), the Client Vocal Quality Classification System (Rice et al., 1979), and the Structural Analysis of Social Behavior Model (Benjamin, 1974) were used to specify the client process components of "values and standards" expressed from the other chair, "felt wants" expressed from the experiencing chair, and "softening" expressed from the other chair. For a statement to be identified as representing the "values and standards" component, rating on the Experiencing Scale had to be level 3, indicating a personal reaction to an external event. Voice quality had to be rated focused (F), indicating inner direction and exploration, as opposed to external (X), indicating an external "lecturing at" quality. Finally, the social interaction dynamic had to be rated 137 or 138, indicating a nonaffiliative and controlling focus toward the other, which is an "enforcing of conformity" or a "blocking or restricting" of the other.

For a statement to be considered representative of the "felt wants" component, the rating on the Experiencing Scale had to be level 4 or above, indicating a description of feelings and personal experiences. Voice quality had to be rated focused (F), indicating inner direction and exploration, and the social interaction dynamic had to be rated 215, an affiliative and independent "open disclosure of personal feelings" and "experiences related to self-development." In summary, using this precise process as language, the state of "softening" of the internal critic was recognized by the patterned component of "focused, 215 at level 5 experiencing"; the state of "felt wants" expressed by the experiencing side was recognized by the patterned component of "focused, 217 or 243 at level 4 experiencing or above"; and the state of "values and standards" expressed from the internal critic was recognized by the patterned component of "focused, 137 or 138 at level 3 experiencing."

Rating Procedures

Two independent raters were used for each of the three measuring instruments (Experiencing Scale, Client Vocal Quality System, and Structural Analysis of Social Behavior Model) and for the selection of the client statement units to be rated.

Two raters initially selected statements representing "dialogue between the chairs" by discriminating these statements from those representing parenthetical comments by the client to the therapist. The six raters used audiotapes and typewritten transcripts of the specific dialogue statements selected for rating. Each of the raters rated two thirds of the data, providing an overlap of one third for a reliability check. Each of the process measure raters had a minimum of 15 hours of training on the relevant rating system, and each was trained in accord with the rules of the particular process classification manual.

Reliability scores were high across all ratings. The dialogue-unit selectors had 98% agreement. On the statement-by-statement ratings, the experiencing raters obtained a Pearson product moment correlation coefficient of $r = .84$; the voice raters obtained a Cohen's kappa of .63; and the SASB raters, a Cohen's kappa of .86.

Results

Resolvers' and nonresolvers' performance patterns (see Figure 2.2 and 2.3) were compared on the frequency of occurrence of the "softening," "values and standards," and "felt wants" patterned components. The figures show the 10 statements in the other chair before the client identified the most significant moment, the five statements after this point, and the five statements in the experiencing chair before this point. The process patterns of the critical components are also shown in these figures.

Table 2.1   Between-Group Comparison on Attainment of the Different
Performance Patterns

	Resolution	Nonresolution
Softening	9	0*
Values & Standards	8	3*
Felt Wants	8	0*
Combined Values & Standards & Felt Wants	9	2*

*$p < .05$

With the use of Fisher's Exact Test, the two groups were found to be significantly different on the occurrence of the "softening" pattern ($p < .05$; see Table 2.1). In fact, all clients in the resolution group showed the "softening" pattern, while none of the individuals in the control group did. When Fisher's Exact Test was applied throughout, the two groups were also found to be significantly different (a) on the presence of the "values and standards" pattern, ($p < .05$), with eight of the nine resolvers and three of the nonresolvers manifesting this pattern (see Table 2.1); (b) on the "felt wants" pattern ($p < .05$), with eight resolvers and no nonresolvers showing this pattern in the 20 statements rated (see Table 2.1); and (c) on the attainment of the combined patterns prior to "softening" ($p < .05$), with seven resolvers and no nonresolvers showing the combined pattern of "values and standards" and "felt wants" (see Table 2.1). In addition, all nine resolvers indicated in the IPR that the most significant moment was during "softening": Five clients indicated the moment co-occurred with the presence of the rated "softening" pattern; three indicated the moment occurred one statement prior to the occurrence of the "softening" pattern; and one client indicated the moment occurred three statements after the "softening" pattern.

Furthermore, assessment of these components on the client perceptual processing system was found to enhance the pattern analysis of the components by capturing additional subtleties of the process. These LCPP ratings, which were done after the hypothesis testing phase of the study was completed, provided additional evidence of a descriptive nature supporting the view that differences in process do in fact exist between resolvers and nonresolvers.

All nine of the softening components were rated as Level V or higher on the LCPP, indicating that the critic is processing at a more internally differentiated level and is reevaluating and integrating information. Only four nonresolvers attained this score in the five statements in Chair 2 preceding the change point. Similarly, all the "feelings and wants" components were rated at V or VI, indicating that this chair is also more internally differentiating and reevaluating in its focus. In addition to helping discriminate between the groups, the measure suggested the possibility of a new process occurring between "standards and values" and "softening." It appears that more resolvers than nonresolvers engage in a process of reevaluation, as rated by the LCPP, Category VI, indicating that the new softening stance may emerge through the process of reevaluating options. This instrument was the only measure that discriminated a meaningful difference between the groups at this point in the dialogue.

Discussion

This study supports the hypothesis that values and standards and feelings and wants patterns appear to precede reliably the softening pattern in two-chair conflict resolution dialogues. Eight of the resolution performances and three of the nonresolution performances attained the "values and standards" pattern in the other chair. Eight of the resolution performances attained the "felt wants" pattern in the experiencing chair. In the one resolution case in which the other chair did not meet our criteria for consideration as a "values and standards" pattern due to the absence of focused voice, inspection of the entire dialogue did reveal that the pattern occurred earlier in the session. The fact that three of the nonresolution performances also attained this patterned component indicates that clients who fail to resolve their conflicts may achieve some of the early components necessary for resolution but become stuck at a later stage in their attempt to resolve their conflict.

The attainment of the "values and standards" component more often appeared to precede than to follow the attainment of the "felt wants" component in the resolution performances. This, plus its appearance on three occasions in the nonresolution performances, suggests that these two components may show some sequential ordering, with values and standards preceding felt wants.

The values and standards component is characterized on the SASB as disaffiliative, restricting, and enforcing of conformity. It is communicated in a focused voice at a moderately low level of experiencing, indicative of personal reactiveness. The change to focused voice in this component, from the external voice of the harsh critic, seems to be the critical feature of the expression of values and standards. No longer is there the "lecturing at" quality of severe criticism but a sense of fit with the person's own values and an experience of the real objections to the experiencing chair. The felt wants component is characterized on the SASB as an affiliative assertion toward the other chair. It is communicated in a focused voice at a moderate to high level of experiencing, indicative of description of feelings and personal experiences.

Examples of the "values and standards" statements in the other chair and the "felt wants" in the experiencing chair from three cases are provided below.

Case 1

"Values and Standards"

Cause you're, you're torn. You want to lay back, but you also have a need you know to make a contribution or, or to be famous or something. It's not quite giving. Who do you want to be . . . do you want to be famous or don't you want to be famous, . . . please be clear with me.

"Felt Wants"

Statement 1. What I really want to say is too bad. If I want to relax you know . . . sometimes I have this vision instead of a neat-as-a-pin house, that I have a house that is piled high with dirt, and mess . . . and I would really like to be happy with that . . . I'm so tired of being run by expectations and I'm not even sure that they're my expectations and that's what I'm starting to get in touch with.

Statement 2. Yeah, I'd just like to be, and I want the time to be—and I'm going to start to remove various expectation I don't think I'm quite ready to quit my job but soon and I may go back to school or do what I want to do.

Case 2

"Values and Standards"

Statement 1. Don't let down because ah, if you do well, number one if you do, it might scare him off/ Hmm don't trust him. Hold back and, ah, don't fall in love with him.

Statement 2. You know you can't, you shouldn't depend on him again. You shouldn't have, ah, expectations. I mean, you know. He's just as likely to leave the job at the drop of a hat and that overrebellious streak he has, ah, that can be dangerous so be careful.

"Felt Wants"

I want you to back off just back off. Just stay in the background OK fine. I you know I realize you're not going to disappear but just keep your mouth shut and, ah, if I need you I'll call you. Yeah wait a minute, there's more than that. Um yeah, I want to know that you will stay there and you will be there if I need you.

Case 3

"Values and Standards"

Um, um let that go, just just get rid of that [feeling sorry for herself] because (sigh) it hasn't done you any good. It hasn't made you any friends. It hasn't um created anything.

"Felt Wants"

Statement 1. What would I like? Well some forgiveness really for um for the gray parts you know that and some acceptance for the gray part, really.

Statement 2. Would you accept the gray parts as well as the pink parts? And I think we could be better friends and I admire the strength there but I also would like some compassion.

The results of this study, as well as providing evidence on values and standards and felt wants, also replicated the finding that softening appears to be a necessary condition of resolution. All nine resolution performances and none of the nonresolution performances attained the "softening" pattern in the other chair. This patterned component is characterized by an open disclosure of feelings, representing a shift from a previously disaffiliative and controlling attitude to one of affiliation and independence. This disclosure is communicated with a focused voice and occurs at a high level of experiencing indicative of the statement of a problem or proposition and the subsequent exploration and elaboration of that issue with reference to feelings and personal experience.

Examples of "softening" of the critic from the above three cases are given below.

"Softening"

Case 1: (Pause) See I don't know where you're going to take me (laughter), and that's scary for me, because it's a whole area I don't have very much experience with, I can tell you how to think, and I can tell you—how to do things, and what you should be doing, but when it comes to feelings . . . and yet I sense you being very strong in your feelings, you know, but they probably rule you many ways that I ruled you, and you haven't made such bad judgements, if it, if it's been judgments based on your feelings in the past, so maybe I, maybe I should trust you, but it's, I'm very tentative.

Case 2: Well. I'm kind of fearful I, I experience myself kind of backing up in a way, but I'm watching um yeah I'm really scared for you that you'll get hurt.

Case 3: (Sigh) About your . . . fearfulness, and about your . . . um . . . holding back. And ah . . . not thinking that . . . you do not have the strength . . . to get out, and to . . . rise above all that . . . um . . . all that fearfulness and cowardness and just hiding in a little corner . . . Ah . . . I would like to um . . . sometimes give you permission to just be that way if you are in that space . . . And, also . . . and (T: uh-huh) have the assurance that . . . you're not going to stay in that corner all the time. You are coming out of that corner at times and . . . and so . . . I will–would only like to say keep trying (T: umm) and . . . and . . . give it, you know . . . I have some . . . have some compassion for whatever is happening there . . . and I also see a bit . . . that it isn't all gray, and that it's becoming also a bit rosy at the edges . . . ah . . . . It's really great to see that um . . . and you have a lot of courage you know a lot of strength there . . . I feel a lot of compassion for that (cries).

The fact that all nine of the resolvers chose the softening experience as their most significant experience of change adds further support to the view that the "softening" client performance pattern is a key resolution component in resolving conflict in Gestalt two-chair dialogue. It appears that, by selecting the softening experience, clients are affirming that a change in relationship between parts of the self is crucial to change and conflict resolution.

The following are three examples from clients' IPR comments about their experience of "softening":

Case 4: When she [other chair] said, "I saw you there," at the time I was so emotional about it, but I think now I'm grasping it. That's where I change . . . really. For the first time I felt compassion [toward the experiencer].

Case 6: That's actually where I was starting to feel a lot stronger. My criticizing part of me was saying, "OK, you know, I'm feeling a little bit more compassionate for you. I'm beginning to understand you a bit more . . . um . . . and therefore, I guess I'll fade into the background a bit and let you take charge of your life by giving you more positive energy." So that was actually what I was saying about the outline of the critical part of me disappearing. I really feel that it was and that it was a really big breaking point. . . . It felt so real to me. I was really feeling happy at this point—really happy. It just seemed like a . . . big . . . relief.

Case 7: At this point I'm feeling softer, kind of melting inside. It's at this point that I feel really connected with myself again . . . in a very positive way. It's so clear . . . so very clear . . . I really had been expecting too much . . . or rather, my expectations had been off. I have a deep clear sense of just being myself . . . and the absence of criticism.

The fact that the co-occurrence of the three process components called "values and standards," "felt wants," and "softening" discriminated the resolution from the nonresolution performances supports consideration of these three patterned components as identifiable and essential components of the in-therapy task of resolving conflict splits. From the results of this study, it appears that the essence of the conflict resolution performances using two-chair dialogue can be characterized as follows: The person's implicit values and standards are articulated and are challenged by a deeply felt assertion of "wants" and "needs" from newly experienced and previously unacceptable aspects of the self. This dialetical confrontation triggers a softening in attitude of the previously harsh inner critic, thus enabling an integration of these two previously disparate aspects of self and a greater sense of self-acceptance.

Conclusion

The method of searching intensively for performance patterns in change events used in this study allows the investigator to track the moment-by-moment process of change. Pattern observation and description of this sort aids one of the fundamental goals of science: explanation (Harré, 1983). As we have shown, continued explorations of the subtleties in the patterned components, through the use of the LCPP or other process measures, could further illuminate the nature of the processes involved in conflict resolution. Once recurring patterns in change events can be reliably measured, these patterns can be interpreted to help explain how change takes place in counseling and therapy. Improved understanding and explanation of this type can enhance practice as well as help predict what processes lead to change.

References

Barrett-Lennard, G. (1962). Dimensions of therapist response as causal factors in therapeutic change. *Psychological Monographs, 76*(43, Whole No. 562).

Battle, C. C., Imber, S. D., Hoehn-Saric, R., Stone, A. R., Nash, E. II., & Frank, J. D. (1966). Target complaints as criteria of improvement. *American Journal of Psychotherapy, 20*, 184-192.

Benjamin, L. S. (1974). Structural analysis of social behavior. *Psychological Review, 81*, 392-425.

Benjamin, L. S. (1981). *Manual for coding social interactions in terms of structural analysis of social behavior (SASB)*. Madison: University of Wisconsin Press.

Bordin, E. (1979). The generalizabiity of the psychoanalytic concept of the working alliance. *Psychotherapy: Theory, Research and Practice, 16*, 252-260.

Clarke, K., & Greenberg, L. (1986). The differential effects of the Gestalt two-chair intervention and cognitive problem solving on decision making. *Journal of Counseling Psychology, 33*, 11-15.

Elliott, R. (1979). *Interpersonal Process Recall (IPR) as a research method for studying psychological helping process: A research manual*. Unpublished manuscript, University of Toledo.

Elliott, R. (1986). Interpersonal Process Recall as a psychotherapy research method. In L. Greenberg & W. Pinsof (Eds.), *The psychotherapeutic process: A research handbook* (pp. 503-527). New York: Guilford.

Ericsson, K. A., & Simon, H. A. (1984). *Protocol analysis: Verbal reports as data*. Cambridge: MIT Press.

Fischer, K. W., & Pipp, L. S. (1984). Development of the structures of unconscious thought. In K. S. Bowers & D. Meichenbaum (Eds.), *The unconscious reconsidered* (pp. 88-148). New York: John Wiley.

Greenberg, L. (1979). Resolving splits: Use of the two-chair technique. *Psychotherapy: Theory, Research & Practice, 16*, 310-318.

Greenberg, L. (1980a). The intensive analysis of recurring events from the practice of Gestalt therapy. *Psychotherapy: Theory, Research & Practice, 17*, 143-152.

Greenberg, L. (1980b). Training counsellors in Gestalt methods. *Canadian Counsellor, 15*, 174-180.

Greenberg, L. (1983). Toward a task analysis of conflict resolution. *Psychotherapy: Theory, Research & Practice, 20,* 190-201.

Greenberg, L. (1984). Task analysis of intrapersonal conflict resolution. In L. Rice & L. Greenberg (Eds.), *Patterns of change: Intensive analysis of psychotherapeutic process* (pp. 67-123). New York: Guilford.

Greenberg, L. (1991). Research in the process of change. *Psychotherapy Research, 1*(1), 14-24.

Greenberg, L., & Dompierre, L. (1981). The specific effects of Gestalt two-chair dialogue on intrapsychic conflict in counselling. *Journal of Counseling Psychology, 28,* 288-294.

Greenberg, L., & Pinsof, W. (1986). *The psychotherapeutic process: A research handbook.* New York: Guilford.

Greenberg, L., & Safran, J. (1987). *Emotion in psychotherapy.* New York: Guilford.

Greenberg, L., & Sarkissian, M. (1984). Evaluation of counselor training in Gestalt methods. *Counselor Education & Supervision, 23,* 328-340.

Greenberg, L., & Webster, M. (1982). Resolving decisional conflict: Relating process to outcome. *Journal of Counseling Psychology, 29,* 468-477.

Harré, R. (1983). *An introduction to the logic of the sciences* (2nd ed.). London: Macmillan.

Horvath, A., & Greenberg, L. (1986). The development of the Working Alliance Inventory. In L. Greenberg & W. Pinsof (Eds.), *The psychotherapeutic process: A research handbook.* New York: Guilford.

Husserl, E. (1973). *Experience and judgement.* Evanston, IL: Northwestern University Press.

Klein, M., Mathieu, P., Gendlin, E. T., & Kiesler, D. (1970). *The experiencing scale: A research and training manual* (vol. 1). Madison: University of Wisconsin, Extension Bureau of Audiovisual Instruction.

Malan, D. H. (1976). *Toward the validation of dynamic psychotherapy: A replication.* New York: Plenum.

McDonald, L. (1985). *Essential process components of conflict split resolution.* Unpublished master's thesis, University of British Columbia, Vancouver.

Newell, A., & Simon, H. (1972). *Human problem solving.* New York: Prentice-Hall.

Pascual-Leone, J. (1980). Constructive problems for constructive theories: The current relevance of Piaget's work and a critique of information-processing simulation psychology. In R. Kluwe & H. Spada (Eds.), *Developmental models of thinking* (pp. 263-296). New York: Academic Press.

Pascual-Leone, J. (1989). An organismic process model of Witkin's field-dependence-indendence. In T. Globerson & T. Zelniker (Eds.), *Cognitive style and cognitive development* (pp. 36-70). Norwood, NJ: Ablex.

Perls, F. (1969). *Gestalt therapy verbatim.* New York: Bantam.

Perls, F., Hefferline, R., & Goodman, P. (1951). *Gestalt therapy: Excitement and growth in the personality.* New York: Delta.

Rice, L. N., & Gaylin, N. L. (1973). Personality processes reflected in client vocal style and Rorschach performance. *Journal of Consulting and Clinical Psychology, 40,* 133-138.

Rice, L., & Greenberg, L. (1984). *Patterns of change.* New York: Guilford.

Rice, L., & Kerr, G. (1986). Measures of client therapist vocal quality. In L. Greenberg & W. Pinsof (Eds.), *Psychotherapeutic process: A research handbook* (pp. 73-105). New York: Guilford.

Rice, L., Koke, C., Greenberg, L. S., & Wagstaff, A. (1979). *Manual for client vocal quality*. Toronto: York University Counselling and Development Centre.

Rice, L. N., & Wagstaff, A. K. (1967). Client vocal quality and expressive style as indexes of productive psychotherapy. *Journal of Consulting Psychology, 31*, 557-563.

Simon, H. (1979). Information processing models of cognition. *Annual Review of Psychology, 30*, 363-396.

Toukmanian, S. (1986). A measure of client perceptual processing. In L. S. Greenberg & W. Pinsof (Eds.), *Psychotherapeutic process: A research handbook* (pp. 107-130). New York: Guilford.

3

Conceptually-Based Interpersonal Process Recall (IPR) of Change Events

What Clients Tell Us About Our Micro Theory of Change

HADAS WISEMAN

This chapter will present a conceptually based approach to the use of Interpersonal Process Recall (IPR) for studying clients' recollection of their experiences in therapy. After providing the background for the development of this tape-assisted recall procedure, the approach will be described, and its utility for testing micro theories of change events will be demonstrated in a study of a particular affective change event in client-centered therapy. In describing this study, the kind of hypotheses that can be tested and the type of data obtained by this method will become apparent. Procedural and methodological problems associated with this method will be discussed, along with the place of a Conceptually-Based IPR in an integrated paradigm of change process.

AUTHOR'S NOTE: This chapter is based in part on my doctoral dissertation and was supported by a Medical Research Council of Canada Studentship. I am indebted to L. Rice, R. Elliott, J. Watson-Lowenstein, D. Sander, and C. Classen for their assistance in the realization of this work, and to the clients of the Counselling and Development Centre at York University for their participation in this research.

51

Background: The Conceptually-Based IPR Methodology

The Conceptually-Based IPR methodology to be described and illustrated in this chapter was developed for the purpose of testing models of therapeutic change events. It evolved as an offshoot of previous work, conducted within the events paradigm, which has used the IPR procedure and the method of task analysis to study change events in experientially oriented approaches to psychotherapy. Before presenting this IPR method, it will be necessary to define the concepts that are relevant to this procedure.

IPR, Events Paradigm, and Task Analysis

The use of video tape recordings to assist clients and therapists in describing their experiences during particular moments of a therapy session was originated by Kagan (1975) in the 1960s. The technique, known as *Interpersonal Process Recall* (IPR), was first employed by Kagan in the training and supervision of counselors and therapists (e.g., Kagan, 1980). In recent years, Elliott (see Elliott, 1986, for a review) has adapted, systematized, and used this method as a tool for psychotherapy process research within the context of the *events paradigm*. This paradigm focuses on the investigation of clinically significant and relatively homogeneous classes of change events (e.g., insight events, decisional conflict events) to provide a description of the stages or "pathways" by which clients carry out specific cognitive-affective tasks (Elliott & Shapiro, 1988; Rice & Greenberg, 1984). Thus the goal of the events paradigm is to develop and refine "clinical micro theories" of therapeutic change (Elliott, 1983; Greenberg, 1986; Rice & Greenberg, 1984; Stiles, Shapiro, & Elliott, 1986). In this context, the method of *task analysis* is used as a means of arriving at a performance model, or a clinical micro theory, which specifies the steps that need to be taken by the client for successful task resolution (Greenberg, 1984, 1986; Rice & Saperia, 1984). This performance model is subsequently subjected to verification by relating the client's in-therapy processes to both task resolution and final treatment outcome (Greenberg, 1984) as well as by testing the kind of therapist interventions that best facilitate these processes in the client (Wiseman & Rice, 1989).

IPR for Testing Models of Change Events

In a "discovery-oriented" approach to psychotherapy process research, the IPR method is used for the identification and description of significant therapeutic change events (Elliott, 1984; Elliott, James, Shulman, & Cline, 1981). Within a task analytic context, the Conceptually-Based version of IPR (C-B IPR) can be used effectively as a tool to verify the stages of a performance model by obtaining the clients' perspectives on the pathways to resolution (Wiseman, 1985). In other words, rather than employing the IPR first to discover significant change events and then to describe them intensively, the starting point for the C-B IPR is a client performance model of a particular class of change events that is of interest to the researcher. The approach thus combines model-based hypotheses on client processes involved in cognitive-affective tasks and clients' own reports of their in-therapy experiences. Its aim is to bring the client's perspective to bear on the clinician-researcher's micro theory of a therapeutic change event.

Development and Description of the Conceptually-Based IPR

The Conceptually-Based IPR procedure was originally developed to obtain clients' reports of their experiences during the unfolding of problematic reactions (Wiseman, 1984, 1985). In an attempt to adapt the IPR procedure for model testing, our research team at York University conducted a trial recall of a Problematic Reaction Point (PRP) change event (to be defined later) in which one of the members of the team was the therapist and another was the client. Our goal was to find a way to get at the specific processes that we believed took place during the evocative unfolding of problematic reactions. This collaborative attempt led us to develop a method of obtaining clients' reports of shifts in mood that we believed reflected the hypothesized steps of the PRP model. Subsequently, I carried out a pilot study in which IPRs were conducted on the PRP sessions of clients in a study by Lowenstein (1985). The results of this study indicated that mood ratings could be obtained easily from clients and that (as will be explained later) the ratings were highly relevant to our change model. In addition, the study led us to adopt a more structured method for obtaining clients' recall as advocated by Elliott (1985) and Hill (personal communication, 1984; Hill & O'Grady, 1985).

The C-B version of IPR (Wiseman, 1986) consists of two major components, the *Mood Rating Scale* and a list of *Client Impacts* (that is, impacts on the client). The Mood Rating Scale was developed (as described earlier) to assess the client's moment-to-moment mood. It is an 11-point scale ranging from −5 through 0 to +5. Ratings on the negative side of the scale indicate a negative mood, with -5 representing an extreme in this direction. A rating of zero represents a neutral mood (neither negative nor positive). Ratings on the positive side of the scale indicate a positive mood, with +5 representing an extreme in this direction. Hypothetically, shifts in mood can range from 0 to 10 points. In addition to providing a rating of their mood at the particular moment in the session, clients are asked to specify the quality of their mood in their own words (e.g., sad, anxious, frustrated, relieved, pleased). Following their responses to the Mood Rating Scale, clients are asked to choose from a list of Client Impacts the impact or impacts that best fit their experience at the time. The list of client impacts for the conceptually based version was adapted from Elliott's (1985) "immediate therapeutic impacts" and Hill's (personal communications, July 1984, 1985) list of "client reactions." Their lists were modified to include impacts that were assumed to tap the kind of change that is hypothesized to occur according to the PRP model (e.g., reexperiencing). In addition to the above, each client is asked to rate particular therapist responses on the Helpfulness Rating Scale (Elliott, 1979, 1986) and to choose from a list of helpful and hindering effects the one that describes his or her reaction to the therapist's response. In the study to be described, this latter information was collected for exploratory purposes. Table 3.1 presents the list of client impacts.

Although the C-B version of IPR was originally developed to test model-specific stages in the resolution of the PRP change event, this procedure could easily be extended to apply to other change events. The features that are unique to this IPR procedure are the following: (a) it is applied to sessions in which a well-identified change event took place; (b) an already existing micro theory or model of the change events dictates a priori the segments that will be replayed to the client (in addition to including control segments); (c) the information that is elicited during the structured recall refers to the kind of data (e.g., impacts, moods) that the researcher-clinician deems relevant to the steps of the model and the kind of change that is hypothesized to occur in the change event under study; and (d) it focuses primarily on the client's performances and views the therapist's interventions in terms of the client processes that these interventions attempt to facilitate rather than in terms of the therapist's techniques per se.

Table 3.1   List of Client Reactions

I. What was going on for you at this point in the session?

HELPFUL REACTIONS

1. *Re-experiencing feelings:* My feelings were evoked, I reexperienced a feeling.
2. *Awareness of feelings:* I became aware of my feelings, or identified exactly what I was feeling.
3. *Awareness of one's own perceptions:* I became aware of the way I perceive(d) a situation, another person, or the world, or what stood out for me.
*4. *Awareness of thoughts:* I got in touch with thoughts that went with a feeling.
5. *Started a real exploration:* I felt like I was getting into a worthwhile exploration.
*6. *Negative self evaluation:* I became aware of viewing myself in a critical way.
7. *New self understanding:* I realized something new about myself or myself in relation to others, or made a new connection.
7a. *Reexamination:* I re-examined my beliefs, shoulds and oughts, or what I need or want.
8. *Clarification of problem:* I identified a problem (or saw it differently), or got a clearer sense of what I need to work on in therapy.
*9. *Alternative perspective:* I began to see that there is another way of looking at things.
10. *Problem solution:* I got a clearer sense of what alternative options I have to deal with a problem or situation.
Other

HINDERING REACTIONS

11. *Felt scared:* Felt scared of what I was finding out, or that things are moving faster than I can handle.
12. *Felt embarrassed:* Felt embarrassed to express what I was really feeling or thinking.
13. *Felt confused:* I felt confused by what I was saying or feeling.

Continued

Table 3.1   Continued

14. *Felt stuck:* I felt blocked like I didn't know what to do or say next.
15. *Felt lost:* I didn't know what to focus on.
Other

II. How did this therapist's response affect you at the time?

HELPFUL EFFECTS

1. *Felt understood:* Therapist really understood what I was saying.
2. *Felt supported:* Felt accepted, reassured and cared for.
3. *Involvement:* I got more involved in therapy.
4. *Personal contact:* I felt that my therapist and I were really working together as a team.
Other

HINDERING REACTIONS

5. *Felt misunderstood:* My therapist just doesn't or can't understand me or what I am saying.
*6. *Felt worse about self:* Felt worse about self as a result of what the therapist said or did; felt judged or attacked.
7. *Felt distracted:* Felt side-tracked or interrupted by therapist.
8. *Confused by therapist:* Felt confused by what my therapist said or did.
9. *Repetition:* Felt bored or impatient with what my therapist was doing.
10. *Lack of direction from therapist:* Felt that too much is left up to me, didn't know what to focus on.
Other

SOURCE: Elliott (1985). Reprinted by permission.
*Impacts suggested by Safran (Personal communication, December 1984).

Testing from the Client's Perspective: The PRP Model of Change

The study described below demonstrates the application of the Conceptually-Based IPR to the analysis of the processes involved in change events in psychotherapy. The term *process* refers to the client's and therapist's context-specific behavior and experience involved in the client's in-session and out-of-session therapeutic changes or shifts. In this research, the IPR methodology was applied to the investigation of a particular class of therapeutic change events in client-centered therapy; this class of events is called the resolution of "problematic reactions" (PRP; Rice, 1974, 1984a). Thus the term *therapeutic change*, in this context, refers to the successful completion of the model-specific steps (to be described below) of the PRP change event, as indicated by nonparticipant observational coding systems *and* by the client's recall of his or her in-session experiences. In a sense, the question we set out to explore in this study was this: *What do clients tell us about our micro theory of change?*

The PRP Change Event: Definition and Micro Theory

The PRP change event begins with a client's statement of a "problematic reaction point" (PRP), that is, a point at which the client recognizes that his or her own reaction to a particular situation is puzzling, unexpected, or otherwise problematic in some way. The client's statement on the PRP is the "marker" signifying to the therapist that the client is in a particular problem space, which, at that moment, is amenable to intervention (Greenberg, 1986). The series of therapist interventions designed to promote change at the PRP marker is referred to as "systematic evocative unfolding." The effectiveness of these interventions in resolving problematic reactions was demonstrated in an analog study (Rice & Saperia, 1984). A task analysis of the moment-by-moment performances of clients engaged in resolving problematic reactions was conducted, and a performance model (i.e., clinical micro theory) of the client processes leading to task resolution was developed (Rice & Saperia, 1984). Preliminary tests of the validity of this performance model were conducted by Lowenstein (1985).

Given that the kinds of client processes essential for task resolution have been specified and tested in the above studies, we were then interested in obtaining the client's perspective on the processes that lead to successful resolution. In other words, we were interested in using the conceptually based version of the IPR to elicit the clients' recall of the therapeutic steps or pathways to resolution as an approach to verifying the stages of the PRP performance model.

A brief description of the four steps of the model is provided below to define the hypothesized processes leading to therapeutic change according to the clinical micro theory (Rice, 1984a; Rice & Greenberg, in press) and to orient the reader to the kind of recall we expected to receive from clients for each stage.[1]

Stage I: Vivid Reentry. This step begins with the therapist asking the client to describe the situation just before the problematic reaction occurred. This includes the client's perception both of the scene and of his or her inner state just before the reaction was triggered. The therapist helps the client to build the incident as vividly as possible, to reevoke the sights and sounds and feelings experienced at the time. This phase is successfully completed when the client "reenters" the scene, reexperiencing freshly the subjective moment when the reaction was first triggered.

Stage II: Salience. At this stage, the therapist attempts, by means of open-ended reflections, to get the client to recognize what it was about the stimulus situation that was salient for him or her at the time the reaction was triggered.

Stage III: Meaning Bridge. In this stage, the client discovers the "bridge" (link) between the stimulus impact as construed and the nature of the puzzling reaction that was triggered. When this step is completed successfully, the client discovers the potential impact of his or her own subjective construal of the eliciting stimulus and recognizes self as agent in this construal.

Stage IV: Resolution. This stage involves an exploration of one's own mode of functioning by broadening, deepening, and owning it. The process is completed when the client reaches a "resolution" of the affective task, that is, "a new awareness of important aspects of one's own mode of functioning in a way that restructures the issue. Though still experientially involved, one now has a sense of what one wants to change and a sense of having the power to instigate the change" (Rice & Greenberg, in press).

Formulating Model-Based Hypotheses

The work of Lowenstein (1985) guided the selection of process measures to assess the completion of the above four steps in the PRP performance model. The first three stages were determined on the basis of three process measures:[2] (a) the Client Vocal Quality system (Rice & Kerr, 1986; Rice, Koke, Greenberg, & Wagstaff, 1979), (b) the Experiencing Scale (Klein, Mathieu-Coughlan, & Kiesler, 1986; Klein, Mathieu, Gendlin, & Kiesler, 1969), and (b) the Task Relevant Process System (Rice & Saperia, 1984). The completion of the fourth stage of the model was also determined on the basis of an expert clinical judge's indication of the point of resolution. Thus the configuration of indicators for the resolution stage, for example, consisted of the following (cf. Greenberg, 1984):

1. Client Voice Quality System: focused (at least one response in this segment);
2. Experiencing Scale: stage 6 (peak);
3. Task Relevant Process System: disembedded owning of personal style (Classen, 1989); and
4. expert clinical judgment of the point of resolution.

The client's pathway to resolution was retrospectively reconstructed on the basis of the client's recollection of impacts and of mood during the change event. To test the fit between the performance model and the client's own perspective of the unfolding of the PRP change event (a) the relationship between the steps of the performance model and the list of client impacts was examined, and (b) the client's recall of shifts in mood was analyzed in relation to the particular steps in which he or she was engaged. Using these two vantage points, the following two model-based hypotheses were formulated:

Hypothesis 1. It was predicted that each stage of the model would be characterized by particular kinds of impacts (experienced by the client as revealed during the IPR) at the corresponding point of recall. Specifically, predictions were made for each step (see Table 3.2).

Step of the Performance

Hypothesis 2. It was predicted that each stage of the model would be characterized by particular patterns of client mood ratings on the IPR Mood Rating Scale. Specifically, predictions were made for each step (see Table 3.2).

The Study

The Conceptually-Based IPR was employed for model testing in a series of single case studies involving the resolution of problematic reactions in short-term client-centered therapy (Wiseman, 1986). The series was conducted at the Counselling and Development Centre at York University.

Table 3.2   Hypothesis 1

Step of the Performance Model	Recalled Impacts
I. Vivid Reentry	Started real exploration, reexperiencing, and awareness of feeling
II. Salience	Awareness of own perceptions, awareness of thoughts, and reexperiencing
III. Meaning Bridge	Clarification of problem: new self-understanding, alternative perspective
IV. Resolution	New self-understanding, clarification of problem, problem solution, and alternative perspective

Table 3.3   Hypothesis 2

Step of the Performance Model	IPR mood ratings
I. Vivid Reentry	A negative shift in mood (of at least 1)
II. Salience	No prediction
III. Meaning Bridge	A mood rating that is (at least +1) higher than the mood rating at the Vivid Reentry point
IV. Resolution	A positive shift in mood and a positive rating that is higher than the mood rating for the Meaning Bridge

The sample consisted of five clients who ranged in age from 21 to 27 years ($M = 23.8$, $SD = 2.49$). Clients were white female undergraduate students. They all met selection criteria for brief psychotherapy (see Malan, 1976). The presenting problems of the five clients focused on interpersonal issues (related to parents, spouses, fiances, boyfriends, and peers), and they suffered from moderate to high anxiety and mild to moderate depression (see Wiseman & Rice, 1989).

The clients were randomly assigned to one of two female therapists. The therapists were advanced doctoral students in clinical-counseling psychology with at least two years of supervised experience in psychotherapy. In particular, they had received intensive training and supervision in systematic evocative unfolding of problematic reactions as well as in client-centered therapy.

The two therapists and a third advanced graduate student served as recall consultants. The therapists did not conduct the recall sessions for their own clients but for each other's clients. They followed the manual for the Conceptually-Based IPR (Wiseman, 1984) and trained together. The structured procedure for conducting this method of IPR ensures a relatively high degree of standardization.

The clients were seen for 10 to 15 ($M = 12.2$) one-hour weekly sessions. Two of these sessions, in which the client was asked to present a PRP, were designated as the "task sessions." To qualify as a PRP marker, the client's statement had to contain the following three elements: (a) a particular situation; (b) the client's own reaction either as a feeling or a behavior, or both; and (c) an indication that this reaction was problematic (Rice & Saperia, 1984). The appearance of these three elements in the task sessions was later reliably established by two judges. The therapist responded to the marker according to the *Therapist Manual for Unfolding Problematic Reactions* (Rice, 1984b). To ensure that the therapists responded to the marker according to the interventions prescribed by the manual, an Integrity Checklist was applied to one randomly sampled PRP task session and one randomly sampled nontask session for each client.

The Conceptually Based IPR Procedure

In the conceptually based version of the IPR procedure, a research assistant (who is often the recall consultant) reviews the videotape of the just-completed PRP session and selects the segments to be replayed later to the client. The PRP client performance model forms the basis for the selection of segments. In general, segments include the specified steps as well as responses by the client that are not part of these hypothesized steps; the latter serve as control segments (Wiseman, 1984).

In this study, when clients gave their informed consent to participate in the research project, they were told that they would be videotaped and would be asked to participate in two recall sessions. It should be noted, however, that a video camera was present in the therapy room during all the therapy sessions, and clients were not informed ahead of time that this would be a session for which they would be asked to participate in a recall procedure.

Typically, the first of the two PRP sessions was the session to which the IPR procedure was applied. In one case, because the first PRP had not been clearly unfolded (i.e., client did not complete stages I and II of the model), the IPR procedure was carried out in the second task session. Two clients who volunteered to do so had an IPR for both of their task sessions. Thus the recall data on the PRP sessions consisted of seven IPR sessions. These sessions usually took place the next day following the therapy session or at most up to 48 hours following the session. The recall sessions lasted between 1.5 and 2 hours. The recall consultants recorded the information provided by the client on the recall sheet, and the recall sessions were also audiotaped.

The Configuration of Client Process Measures

The PRP sessions were rated using the Client Vocal Quality system, the Experiencing Scale, and the Client Task Relevant System by three pairs of independent judges with adequate interjudge reliabilities (Wiseman, 1986; Wiseman & Rice, 1989). The clinical judgment of resolution was also made independently of the other ratings.

The Client Vocal Quality classification system (Rice, Koke, Greenberg, & Wagstaff, 1979) was used to assess the client's response-by-response deployment of attentional energy during the PRP task sessions. The CVQ is a nominal measure consisting of four mutually exclusive vocal patterns: Focused, Emotional, Externalizing, and Limited. Focused voice indicates a turning inward of attentional energy in the tracking of inner experience. The CVQ has been shown to possess satisfactory interjudge agreement. Studies relating the CVQ to outcome in client-centered therapy have shown that Focused voice is a reliable index of productive client process (Rice & Kerr, 1986; Rice et al., 1979).

The Experiencing Scale (Klein et al., 1969; Klein et al., 1986) was used to assess the client's response-by-response experiential involvement during the PRP task session. The Experiencing Scale is a 7-point, annotated, and anchored rating device. The scale assesses a progression from impersonal references to self, to an inner description of feelings, to a felt shift and newly emergent experiencing with a step toward resolution of an issue. Evidence of reliability and validity is reviewed in Klein et al. (1986).

The Task Relevant Process System was developed by Rice and Saperia (1984, p. 52) to label at "a molar descriptive level the internal processes in which the client appeared to be engaged" during the unfolding of a PRP. In the current study, this measure was employed to determine whether or not clients had performed the specified steps of the PRP model. This system consists of mutually exclusive observational categories.

Findings

Clients' Endorsements of Hypothesized Impacts

To test the stages of the PRP performance model from the client's perspective, an examination was made of the fit between the stage of the model in which the client was engaged and the particular impact that the client endorsed at the corresponding point of recall. The completion of the stages of the model for each PRP session was established by employing the above configuration of process measures. The client, it should be noted, was clearly *unaware* of the model and was not expecting certain steps. For each of the four steps of the model, the frequency with which the predicted impacts were endorsed by the clients via IPR (in the seven PRPs) was obtained, and the percentage was calculated. Clients chose these impacts out of the 18 possible impacts (12 helpful and 6 hindering impacts). In addition, a more stringent test was provided by the indication that the predicted impact was not endorsed by the client at any preceding recall point. For example, the impact of "new self-understanding" should thus be endorsed for the first time during recall at the point that, according to the objective ratings on the configuration of process measures, is the Meaning Bridge.

The relationships predicted in Hypothesis 1 between the client's recall of impacts and the four stages of the model were generally supported.

At the Vivid Reentry stage, six out of the seven clients indicated the predicted impacts. The one client who recalled a different impact than those predicted indicated that she "felt scared" and "was not sure what was going on." Of the clients, 57% endorsed the predicted impacts at this point for the first time during recall (i.e., the more stringent criterion).

The findings for the Salience step were somewhat weaker. For one client, this step was missing. For the remainder, four out of six indicated the predicted impacts. An additional client indicated a predicted impact as "also present." Yet one client endorsed a hindering impact (i.e., "felt stuck"). Further, of the six clients who recalled experiencing the predicted impacts, only two of these fulfilled the more stringent criterion of first endorsement.

Stronger evidence was found for the Meaning Bridge step of the model. The predicted impacts were endorsed during recall for six out of the seven PRPs, and all of these were first endorsements. The seventh client indicated that what she discovered at this point in the session (which corresponded to the Meaning Bridge stage of the unfolding) was new, but she recalled the impact of "felt scared."

Finally, the findings for the Resolution stage of the model were the most convincing. The predicted impacts were endorsed by all three resolvers (i.e., 100%), and all were first endorsements. The impact of "problem clarification" that was indicated by one resolver at the Meaning Bridge point, and by another at the Resolution point, was probably qualitatively different at these two steps. The implications of this difference will be discussed later. The client who achieved what was referred to as an "options resolution" indicated that she "felt scared." It is of interest to note that, for the three other performances in which clients did not achieve a full resolution, the predicted impacts were indeed endorsed during recall at the point of the unfolding that corresponded to the clinical judge's indication of "partial resolution" or "a kind of resolution." The pathway to resolution from the client's point of view and the corresponding stages of the model for one resolver are presented in Table 3.4.

IPR Mood Ratings

Mood ratings obtained during the IPR session were examined in relation to the stages of the model. Shifts in mood were calculated, for each of the four steps, on the basis of the actual mood ratings at the point of recall that corresponded to the completion of that step as well as at the point just before it. The predicted negative shift in mood at the Vivid Reentry step was verified for all seven PRP performances. This negative mood shift, which for half of the performances was of three units or more, provided evidence from the client's perspective that a process of reentering the scene with a high level of arousal, as predicted by the model, was indeed taking place.

The clients' ratings of mood at the Meaning Bridge step failed to support the predicted shift in mood. First, the ratings by all of the clients were rather low (ranging from −4 to −1). Second, for two of the PRP performances, the mood rating at the Meaning Bridge was lower than the one at the Vivid

Table 3.4   Client's Pathway of the Resolution of Problematic
Reaction Point: CS7h

Client Impact (recalled during IPR)	Stage of the Model
Other (started to get into problem)	
Started real exploration	
Felt scared (didn't understand what was going on)	VIVID RE-ENTRY
Started real exploration	
Other (hard to talk about)	
Re-experiencing feelings	SALIENCE
Awareness of feelings	
[1]ap: Awareness of perception	
Re-examination	
Other (new awareness of reason for behaviour)	
Re-experiencing feelings	
Other (new to talk about)	
Started real exploration	
New self-understanding	MEANING BRIDGE
Alternative perspective	
Other (continued exploration)	
New self-understanding	
Other (realized there was a problem)	
Clarification of problem	RESOLUTION
ap: Alternative perspective	

[1]ap—also present impact

Reentry point, and, for two others, the mood ratings at both steps were identical.

At the point of Resolution, the predicted positive shift in mood was found in all three resolution performances. For the "options-resolution" client, the rise in mood appeared at the very end of the session, when she recognized "wants" and "needs." Two other clients who achieved partial resolution performances indicated the predicted rise in mood, although the third client who gained some new self-understanding indicated no shift in mood. The clients' ratings of mood at different points of the unfolding of the PRP, as recalled in the IPR, are presented graphically for two resolvers in Figures 3.1 and 3.2.

Summary of the Client's Perspective on the PRP Model

In the main, there was support for the predicted relationships between the steps of the performance model and the client's recall of impacts and shifts in mood during the unfolding of the problematic reaction. The information obtained from the clients by means of the conceptually based version of Interpersonal Process Recall (IPR) provides further verification of the steps of the model. The fit between the completion of the step of *Vivid Reentry,* as judged by the configuration of process measures, and clients' indication during recall of "reexperiencing of feelings" and "awareness of feelings," as well as a negative shift in mood, indicates that at this essential step the client reenters the scene and reexperiences the problematic feelings that arose in the situation. There is a caveat, however: If the therapist builds the scene in a rather technical manner and loses the exploratory stance, this could have a hindering impact on the client, as was the case for the client who indicated that she felt scared and was unsure about what was going on at that point in the session (see Table 3.4).

The data regarding the step of *Salience* were less clear. Although there was some indication that at this stage clients became aware of their own perception and thoughts, or reexperienced feelings, the criterion of the first endorsement was more difficult to achieve at this step of the model. In relation to this step, an unstructured recall format perhaps would have yielded more interesting results. No prediction was made regarding the ratings on clients' mood. A post hoc examination of the data, however, indicated that there were two clients who recalled higher mood at Salience than at Vivid Reentry and four clients who recalled the same mood rating or a lower rating (for one client, recall was unavailable for Salience). This suggests that, when clients become aware of what stood out for them in the situation and of their construal of it, they still tend to feel as they did in the original situation. Some also tend to continue to feel puzzled by their subjective construal or, as one client indicated, she "felt stuck" and was "questioning her reaction."

The findings on the IPR impacts for the Meaning Bridge indicate that at this step, in which, according to the model, the client becomes aware of the self-relevant impact of her own construal and/or inner reaction, clients recall that for the first time in the session they achieved a "new self-understanding." Similarly, they report the impacts of "alternative perspective" and "problem clarification." These client impacts support the conceptualization of the Meaning Bridge as the "point

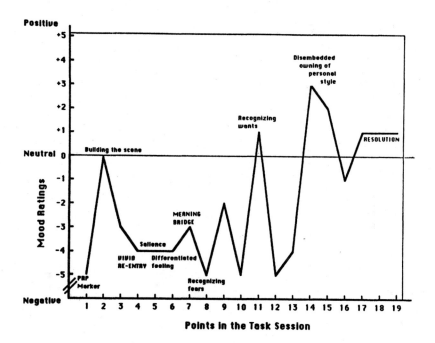

Figure 3.1. IPR Mood Ratings: CSIJ-PRP2

of no return," in the sense that some important new awareness that is relevant to the question posed by the problematic reaction has emerged. Nevertheless, the mood ratings indicate that, contrary to the prediction, clients still experience very little relief at this stage of the unfolding. Although some clients reported a decrease in negative feelings, others reported no change, and for some the discomfort increased.

In contrast, at the point of Resolution, the predicted shift in mood occurred and clients reported feelings of relief and optimism. This finding supports the notion that, even though clients do not necessarily feel that they have reached a problem solution, the new awareness and ownership of their mode of functioning and the process of stepping back and seeing it in the context of their life are experienced as an affective shift; this shift leaves them with the feeling that they have the power to change and grow. In addition, when clients experience a "problem clarification" at the Meaning Bridge, they most likely perceive the problem in a narrower context than at the point of Resolution and probably still feel over-

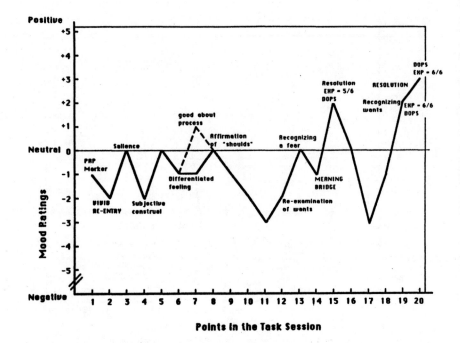

Figure 3.2. IPR Mood Ratings: CS7H-PRP2

whelmed and enmeshed in the issue. In contrast, the experience of problem clarification, when resolution has been achieved, is one in which there is a sense of having the power to come to grips with the problem.

In summary, the conceptually-based version of IPR provided a useful means for verifying the PRP performance model from the client's perspective. This demonstration that clients, who of course have no knowledge of the model, recall their experience in ways that fit the conceptualization of the processes leading to task resolution adds a certain degree of validity to the model.

Procedural and Methodological Issues and Problems

The Conceptually Based IPR methodology involves a number of procedural considerations. The first relates to the length of this procedure. Although the IPR session itself takes about 90 to 120 minutes and is not as time-consuming as Elliott's (1979) original procedure for identifying and describing significant events, the C-B IPR requires approximately two additional hours for the sampling of recall segments. In preparing for the IPR, a research assistant, who is knowledgeable and familiar with the model/micro theory of the change event, must view the whole task session, sample the segments (to be replayed to the client later), and indicate on the recall sheet the footage of where they appear on the tape. This process could be expedited, however, with experience and with greater familiarity with the model.

The second issue refers to the clients' choice of impacts. Although the list of impacts in our study provided a relatively structured way of obtaining the client's experience, sometimes it seemed unclear whether the client was using these impacts to mean what we understood them to mean. Furthermore, it remains unspecified as to the extent to which impacts that were endorsed more than once had the same flavor or degree of impact on the client at different points. To overcome this problem, it would be useful to ask clients to rate degree of impact on a 5-point rating scale, as was done in a recent study by Elliott and Shapiro (1988).

Finally, the use of the conceptually-based version of the IPR procedure may at times hinder the client's spontaneity of recall. In our work, it was found, for example, that, although some clients engaged more easily in recalling their experience of their own responses (e.g., "at that point I began to feel how much it affected me what happened the other day"), others were better able to recall their experiences of the therapist's intervention (e.g., "she really was able to zoom in on the problem"). Nevertheless, most clients in this research seemed to be able to refocus on themselves once they were so directed by the recall consultant. It should be noted, however, that in this study the change events were examined through the IPR method after the therapeutic working alliance (Bordin, 1979) seemed to have been established. Thus, in cases where the client-therapist relationship is at issue, it would make less sense to focus on model-specific client performances for their validation and analysis.

From a methodological standpoint, there is the issue of the reliability and validity of the IPR method. In a recent review of the literature, Elliott (1986, p. 523) concludes that IPR measures of therapist response quality and intentions are psychometrically adequate, but that they "are not as 'clean' as might be desired by methodological purists." To date, the reliability of the C-B version of the IPR has not been established. Although we followed a relatively standardized and structured procedure, there was still room for some variation both in the sampling and in the recall procedures. It is advisable therefore that future researchers use well-trained recall assistants who have had similar experiences with both the model and the procedure. Another factor is that assistants' interviewing styles need to be compared by listening to the audio recordings of the recall session. It probably would be infeasible to have clients undergo a recall session with two independent assistants for the purpose of obtaining interjudge reliability. It would be possible, however, to have the sampling procedure done by independent raters to establish its reliability across judges.

The validity of the C-B version of the IPR similarly has not yet been systematically studied. One possible direction suggested by the current research is that IPR ratings be obtained in conjunction with external judges' ratings of therapy process. For example, in this study, independent ratings of client's vocal quality (Focused voice), Experiencing (at level 6), and resolution were obtained for the same recall point at which the client indicated an impact of "new self-understanding" and a sharp rise in mood. This provided some support for the construct validity of the data derived from the C-B IPR method. The convergence between client judged impacts mediated through IPR and process ratings by external judges could, in turn, be viewed as providing evidence for the construct validity of the Client Vocal Quality system and the Experiencing Scale.

Finally, it should be noted that participation in an IPR session may affect the mental set of the respondent, who, in this case, is the client. Indeed, as will be discussed later in this chapter, the reactive aspect of this method may have some interesting clinical payoffs for the clients. Nevertheless, when employing the IPR method in an outcome study, it would be important to control for its possible effects by, for example, having clients in all conditions undergo the IPR procedure.

The Place of the Conceptually-Based Approach to IPR in an Integrated Research Paradigm

The conceptually-based approach to obtaining clients' own accounts of their in-therapy experiences via IPR was developed within the task-focused approach to the study of change events (Rice & Greenberg,

1984). In this approach, the clinician-researcher's micro theory of change provides the basis for the formulation of hypotheses regarding particular in-therapy client and therapist processes (Wiseman & Rice, 1989). In this sense, the C-B approach to IPR is primarily a theory-guided method for psychotherapy process research.

In using this approach to study the client's experience during the unfolding of problematic reactions, we were guided by the component steps or processes of change specified by the PRP model. Verification of these steps by the impacts and mood ratings endorsed by the client during recall, however, is only one part of the story that the client has to tell on the change event, whether or not it is the one we would like to hear. In other words, the "whole story" cannot be fully explored by a theory-guided approach alone. Although the clients in our study did provide independent confirmation that they indeed vividly reexperienced the troubling reactions triggered in the original situation, and that they reached a new self-understanding at resolution point, the question of whether or not clients perceived the steps of the model as necessary and important still remains unanswered.

In an attempt to answer this question and become aware of the client's "inner world" during the course of significant change events, Lowenstein (1989) used the grounded theory approach to analyze the tape-assisted recollections (see Rennie, this volume) of two PRP and two interpersonal conflict events. In this approach, clients are asked, at the beginning of the recall interview, to identify significant moments during the session when they may have perceived something differently or may have experienced a shift or, alternatively, may have felt hindered or impeded in their task. It is interesting that, for Lowenstein (1989), for all clients, the significant moment identified by the client was also the one identified by both the therapist and an expert clinical observer as representing resolution (or the closest approximation to resolution). This kind of evidence suggests that the study of clients' accounts of their phenomenological experiences (Rennie, 1990, this volume) could be an important source contributing to a more comprehensive understanding of the mechanisms underlying client change.

The conceptually based approach to the study of client's experiences of change events appears to fall in the middle of the continuum between the purely theory-based and purely client experience-based strategies of psychotherapy process research. It is guided by a micro theory of change and, as such, it is deductive; it is also somewhat more quantitative rather than qualitative in nature. In its pursuit of the client's experience, this approach is particularly appropriate for studies that set out to test model-based hypotheses, in either a group design or a small N study (Greenberg & Pinsof, 1986).

The methods presented in this chapter also could be employed to study similarities and differences between change events in different therapy orientations from the vantage point of the client's experience. Specifically, the list of client impacts could be expanded to include impacts that seem relevant to the study of particular micro theories of other change events (e.g., Greenberg & Safran, 1987) in other therapy orientations. Moreover, the Mood Rating Scale could be a potentially useful tool for the study of emotion in psychotherapy (Greenberg & Safran, 1989).

Implications for Clinical Practice

There are at least four distinct implications of the C-B IPR for clinical practice. The first is related to Kagan's original use of the IPR method as a tool for supervision. Reviewing the feedback received from clients via IPR was most enlightening to therapist-trainees struggling to master the techniques prescribed by the *Therapist Manual for Unfolding Problematic Reactions* (Rice, 1984b). At times, this feedback was encouraging and showed that skillful practice of the techniques led the client to successfully reexperience her reaction. At other times, however, it was painfully discouraging to find that the therapist failed to capture vividly the flavor of the client's experience or that the former was completely on the wrong track.

The second implication stems from the evidence we obtained from the mood scale, which confirms the effectiveness of evocative interventions (Rice, 1974) in getting clients to reexperience vividly feelings that were triggered in past problematic situations. The reevocation of the sights and feelings, initially experienced by the client, seems to activate an emotional schema that in turn elicits information that was not remembered before (Greenberg & Safran, 1987) and subsequently leads to the path for a real experiential search (Rice & Greenberg, in press).

The third implication relates to clients' accounts at the point of resolution. In contrast to the divergence across therapy orientations regarding techniques for achieving change, there seems to be more convergence regarding the conceptualization of what constitutes change or what it is that changes for the client in therapy. Goldfried and Padawer (1982, p. 16) suggest that a common clinical ingredient shared by all forms of therapy is that of helping clients/patients arrive at "an alternate way of looking at themselves, their behavior, and the world around them." The impacts that clients in the current study chose to describe the point of resolution are consistent with the above view of therapeutic change. Moreover, the IPR findings regarding clients' rise in mood, and their experience of feelings of relief and optimism at the point of resolution, support the notion that resolution involves a sense of having the power to change and grow. This ingredient of change has been discussed by theorists from diverse therapeutic orientations. For example, Luborsky (1984) refers to a similar process as an "increase in mastery." As one of the clients in the current study indicated during the IPR session: "I felt strength . . . satisfaction . . . I felt in control."

The final implication relates to the possible clinical payoff involved in using the IPR method with therapeutic change events. In my experience, viewing the videotape of a just-completed therapy session in which the PRP change event culminated in a resolution seemed to have a productive impact on the client. During the recall of resolution segments, some clients spontaneously reported to the recall consultant that, in viewing the tape, they became clearer about the discoveries they had made during the session. Similarly, some clients reported to their therapist in the session following the IPR that the recall session had consolidating effects on their experience. It would seem, therefore, that the high arousal and the relatively fast pace with which the PRP session is experienced (especially at the resolution point) make it difficult for some clients to process fully the new awareness that was achieved in the therapy session. Thus, in addition to being a productive research method, the IPR procedure may, with further work, also prove to be clinically useful as a means of getting clients to reprocess significant experiences in therapy.

Notes

1. Rice and Greenberg (in press) refer to five steps in the PRP model, the first one being "staying with the primary reaction."

2. The configuration in Lowenstein's (1985) study also included the Levels of Client Perceptual Processing (Toukmanian, 1986) as a fourth process measure.

References

Bordin, E. S. (1979). The generalizability of the psychoanalytic concept of the working alliance. *Psychotherapy: Theory, Research and Practice, 16*, 252-260.

Classen, C. (1989, June). *Self disembedding: A mechanism of change in psychotherapy.* Paper presented at the annual meeting of the Society for Psychotherapy Research, Toronto, Ontario.

Elliott, R. (1979). How clients perceive helper behaviors. *Journal of Counseling Psychology, 26*, 285-294.

Elliott, R. (1983). Fitting process research to the practicing psychotherapist. *Psychotherapy: Theory, Research and Practice, 20*, 47-55.

Elliott, R. (1984). A discovery-oriented approach to significant change events in psychotherapy: Interpersonal Process Recall and Comprehensive Process Analysis. In L. N. Rice & L. S. Greenberg (Eds.), *Patterns of change: Intensive analysis of psychotherapy process* (pp. 249-286). New York: Guilford.

Elliott, R. (1985). Helpful and nonhelpful events in brief counseling interviews: An empirical taxonomy. *Journal of Counseling Psychology, 32*, 307-322.

Elliott, R. (1986). Interpersonal Process Recall (IPR) as a psychotherapy process research method. In L. S. Greenberg & W. M. Pinsof (Eds.), *The psychotherapeutic process: A research handbook* (pp. 503-527). New York: Guilford.

Elliott, R., James, E., Shulman, R., & Cline, J. (1981, June). *Significant events in psychotherapy: A systematic case study.* Paper presented at the annual meeting of the Society for Psychotherapy Research, Aspen, CO.

Elliott, R., & Shapiro, D. A. (1988). Brief structured recall: A more efficient method for studying significant therapy events. *British Journal of Medical Psychology, 61*, 141-153.

Goldfried, M. R., & Padawer, W. (1982). Current status and future direction in psychotherapy. In M. R. Goldfried (Ed.), *Converging themes in psychotherapy* (pp. 3-49). New York: Springer.

Greenberg, L. S. (1984). A task analysis of interpersonal conflict resolution. In L. N. Rice & L. S. Greenberg (Eds.), *Patterns of change: Intensive analysis of psychotherapy process* (pp. 67-123). New York: Guilford.

Greenberg, L. S. (1986). Change process research. *Journal of Consulting and Clinical Psychology, 54*, 4-9.

Greenberg, L. S., & Pinsof, W. M. (1986). Process research: Current trends and future perspectives. In L. S. Greenberg & W. M. Pinsof (Eds.), *The psychotherapeutic process: A research handbook* (pp. 3-20). New York: Guilford.

Greenberg, L. S., & Safran, J. D. (1987). *Emotion in psychotherapy: Affect, cognition, and the process of change.* New York: Guilford.

Greenberg, L. S., & Safran, J. D. (1989). Emotion in psychotherapy. *American Psychologist, 44*, 19-29.

Hill, C. E., & O'Grady, K. E. (1985). List of therapist intentions illustrated in a case study and with therapists of varying theoretical orientations. *Journal of Counseling Psychology, 32*, 3-22.

Kagan, N. (1975). *Interpersonal Process Recall: A method of influencing human interaction.* Unpublished manuscript. (Available from N. Kagan, Farrish Hall, University of Houston, Houston, TX, 77004)

Kagan, N. (1980). Influencing human interaction: Eighteen years with IPR. In A. K. Hess (Ed.), *Psychotherapy supervision: Theory, research and practice*. New York: John Wiley.

Klein, M. H., Mathieu, P. L., Gendlin, E. T., & Kiesler, D. J. (1969). *The Experiencing Scale* (Vol. 1). Madison: Wisconsin Psychiatric Institute.

Klein, M. H., Mathieu-Coughlan, P. L., & Kiesler, D. J. (1986). The Experiencing Scales. In L. S. Greenberg & W. M. Pinsof (Eds.), *The psychotherapeutic process: A research handbook* (pp. 21-71). New York: Guilford.

Lowenstein, J. C. (1985). *A test of a performance model of problematic reaction points and an examination of differential client performances in therapy*. Unpublished master's thesis, York University, Toronto.

Lowenstein, J. C. (1989, June). *Change events in two experiential therapies: Preliminary returns from a qualitative analysis*. Paper presented at the annual meeting of the Society for Psychotherapy Research, Toronto, Ontario.

Luborsky, L. (1984). *Principles of psychoanalytic psychotherapy: A manual for supportive-expressive treatment*. New York: Basic Books.

Malan, D. H. (1976). *Toward the validation of dynamic psychotherapy: A replication*. New York: Plenum.

Rennie, D. L. (1990). Toward a representation of the client's experience of the psychotherapy hour. In G. Lietaer, J. Rombauts, & R. Van Balen (Eds.), *Client-centered and experiential therapy in the nineties* (pp. 155-172). Leuven, Belgium: Leuven University Press.

Rice, L. N. (1974). The evocative function of the therapist. In D. A. Wexler & L. N. Rice (Eds.), *Innovations in client-centered therapy* (pp. 289-312). New York: John Wiley.

Rice, L. N. (1984a). Client tasks in client-centered therapy. In R. Levant & J. Shlien (Eds.), *Client-centered therapy and the person-centered approach: New directions in theory, research and practice* (pp. 182-202). New York: Praeger.

Rice, L. N. (1984b). *Therapist manual for unfolding problematic reactions*. Unpublished manuscript, Counselling and Development Centre, York University, Toronto.

Rice, L. N., & Greenberg, L. S. (Eds.). (1984). *Patterns of change: Intensive analysis of psychotherapy process*. New York: Guilford.

Rice, L. N., & Greenberg, L. S. (1991). Two affective change events in client-centered therapy. In J. Safran & L. S. Greenberg (Eds.), *Emotion, psychotherapy and change* (pp. 197-226). New York: Guilford.

Rice, L. N., & Kerr, G. P. (1986). Measures of client and therapist vocal quality. In L. S. Greenberg & W. M. Pinsof (Eds.), *The psychotherapeutic process: A research handbook* (pp. 73-105). New York: Guilford.

Rice, L. N., Koke, C. J., Greenberg, L. S., & Wagstaff, A. K. (1979). *Manual of client vocal quality* (Vol. 1). Toronto: York University, Counselling and Development Centre.

Rice, L. N., & Saperia, E. P. (1984). Task analysis and the resolution of problematic reactions. In L. N. Rice & L. S. Greenberg (Eds.), *Patterns of change: Intensive analysis of psychotherapy process* (pp. 29-66). New York: Guilford.

Stiles, W. B., Shapiro, D. A., & Elliott, R. (1986). Are all psychotherapies equivalent? *American Psychologist, 41,* 165-180.

Toukmanian, S. G. (1986). A measure of Client Perceptual Processing. In L. S. Greenberg & W. M. Pinsof (Eds.), *The psychotherapeutic process: A research handbook* (pp. 107-130). New York: Guilford.

Wiseman, H. (1984). *Manual for the conceptually-based version of Interpersonal Process Recall (IPR)*. Unpublished manuscript, Department of psychology, York University, Toronto.

Wiseman, H. (1985, June). *Conceptually-Based Interpersonal Process Recall*. Paper presented at the annual meeting of the Society for Psychotherapy Research, Evanston, IL.

Wiseman, H. (1986). Single-case studies of the resolution of problematic reactions in short-term client-centered therapy: A task-focused approach. *Dissertation Abstracts International, 47*, 4669B.

Wiseman, H., & Rice, L. N. (1989). Sequential analyses of therapist-client interaction during change events: A task-focused approach. *Journal of Consulting and Clinical Psychology, 57*(2), 281-286.

4

Studying the Client's Perceptual Processes and Their Outcomes in Psychotherapy

SHAKÉ G. TOUKMANIAN

For more than a decade, diverse concepts advanced within the general framework of the information processing paradigm have been used in an attempt to clarify and/or describe the components and procedures of existing methods of psychotherapy in the language of cognitive psychology (e.g., Goldfried & Robins, 1983; Ingram & Hollan, 1986; Turk & Spears, 1983; Wexler & Rice, 1974; Winfrey & Goldfried, 1986). The potential of this paradigm as a conceptual tool or as a "methodology for theorizing" (Anderson & Bower, 1973, p.136) about the change processes occurring within the client's perceptual-processing system and about the ways in which therapists affect these processes on a moment-to-moment basis in experiential therapies has, however, not yet been fully explored in the realm of therapeutic psychology.

The objective of this chapter is to present a theory-guided program of psychotherapy research conducted within the framework of a schematic processing model of client perceptual organization and change. The chapter begins with a brief description of this model, followed by a portrayal of how it can be implemented to generate testable hypotheses in studies designed to explore the internal processes of client

77

change. The presentation then centers on data derived from research methods and strategies used to test the core assumptions of the model. The final section of the chapter deals with the implications of the findings for clinical practice and for future investigations along this line of process research.

Theoretical Framework

The construction of the perceptual-processing model of client change has been influenced by several information processing formulations advanced in experimental cognitive psychology and social cognition for the examination and understanding of the processes underlying a wide range of cognitive-affective phenomena (e.g., Anderson, 1981; Craik & Lockhart, 1972; Fiske & Taylor, 1984; Hayes-Roth, 1977; Neisser, 1976; Weimer, 1977). Although these approaches differ in focus and in type of constructs invoked to conceptualize various mental functions, collectively they represent a perspective on human functioning that is congruent with the basic tenets of phenomenological and constructivist perspectives on human change processes (e.g., Guidano & Liotti, 1983; Kelly, 1955; Mahoney, 1985).

An inherent feature common to most of these formulations is the belief that only a unitary, interactive, and constructive view of mental activity can lead us "to understand cognition as it occurs in the ordinary environment and in the context of natural purposeful activity" (Neisser, 1976, p. 7). A further suggestion in this regard is that the mental activity that performs this critical integrative function is perception (e.g., Craik & Lockhart, 1972; Leventhal, 1982; Linville, 1985; Neisser, 1967, 1976). Neisser (1976) contends, for example, that perceiving is the most fundamental cognitive act and maintains that the constructive nature of mental activity is the direct function of *schemata*, the dynamic structures of cognition that develop progressively through people's continuous interactions with the environment. From this perspective, perception is seen as a constructive developmental process that, at any given moment in time, reflects the perceiver's cognitive capability to detect, integrate, and give meaning to information on the basis of his or her past transactions with the world. These transactions, according to Neisser (1976, p. 11), "do not merely inform the perceiver, they also *transform* him" and as such they are seen to be the perceiver's own creation or construction of his or her experience of "reality."

In the perceptual-processing model, *perceiving* is broadly defined to refer to the act of construing and representing one's own view of "reality." In other words, it is maintained that the perceptual-processing system is where people's meanings regarding self and the world develop. In this sense, the model is consistent with constructivistic formulations of cognition (e.g., Guidano, 1984; Kelly, 1955; Mahoney, 1988; Weimer, 1977) in two important ways. First, it argues that *potentially* meaningful information is available in the environment—that events have an "affordance structure" (Gibson, 1966)—but that the meaning *of that information* is constructed by the individual. What is perceived therefore is not the object or the event per se but the meaning that a particular object or event has for the perceiver. Second, the model adopts a schematic developmental view of perception wherein perception is seen as a schema-driven construction that develops as its basic units (i.e., constructs or schemata), and links among these units develop, through experience, into qualitatively different cognitive meaning structures that have adaptive consequences for the perceiver (e.g., Fiske & Dyer, 1985; Hayes-Roth, 1977; Kelly, 1955; Taylor & Crocker, 1981).

Beyond this general proposition, the perceptual-processing model maintains that what people "see," or how they organize and integrate the elements of a given event into a cognitive representation, is the function of two interactive components of perceptual activity.[1] The first relates to the perceiver's schematic or "perceptual readiness," that is, the network of preexisting schemata invoked for the construction of the target event (e.g., Broadbent, 1977; Neisser, 1976); the second, to the particular mode of information processing that the perceiver brings to bear on the elements of the situation when formulating his or her experience of the event. From this perspective, perceptual development and change are seen to entail schematic or "structural transformations" (Mahoney, 1988) that *result from* the perceiver's enactment of qualitatively different mental operations on the information being processed. These operations range from the simple scanning and recognition of some features of a given event to operations that serve to elaborate, differentiate, and integrate information into more complex (i.e., conceptual, imagistic, and symbolic) cognitive representations of that event (e.g., Craik & Lockhart, 1972). The contention is that bringing a variety of mental operations to bear on the processing of information (internal or external) with respect to an event increases the probability for schemata associated with that event to undergo structural changes that in turn set the stage for further perceptual development along lines that "reality" offers.

The Role of Schemata in the Perceptual-Processing System

Schemata are typically thought of in the literature as hierarchically organized and interconnected networks of knowledge structures and/or content-free rules and procedures that people derive from experience and use for the anticipation and processing of new information (e.g., Fiske & Taylor, 1984; Winfrey & Goldfried, 1986). Although modern schema theories vary in their postulations of the specific nature and functions of schemata, there seems to be a general agreement that "schemata truly are the fundamental elements upon which all information processing depends" (Rumelhart, 1984, p. 162). In the current context, the term *schemata* refers to the structures underlying people's internal or mnemonic representations of prior experiences that serve as loosely organized frameworks for the anticipation of information specific to varying domains of experience.

A basic assumption of the model is that people begin life with some innate but crude and undifferentiated schemata that are responsible for the simple orienting responses observed in newly born infants (Neisser, 1976). Once individuals start interacting with the environment, these anticipatory structures become progressively embedded within each other to form complex and hierarchically organized constructions (see Kelly, 1955), each representing a different but related aspect of the particular event or situation experienced by the person.

A further contention is that schemata, activated by a given situation, prepare the individual to anticipate certain kinds of information for exploration. In this sense, schemata function to provide the individual with certain *possibilities* as to the nature of information that can be picked up from the field for processing. For example, perceiving somebody talking involves, in addition to the schema of someone talking, a variety of other anticipations, such as the authority of the speaker, facial expressions and gestures, and the environment surrounding the speaker. Each perceptual activity, set simultaneously in motion by these schemata, supports the others with the more extensive one often determining the direction and course of exploration and information that is picked up. In our example, if the schema of someone talking involves the anticipation of "seeing" more than a person moving his or her lips or making gestures (e.g., an internal representation of a speaker at a political rally), then that schema will direct exploration and information gathering for a different but overlapping set of anticipations. Thus the more complex the schematic structures with respect to an event, the broader will be the range of a person's explorations and consequently the higher the probability of noticing more of the available information. What individuals "attend to" and "select from" in a given context and at any given moment in time depends therefore on their schematic readiness, or on the network of structures that is available to them.

Modes of Perceptual Processing

Perceiving, like any other phenomenon, occurs within a time frame. As such, the time allotted to the processing of a given event for its representation as a unitary experience is an important dimension underlying the functioning of an individual's perceptual system. While the time required to perceive an event varies depending upon the characteristics of the individual (complexity of available schemata) and of the stimulus event, once established, the process becomes part of the perceiver's mode or manner of construing the event on subsequent occasions.

This perspective rests on two important considerations. First, it is postulated that people potentially are capable of engaging in a variety of mental activities that are learned and refined with experience (Neisser, 1967). These activities may be thought of as qualitatively different mental operations (e.g., scanning, elaboration, differentiation, integration) that, when brought to bear on information anticipated by schemata relevant to an event, influence how that event is construed or perceived by the individual. In this sense, the term *perceptual processing* refers to *both* the anticipation as well as the application of one or more of these mental operations to the information being processed.

Second, it is contended that, at any given moment in time, the elements of a given experience are processed in an "automated" or "controlled" manner (Shiffrin & Schneider, 1977). *Automated processing* refers to the very rapid, almost nonreflective, analysis of a few readily discernable elements of an event. This mode requires *minimal time and effort* from the perceiver in that it is carried out without conscious intent and without interfering with other mental activity (e.g., Bargh, 1982; Blumenthal, 1977; Posner, 1978). As such, it provides an efficient or economical way of dealing with highly familiar and redundant information. The controlled mode, on the other hand, is carried out more slowly. Once it is initiated, the perceiver engages in a variety of mental operations and performs a more reflective and deliberate exploration of a given situation; that is, he or she analyzes the information in more depth and develops a fuller or more differentiated representation of an experience. The contention here is that, although both modes are essential to human functioning, it is the controlled mode of processing that is instrumental in enhancing perceptual development and change.

To elaborate, initially most perceptual acts are carried out slowly and deliberately with schemata, activated by relevant information in a given context, setting the stage for the anticipation, exploration, and analysis of information from internal as well as external sources. Some elements of the situation may simply be detected or assimilated (in the Piagetian sense), leading to no major changes in schematic structures. Others may be subjected to different kinds of mental operations forcing "structural transformations" in the original schemata and hence in the construction of the experience analogous to Piaget's "accommodation." In either case, when the construction is repeated with frequent exposure to the same invariant information, perceptual activity becomes habitual. In social encounters, for instance, an extended hand is immediately perceived as a gesture for a handshake and a smile as a cordial greeting. In such situations, the individual engages in the activity "as if" automatically; his or her construction takes place predictably, based on a few readily recognizable cues that are processed very rapidly (within a fraction of a second) and without conscious intent. Automated processes thus may be thought of as perceptual "shortcuts" that render the diversity of available information more manageable for the perceiver. In this sense, they are seen to provide constancy and predictability to people's constructions of momentary experiences, a notion that corresponds to Kelly's (1955) characterization of "tight constructions" as constructs that "lead to unvarying predictions."

Thus, although automated processes are necessary components of perceptual activity, they do not contribute to perceptual development and change. As Blumenthal (1977, p. 14) notes, "The relative effectiveness of human behavior is the result of a varying ability to 'time share' mental operations or to alternate attentional focussings purposely and effectively." What this means is that relatively well-functioning individuals are prepared and able to engage in a variety of operations. Some of the operations provide the rapid detection of familiar or redundant information (i.e., automated processes). Others are performed within a time frame that is broad enough to allow a fuller exploration of the elements of a given situation (i.e., controlled processes). Thus, by bringing a predominantly controlled mode of processing to bear on most of the available information, individuals further their schematic development, leading them to generate a richer perspective when construing similar situations on subsequent occasions.

From this theoretical vantage point, an individual's attained level of perceptual development vis-à-vis a given domain may be thought of as a skill that is acquired and refined with experience. It involves learning to use and "time share" mental operations for the purpose of elaborating and differentiating the relevant structures and expanding the network of existing associations among them. In other words, it is suggested that, while schemata play an important role in determining the kind of information that can be anticipated and accepted into the individual's perceptual system, it is the extent of existing schematic *links* and *associations* that ultimately determines the range of alternative perspectives that the person is capable of generating when interacting with the environment (Toukmanian, 1990). In this sense, the precise course of people's perceptual development in a given domain of experience is seen to be the cumulative product of what they have actually *learned to do* with the information involved in their transactions with the environment, that is, the particular kinds of mental operations and networking strategies that they have learned to use for the construal of events entailed in particular domains of experience.

The Nature of Psychological Dysfunctions

How does the above model of perceptual organization and change contribute to our understanding of the nature of processes that mediate the development of psychological dysfunctions?

As noted earlier, a basic assumption underlying our model is that people's perceptions of everyday life events play a significant role in how they act and interact with their environment. This perspective implies that, by and large, maladaptive behaviors associated with particular classes of intra- and interpersonal events are difficulties related to perceptual dysfunctions; that is, such behaviors are symptomatic of "an underlying perceptual system that is developmentally arrested and restricted in the kind of information that it can accept and the way in which this information is processed" (Toukmanian, 1990, p. 311).

More specifically, the model maintains that the processing capabilities of an individual's perceptual system with respect to certain classes of events will be constrained by schematic and/or processing dysfunctions that may occur at any point in the course of its development. For example, the anticipation of an event based on simple or insufficiently developed schemata will impose limits on the information that can be anticipated and detected and hence on the way in which that event will be perceived and experienced. Similarly, subjecting the detected information to a very rapid or automated mode of processing (Shiffrin & Schneider, 1977), that does not allow the perceiver to analyze the elements of the situation in more depth (Craik & Lockhart, 1972), will maintain the existing schematic structures and the network of associations among them and subsequently hamper their potential development.

Extreme schematic dysfunctions are very rare except perhaps in severely restricted environments, such as in cases of sensory deprivation or social isolation, where there is a limited range of environmentally and internally available information. There are instances, such as a young man's or woman's experience with a first date, however, where no prior information based on an "enactive representation" (Bruner, 1964), or direct contact with the environment, is available to the person. Under these circumstances, the person's construction of the experience will be based on schemata relevant not to dating *per se*—although some anticipations based on "iconic" and "symbolic" representations (Bruner, 1964) may be present—but relevant to interpersonal encounters in general. Thus the less overlap there is between information contained in the dating situation and schemata associated with interpersonal encounters, the more "inappropriate" or limited these structures will be for the construction of the experience. In other words, the individual will be unable to make full use of the available information because of the lack of relevant organizing schemata. His or her perception will be based on a restricted range of information involving a few schemata that are only congruent with some elements of the situation. As such, elements that are contradictory and/or too diverse to be accommodated easily into the existing structures either will be largely ignored or will form the basis of new perceptual cycles that will develop and coexist independently of others, depending on the individual's subsequent experiences with heterosexual encounters. A person's confusion and inability to structure and make sense of seemingly dissonant aspects of an event is an example of the latter kind of perceptual activity.

An individual's perceptual development in a given domain of experience also may be hampered by processing dysfunctions. There are several reasons why the automated processing strategy is detrimental to perceptual development and change. First, because automated processes are "learned" through the perceiver's repeated exposure to familiar or redundant information, they are very difficult to modify unless they are deliberately interrupted or "deautomatized" (Shiffrin & Schneider, 1977). Second, because these habituated processes and the stereotypical behaviors associated with them are circumscribed to specific events and situations, their adaptive value is not generalizable to other events. When they occur out of context, they generally are dysfunctional or inappropriate for the construction of a particular experience. For example, automated processes associated with schemata of "rejection by an adult" learned in the context of parental relationships would lead a person to construe or infer rejection in most other adult interpersonal encounters "automatically," regardless of the particular nature of the situation.

Finally, although by and large adaptive, the construal of an event carried primarily through automated processes, even when it occurs within its appropriate context, restricts the subsequent development of the individual's perceptual system relevant to that event. In the above example, for instance, even when the interpersonal encounter perceived by the individual is truly one of rejection, the fact that the individual's perceptual activity is "short-circuited" or automated will drastically curtail the enactment of different kinds of mental operations on the information that already exists in his or her perceptual system. Consequently, the person's ability to bring about "structural transformations" and new links among these transformed structures will be hampered.

It is important to emphasize at this point that the issue with respect to perceptual dysfunctions is not one of controlled versus automated processing. Rather, it is the extent to which perceptual activity associated with certain kinds of important life events is automatized and the level of perceptual development at which automatization has taken effect (Toukmanian, 1986). The contention here is that, the earlier the onset of automatization, the more inadequate will be the perceiver's construal of an event and therefore the more debilitating his or her perceptual system is likely to be vis-à-vis that event.

The onset of automatization early on in a person's history of perceptual development arrests the elaboration of schematic structures at simple and undifferentiated levels. Perceptions based on such limited constructions are by necessity categorical, incomplete, or superficial and the behaviors associated with them highly routinized and predictable. For example, a student who perceives taking a final examination for a course as a life or death situation and who finds the reaction incomprehensible may be thought of as an individual with such a history of perceptual development. Success or failure at the task has a categorical meaning for the student. There are no other elements in his or her perceptual system regarding the situation and self in the situation to allow him or her to construe the experience more flexibly or differently. In other words, the student lacks the perceptual skills with which to explore the nuances of his or her perceptual field more thoroughly and in a manner that leads him or her to arrive at a potentially more functional perspective.

Automatization also may occur at relatively more advanced levels of perceptual development, in which more elaborated and complex schemata direct perceptual activity. Here there is a broader range of anticipations of environmental and internal information that, nevertheless, are organized and represented repeatedly in the same highly structured and predictable manner. In this sense, although the individual appears to scan the field reasonably well, automatization precludes the introduction of new elements and/or the "flexible networking" of old ones to allow the person to broaden his or her outlook on the event. An example of this kind of perceptual dysfunction is seen in people who manifest an "ability to see" varying aspects of an issue independently but who fail to restructure and integrate these into new or alternative perspectives.

An essential feature of the above conceptualization is that inappropriate or maladaptive behaviors associated with certain classes of events are the function of people's automated and/or invariant constructions. It should be kept in mind that, within this framework, the term *information* refers both to what is available for the individual in the outside world and to the internal representations of his or her past experiences with the world. Of particular importance to the therapeutic context in this regard are people's schematic representations of self and their affective reactions contained in their construal of events across a wide range of situations and contexts. These schematic representations perform the crucial function of linking the individual to his or her external environment. When invoked, they feed into and become inextricably embedded in the person's idiosyncratic representations of intra- and interpersonal events and as such play a significant and often pervasive role in determining how these events will be perceived and experienced. Thus it may be stated that, while the prevalence of automated processes is, by and large, detrimental to people's perceptual development in a particular domain of experience, it is the automatization of perceptual activity associated with the processing of information relevant to *self* and to *internal* arousal states that appears to be the main source of perceptual dysfunctions hampering people's adaptive functioning and, consequently, their personal growth and development.

The processing of self-relevant information. Within the social cognition literature, the "self" is commonly conceived of as a complex system of hierarchically organized networks of cognitive structures that are associated with both the general and the more situation-specific aspects of an individual's representations or conceptions of self. Self-schemata may thus be seen as "personal identity structures" (Guidano, 1984). When invoked, they provide the individual with a rich and consistent source of autobiographical information that is potentially readily available to the person across a wide range of everyday life situations. Because of the apparent "sameness" of these situations (e.g., interpersonal encounters), however, some of these structures run the risk of being repeatedly activated and consequently becoming chronically accessible (e.g., Bargh, Bond, Lombardi, & Tote, 1986; Higgins & King, 1981). The processing of information associated with such structures will be highly susceptible to becoming automated and hence to being resistant to change and development. This in turn will sustain the person's self-referenced impressions, evaluations, and judgments, independent of situation and context. Thus, in spite of the availability of other more varied and idiosyncratic self-representations, the individual will tend to act upon and interact with the environment only through a few relatively undifferentiated and restricted networks of personal identity structures. And when events are formulated from this limited and ostensibly external frame of reference, the individual's construals typically will be devoid of his or her felt sense of the *I* or *me*, resulting in experiences that are less than personally meaningful or satisfying.

The processing of emotion. Consistent with recent theoretical formulations, the perceptual-processing model maintains that emotions represent a class of schemata that are associated with internal arousal states. These structures serve to anticipate, organize, and give meaning to information in a given situation that elicits internal reactions; they develop through experience and are inherent in the perceptual-processing system (e.g., Greenberg & Safran, 1987; Leventhal, 1982, 1984; Neisser, 1976). The model further maintains that arousal states, as physiologically based and internally generated information, constitute the "affective component" of the total pool of available information surrounding a given event. When detected and processed along with other elements of the situation, this information becomes an integral part of the individual's construction of the event. Perceptual activity initiated by emotion schemata become embedded within other simultaneously occurring perceptual acts, each representing a different aspect of the event and each feeding into and modifying the event's construction and representation. It is in this sense therefore that the "experience of emotion" is said to be "contextual" (Schachter & Singer, 1962), that is, construed in the context of and in relation to the other components of perceptual activity. Thus, to the extent that emotion schemata are part of an individual's schematic record (i.e., history of past experiences with the same or similar events), they will have a relatively insignificant, moderate, or extensive influence on how a given event will be construed and experienced.

This perspective suggests, therefore, that people's experienced difficulties with certain classes of intra- and interpersonal events inevitably involve perceptual dysfunctions that, partially at least, are associated with the processing of the affective components of their experiences. In other words, the perspective suggests that, when people are frequently exposed to situations that elicit emotions (positive or negative), they will gradually learn to process this rich pool of internally available information "automatically" or with minimum time and effort. As environments provide similar but almost never identical information (internal or external), however, the prevalence of automatization in this respect impedes people's ability to analyze the affective elements of their experiences in more depth, resulting in incomplete construals (e.g., when clients talk about personal problems without an apparent "awareness" of their emotional reactions) or in construals that are "inappropriate" for the specifics of a given situation as, for example, in Rice's (this volume; Rice & Saperia, 1984) characterization of "problematic reactions."

To summarize, the perceptual-processing approach maintains that difficulties experienced by clients are, by and large, the function of their inability to "take in" and process the elements of their experiences more fully and in ways that would help them generate different and potentially more functional perspectives. This inability is seen to stem from perceptual dysfunctions that are associated mainly with the processing of events (both internal and external) in an automated fashion. As this processing strategy impedes the enactment of qualitatively different mental operations, it hinders schematic development and results in rather simple and undiscriminating construals that have limited generalizability and functional value. Being based on developmentally stunted networks of schemata, such construals have neither the breadth nor the flexibility with which to accommodate the exigencies of varying life circumstances. As such, they lead to experiences that are vague, discomforting, devoid of personal meaning, and hence unsatisfactory for the individual.

The Identification of Perceptual Dysfunctions

Before discussing the implications of the above conceptualization for psychotherapy research, it is necessary to show how this perspective can be used to identify dysfunctional patterns of client perceptual processes in therapeutic transactions. The discussion in this section will focus therefore on the following two questions: (a) What is the interface between the model's postulated targets of therapy and clinically relevant factors that are manifest in clients' performances both within and across therapy sessions? and (b) How is therapeutic change defined or what is the unit of analysis that needs to be focused on and studied when investigating this phenomenon in experiential therapy?

It is important to remember that, when evaluating clients' in-therapy level of perceptual functioning, the focus is not on *what* clients perceive but on *how* they perceive or go about formulating their thoughts and feelings when they express themselves in therapy. In this sense, the identification of perceptual dysfunctions may be thought of as a process diagnostic endeavor (Toukmanian, 1983) wherein inferences are made about covert phenomena on the basis of indicators manifested in clients' dialogue in therapy. The approach requires, therefore, that we make two basic assumptions. The first assumption is that clients' internal representations (i.e., images, thoughts, impressions) of disturbing experiences are the *products* (Toukmanian, 1983, 1990; see also Ingram & Kendall, 1986) of their experientially learned *ways* of constructing or perceiving "reality." Second, it is assumed that the manner in which clients talk about their difficulties is the most accessible index of how they organize and make sense of information regarding self and self in relation to significant others and situations in their environments.

The identification of perceptual dysfunctions can be organized in terms of two observable client factors, each reflecting one of the two fundamental activities performed by the perceptual processing system outlined earlier in this chapter: the determination of (a) the nature and/or range of information that clients attend to and use in their reports of a given experience and (b) the kind of mental operations that they use to describe the experience. The first is seen to be related to the network of schemata involved for the *anticipation* of information; the second, to the processing mode or strategy employed for the *transformation* of information into an internal representation. These two client factors can be further subdivided into their respective components and organized into several processing patterns or configurations, each pattern depicting a particular class of information (e.g., self- or other-referenced, diverse, restricted) and type of mental operation (e.g., recognition, scanning, differentiation, evaluation).

To date, seven therapeutically relevant patterns or clusters of these factors have been identified and used in the development of the Levels of Client Perceptual Processing (LCPP) measure. As this work has been presented in some detail elsewhere (Toukmanian, 1986), it will not be reviewed here. Suffice it to say that, in varying combinations, these client "process markers" (Rice & Greenberg, 1984) are discernible from the differential quality of clients' discourse, some being featured more prominently than others at different points during the course of therapy. For example, in early sessions, one is more likely to find a preponderance of patterns involving simple recognition and scanning types of mental operations in conjunction with other-referenced, external, or "factual" information. Configurations of more complex operations (e.g., differentiation, integration) involving internal or affect-related and self-referential information appear, on the other hand, to be more typical of the later stages of productive psychotherapy. Thus, by examining the structural characteristics that are featured predominantly in clients' discourse, it is possible to infer where they are with respect to their level of processing within a given domain.

The marker identification procedure is, however, more than a diagnostic technology. It also represents a conceptually-based method of specifying and/or isolating the basic units of analysis for process research. In other words, to the extent that there is an inferred relationship between the component processes of the model and the manifest features of clients' manner of responding, the approach provides the psychotherapy researcher with a set of model-specified guidelines by which productive and unproductive client in-therapy performances can be contextualized (as events or episodes) for process analysis. The implications of this procedure for psychotherapy research will be the topic of discussion in the section that follows.

Research

The main goal of our psychotherapy research program has been to see whether the above model of client perceptual organization and change is valid as a conceptualization and adequate in its specification of clients' internal processes mediating change in experientially oriented psychotherapies. In this work, we have endeavored (a) to test the core assumptions of the model concerning the process of schematic change and its consequences under both laboratory and naturalistic conditions and (b) to determine whether or not the model's hypothesized processes of client change are entailed in therapeutic episodes that are specified as "significant change events" from the vantage point of perspectives other than the perceptual-processing viewpoint.

Hypothesis Testing Research Strategies

Except for a few laboratory-based studies (e.g., Sander, 1990), most research conducted within this framework has been carried out in the context of the perceptual-processing method of experiential therapy (Toukmanian, 1990). This manualized approach requires that therapists use specific kinds of process-directed interventions at various client "markers" that, according to the model, indicate the presence of different kinds of processing difficulties. The main goal here has been to see whether or not engaging clients in certain kinds of model-specified mental operations does in fact increase the complexity of clients' schematic structures and lead to perceptual modifications that have adaptive consequences.

By and large, the basic strategy used in this type of research has been the pretest-treatment-posttest control group design. From this vantage point, we have been able to investigate the phenomenon of change on three levels of analysis: (a) the structural changes brought about in clients' self-schemata as a result of therapy, (b) the kinds of mental operations associated most often with productive segments or sessions of therapy, and (c) the relationship between clients' acquired level of in-therapy perceptual functioning and treatment outcome.

Research methods and procedures. Our research participants generally have been recruited from the population of self-referred clients at a university counseling center, with the treatment group consisting of recruits from clients seeking individual therapy and the control group from those participating in various self-help and skills-training group programs. All therapists have had specialized training in the perceptual-processing method of therapy, and random "manipulation checks" have been performed to ensure the treatment's integrity.

Typically, our research has involved three broad classes of data collection methods and procedures. First, we have used a standard battery of self-report measures (consisting of the Beck Depression Inventory, the Tennessee Self Concept Scale, the State-Trait Anxiety Inventory, and the Social Adjustment Scale) to obtain global assessments of treatment outcome.

Second, we have employed the Levels of Client Perceptual Processing measure (LCPP) to examine clients' processing strategies and depth of involvement in therapy. The LCPP (Toukmanian, 1986) is a treatment-specific coding system. It consists of seven mutually exclusive categories, each category representing a particular kind of processing pattern referred to earlier in this chapter. These patterns can be observed and categorized, with reasonably high interjudge agreement, from the structural characteristics of clients' in-therapy discourse. In our hypothesis testing studies, the strategy has been to use verbatim transcriptions either of early and late therapy sessions or of sessions nominated by the client and/or an expert clinician as having been productive. Thus, by comparing data obtained from segments of early and late therapy sessions and from segments of nominated versus randomly selected sessions, we have been able to test the appearance of various processing patterns that are predicted by our model to be essential for client change and therapeutic improvement.

Finally, with the assumption that schematic processing and change occur out of awareness and are not fully accessible to self-reports, we have also used various theory-relevant research methods and procedures to evaluate pre- to posttreatment structural changes in clients' self- and other-related schemata. For example, Crockett's (1965) 8-Role Category Questionnaire (8-RCQ), which is derived from Kelly's (1955) theory of personal constructs, has been a frequently used method in our research. As constructs are conceptually similar to the notion of schemata, this instrument has provided a relatively simple way of assessing the therapeutic impact on clients' level of cognitive complexity, that is, the degree of schematic differentiation attained as a result of therapy. This measure requires that respondents describe eight individuals known to them, in point format and within a three-minute period per category. A respondent's cognitive differentiation score is the total number of *different* descriptors used across the eight stimulus persons, with higher scores indicating the presence of a more complex or differentiated cognitive system than lower scores.

A second method has entailed obtaining self-referential ratings from clients on a set of positively and negatively toned adjectives. In this technique, respondents are provided with two five-point rating scales per adjective and are asked first to indicate the degree to which the adjective is descriptive of them and then to rate the same attribute for its perceived degree of helpfulness in interpersonal relationships. Two scores are derived from this procedure. The *self-perception* score is the percentage of positive and negative adjectives that the respondent endorses as being "extremely" or "highly" self-descriptive. The *perceptual congruence* score is the value obtained by correlating, for each respondent, the two sets of ratings across all the adjectives. This score represents the extent to which an individual's own recognized attributes of self (i.e., self-schemata) correspond with his or her general perceptions of them as being functional or dysfunctional in interpersonal contexts. The assumption here is that, when therapy is indeed successful in facilitating the development of clients' self-schemata, there will be (a) a decrease in negative self-schema content and (b) an increase in the value of the congruence score, reflecting a construal of self that is more flexible in recognizing and accepting a broader range of self-relevant information vis-à-vis the interpersonal environment.

We also have attempted to evaluate self-schema change by means of experimental procedures adapted from the recent literature on social cognition. One such strategy has entailed asking participants to make self-referential judgments on a set of positive and negative personal trait adjectives that are randomly presented on a personal computer, programmed to record yes/no decisions and reaction times for each adjective. This procedure yields a frequency score for self-referent decisions and two average reaction time or latency scores, one for each of the positive and negative self-referent judgments. According to the theoretical arguments advanced in the self-schema literature (e.g., Markus, 1977; Markus & Kunda, 1986; Markus & Sentis, 1982), the efficiency or speed with which individuals make self-referential judgments is the function of a well-established system of self-schemata. Thus, when using this procedure prior to and again shortly after a given treatment, the assumption is made that changes in the latency of respondents' self-referential judgments reflect the effects of the treatment, with shorter reaction times indicating a more integrated self-system.

Results. In the main, the pattern of results emerging from our hypothesis testing research has provided support for the model's central tenets concerning the structural and processing changes expected of clients exposed to the perceptual-processing method of therapy. Given the fact that most of our studies have involved relatively small samples of clients (n = 12 to 18), however, the findings summarized in this section should be viewed as tentative and exploratory.

We have found that the complexity of self- and other-relevant schemata and level of self-concept, for clients receiving this treatment, is significantly greater than for those involved in self-enhancement group training programs (Toukmanian, 1988; Toukmanian & Grech, 1991; Toukmanian & Roese, 1989). By and large, we also have found evidence indicating that clients do in fact change their processing strategies in the manner and direction specified by the model. Although our results have shown some individual variations, the patterns emerging from several studies (e.g., Toukmanian, 1986; Toukmanian & Grech, 1991; Zink, 1990) have been consistent in demonstrating that clients process their experiences at a more complex, internally differentiating, reevaluating, and integrating level in later than in earlier therapy sessions. As well, we have found that clients who gain more from their therapeutic experience are more likely to engage in these complex mental operations than those for whom therapy is less successful (Toukmanian & Grech, 1991).

Our response-by-response evaluations of clients' discourse on the LCPP have further revealed that responses reflecting an internally focused differentiation of self- and affect-related information almost always precede responses that are reevaluating and integrating in their focus (Toukmanian & Grech, 1991). This observed sequence of processing supports our model's basic proposition that clients need to learn to differentiate the elements of their own "felt sense" of an experience in a "controlled manner" before they become aware of their perceptual resources and "see" the possibility that they can reconstruct the experience and thus perceive it differently (Toukmanian, 1990).

The Analysis of Therapeutic Episodes

In this line of research, we have used the strategy of the "events paradigm" (Rice & Greenberg, 1984) to study specific types of therapeutic episodes for evidence regarding the kinds of change processes that are postulated by our model of client change. Procedurally, we have worked with this approach in the following way. First, we have selected a theoretical perspective or a source, other than the perceptual-processing model, to identify the "change event" to be studied. Second, we have used quantitative and/or qualitative methods to describe the processes underlying the "event" in as much detail as possible. Finally, we have evaluated the same material on the LCPP and examined the convergence or divergence of key client processes across perspectives.

To illustrate, in one of our recent investigations (Toukmanian & Dunbar, 1991), we sought to determine (a) whether our model's conception of client change, as measured by the LCPP, would discriminate between conflict resolution and nonresolution client performances in Gestalt two-chair dialogue (Greenberg, 1984) and (b) whether the use of this measure would enhance our understanding of the components of the resolution process in this method of therapy. The events studied were the nine resolution and nine nonresolution client performances described by Greenberg in this volume. The 20 client statements contained in each of these 18 two-chair dialogues were previously rated on three process measures (the Experiencing Scale, the Client Vocal Quality Classification System, and the Structural Analysis of Social Behavior). These were then used to analyze and compare resolvers' and nonresolvers' performance patterns with respect to the "standards and values," "felt wants," and "softening" components of Greenberg's (1984) intrapersonal model of conflict resolution. (For details, see Greenberg's chapter in this volume.)

In our study, the same 20 statements from each of the 18 two-chair dialogues were coded on the LCPP by an expert rater. A second trained rater evaluated one third of this material. Both were blind as to the nature and purpose of the study. They worked from typewritten transcriptions that were presented in random order. The absolute proportional agreement between the two judges on the 120 client statements was .71 and the corresponding Kappa coefficient was .67 ($p < .001$).

The analyses revealed that resolution and nonresolution performances were significantly different on the occurrence of a Level V or above rating on the LCPP. We found that "resolvers" as a group engaged in more internally differentiating, reevaluating, and integrating types of mental operations than "nonresolvers." Furthermore, when the LCPP ratings for the "values and standards" performance pattern (statements of the disaffiliative "harsh critic") was compared with the "felt wants" (elaborations of the problem prior to change point) and the "softening" (open expressions of feelings and experiences *following* change point) patterns for "resolvers," it was found that the latter two patterns were significantly different than the former on clients' attained level of perceptual processing ($p < .001$). Results showed that, while none of the responses in the "values and standards" pattern received a rating of Level V or above on the LCPP, a significant proportion of all responses in the "felt wants" and "softening" patterns was rated as internally differentiating, reevaluating, or integrating in focus (i.e., Levels V, VI, and VII, respectively). These findings seem to indicate that the component processes of conflict resolution performances in Gestalt therapy can be identified reliably by the LCPP. They further suggest that the LCPP (and by implication the conceptual framework on which it is based) is tapping some fundamental dimensions of the change process that may also occur at various critical moments in other experiential psychotherapies.

In view of recent evidence indicating that metaphors perform a useful function in psychotherapy, a second study (Sinclair, 1990) in this line of research attempted to see whether clients differed in the way they processed their experiences before, during, and after two types of metaphoric events: conjunctive and disjunctive. Following Angus's specification, the former was defined as a communication involving a metaphor that was elaborated in such a way that it promoted a deepened understanding between client and therapist, while the latter was one that led to a mutual misunderstanding (Angus, 1986, this volume; Angus & Rennie, 1988).

In this study, we used a combination of qualitative and quantitative research methods to collect the data. First, 12 metaphor events were selected, from one of the middle sessions of six therapy dyads, one therapist- and one client-generated per case. The procedure entailed selecting interactions that, on the basis of clinical judgment, appeared to be crucial to the exploration of the client's interpersonal issues and then identifying, within these interactions, a metaphor that encapsulated the issues being explored. Each metaphor sequence contained a metaphor or metaphor phrase plus enough of the interaction preceding and following the metaphor to make the sequence comprehensible as a unit. Client responses in the 12 units selected in this manner were rated on the LCPP. Responses occurring in the two minutes immediately preceding and immediately following the metaphor sequence were also rated and used as control segments. In addition, data on the strength of the therapeutic alliance in these sessions were obtained from both clients and therapists using Horvath's (1981) Working Alliance Inventory (WAI).

The specification of a metaphor sequence as conjunctive or disjunctive was accomplished by means of an Interpersonal Process Recall (IPR) interview (Kagan, 1975) conducted with each participant subsequent to the target session. This method was consistent with Angus's (1986) indication that a metaphoric interaction could be categorized as conjunctive or disjunctive only by gaining access to each participant's implicit meanings associated with such an interaction. Procedurally, both client- and therapist-generated metaphoric units of analysis were replayed for each participant separately, within 24 hours of the target session. After each unit was replayed, the audiotape was stopped and the participant was asked to recall her experience at that moment in therapy. At these points, the interviewer asked a series of open-ended questions designed to elicit the thoughts, impressions, and visual images that occurred to the interviewee during the therapy session in relation to the sections replayed on audiotape.

The analyses revealed that, regardless of whether the source of metaphor was the client or therapist, clients' manner of processing before, during, and after *disjunctive* events was predominantly low, involving only simple recognition and scanning types of mental operations that were external or factual in their focus. Although the processing was similarly low before *conjunctive* metaphoric events, evidence showed that typically clients' exploration of a given experience *during* such events was carried out through internally focused differentiating, reevaluating, and integrating types of mental operations and that there was a spillover of this higher level of processing *after* the event. Results also indicated, however, that this pattern was only consistent in dyads for whom both metaphoric events were either conjunctive or disjunctive. For dyads with mixed types of metaphors, the pattern of client processing tended to be predominantly low regardless of type of metaphoric event. Furthermore, a cursory inspection of the Working Alliance Inventory scores revealed that, in general, conjunctive dyads tended to rate the strength of the therapeutic alliance highly, disjunctive dyads less highly, while conjunctive/disjunctive dyads were mixed in their evaluation of the alliance. These results suggest that, although meaning-conjunctive metaphors appear to play a critical role in facilitating a shift from a predominantly low to a predominantly high level of client processing, this shift may have been mediated by the quality of the therapeutic relationship. More important, however, the findings do indicate that, regardless of the direction of the shift, the LCPP is capturing some of the subtleties of this process and that these are verifiable through the clients' own reports in the IPR interview of the experience of conjunction or disjunction.

Together, the evidence from the above two studies suggests that our model's hypothesized processes of client change are also those that are centrally involved in the processing of at least two different kinds of important episodes of therapy. Furthermore, considering that these processes are conceptualized to represent change on the level of clients' internal mental operations, the evidence also suggests that whatever it is that is being tapped by the LCPP is on the basic level of clients' information processing operations. If this indeed is the case, then their specification in other contexts and in relation to other kinds of change events may greatly enhance our understanding of what actually happens within the client to bring about change in psychotherapy.

Implications

What have we learned from our efforts at conceptualizing and evaluating the processes of client change from the standpoint of the perceptual-processing model of therapy? What are the implications of this work for psychotherapy practice?

Implications for Practice

One of the main advantages of working from the framework of a model of perceptual organization and change has been the conceptual specificity that it has provided for the development of the perceptual-processing method of experiential therapy (Toukmanian, 1990). The therapeutic goals and strategies advocated by this approach stem directly from the model's assumptions about the processes that mediate client change. This interface between theory and method has also proven to be extremely helpful in the development of a training manual and of a coding system for evaluating therapists' adherence, as research participants, to the treatment's recommended strategies.

As a client process-oriented system, this approach to therapy is not constrained by the assumptions of a particular theory of personality requiring, for example, that clients learn to interpret "reality more correctly" or engage in the rational analysis of their "faulty logic" or learn various fact finding strategies to collect evidence to disprove "erroneously" held assumptions about causal relationships (e.g., Beck, 1976; Ellis, 1962). Rather, with its focus on process, this method gives clients a considerable degree of latitude to set their own therapeutic agenda and explore a broad range of life experiences without fundamentally affecting either the goals or the progression of therapy. In fact, informal reports from clients at termination have repeatedly informed us that this "handing over the controls" is one of the most valuable components of their therapeutic experience. Clients also appear to appreciate the fact that, although often frustrating, the therapist's attempts at *getting them to do* their own explorations and discovery of alternative ways of "seeing" and interpreting events in their lives is a "liberating" experience. As one of my clients told me, "I now have the choice of seeing things differently . . . not jumping into conclusions . . . being able to give people the benefit of the doubt . . . even to hold on to some of my old habits . . . views . . . if I choose to . . . yeah . . . that's what I have learned . . . and you know, I think it will work." What the client was alluding to in this instance was an awareness that there was a fundamental change in how she construed self in relation to others and a sense that she could rely on her own inferential capabilities in the future to arrive at satisfactory resolutions of problems.

Research Implications

To date, our conceptually guided research has served us well in a number of important ways. First, it has opened up the possibility of studying the process of therapeutic change on the level of clients' internal mental operations, a dimension that has received scant attention but that needs to be studied more intensely if we are to have a more thorough understanding of the mechanisms underlying client change. Second, it has given us the flexibility to test its validity in a variety of contexts and from the vantage point of different research paradigms. As noted earlier, initially it was important for us to undertake research of the hypothesis testing variety and to use aggregate designs to obtain probabilistic estimates of the processes and constructs being studied. To the extent that this strategy allowed us to confirm the general parameters of our model, we then moved to more focused explorations of its basic assumptions through the analysis of specific kinds of clinically relevant therapeutic episodes. The interplay between these two investigative strategies has generated a wealth of information and a number of challenging new directions for future research, two of which are elaborated below.

We have learned from one of our laboratory studies (Sander, 1990), for example, that the demands put on the perceptual-processing system by positive and negative self-discrepant experiences may differ and that these need to be specified and delineated more clearly by the model. Briefly, this study attempted to evaluate the impact of an experimental manipulation, derived from the model, on the content and processing efficiency of nondepressed and mildly depressed subjects' self-schemata. This involved having participants engage in the guided recall (i.e., controlled processing) of positively or negatively toned personal experiences that were known to be discrepant with their self-perceptions. The expectation based on the model was that participants' deliberate search for and enactment of different kinds of perceptual-processing operations on information that did not fit or was inconsistent with their self-conceptions would increase the positive content and enhance the processing efficiency of their self-schemata. This prediction was upheld, regardless of participants' level of depression, but only for those in the positive self-discrepant recall condition.

Following the arguments advanced by some expectancy models (e.g., Carver & Scheier, 1986; Kanfer & Hagerman, 1981), one can speculate that participants' favorable or unfavorable expectations for the outcome of the task may have played an important role in the processing of these two types of experiences. Although little can be said with certainty, it may be that, when the expectancy of seeing oneself in a situation is self-discrepant but favorable (i.e., positive self-discrepant recall), people are more likely to engage in the processing of a wide range of self-referential information to resolve the discrepancy and achieve positive self-perceptions. When the expectancy is unfavorable (i.e., negative self-discrepant recall), however, they may be more inclined to disengage or refrain from additional processing and consequently maintain their existing self-perceptions (Carver & Scheier, 1986).

The expectancy factor may also have been operative in Sinclair's (1990) disjunctive dyads, described earlier in this chapter. As it will be recalled, her analysis of metaphoric episodes revealed that only meaning-conjunctive metaphors, occurring within conjunctive-only dyads, were associated with the model's specified processes of client change. In other words, when conjunctive metaphors occurred within conjunctive/disjunctive dyads, the clients' patterns of processing were found to be similar to those involved in the processing of disjunctive metaphors. It may be that a client's experience of disjunction, as a perceived instance of being misunderstood by the therapist (e.g., "she does not understand what I am talking about"), is an occasion that, at least temporarily, sets an unfavorable expectancy about the outcome of the therapeutic task (e.g., "what's the use . . . I cannot make myself understood"), thus blocking the client from further attempts at exploring his or her perceptions of a given experience on deeper or more productive levels of analysis.

The above perspective also suggests that a self-regulatory mechanism or an element of intentionality (Martin, this volume; Rennie, this volume) may have been at play in both sets of data. In any event, it is clear that more focused studies that combine quantitative and qualitative research methods are required for an in-depth exploration and understanding of the effects of these variables on the processes of client change. Such efforts may eventually indicate ways in which some of these elements may be incorporated into the perceptual-processing model and suggest possible links between it and other cognitively based process-oriented conceptualizations of psychotherapy (see Martin, this volume).

The second line of research relates to the improvement of our process and outcome assessment procedures. With respect to the former, evidence showing that the LCPP can be applied reliably to capture and represent our model's key process constructs has been extremely encouraging. Inasmuch as client change processes may vary with type of treatment and/or psychological disorder, however, further research is needed to determine whether this instrument can also be used as a valid process measure across different client populations and methods of therapy.

Furthermore, the various patterns of client processing depicted by the LCPP need further research attention. As noted earlier, the categories of this coding system have been designed, in accordance with the model, to capture the strategic shifts in clients' processing of information. We are not satisfied that the measure, as it stands, is sufficiently refined to be sensitive to the total set of qualia acted upon by the cognitive operations represented in it. "Change" occurring at the level of clients' internal mental operations should, by definition, be manifest through a variety of linguistic and paralinguistic acts that probably entail features or characteristics specific to the type of information being processed (e.g., sensory, imagistic, affective, conceptual). Thus, to represent it more completely, we need to develop other model-based coding systems that tap some of the concomitants of these basic processing operations. Once developed, these measures can be used in evaluations of different kinds of clinically meaningful therapy episodes. Data emerging from these instruments then can be analyzed to identify common and specific configurations of these variables across episodes, a strategy similar to Campbell and Fiske's (1959) proposed convergent and discriminant validation procedures. This is a challenging and labor-intensive task but one that potentially may offer a more detailed understanding of the components of the change process and an operationally based representation of this construct.

Further work also remains to be done with respect to our assessment methods of assessing therapy outcome. For example, although data from both the standard and model-relevant measures used in our research have been supportive of the efficacy of the perceptual-processing method of therapy, to date we have found that only the gains on the Tennessee Self Concept Scale and the perceptual congruence measure have been *consistent* in showing a positive relationship with LCPP ratings of client improvement in in-therapy process. In retrospect, this is not surprising considering that the constructs assessed by these two measures (i.e., self-concept and self-schema structure) are indigenous to this treatment's prescribed client outcomes, whereas those assessed by, for example, the State-Trait Anxiety Inventory or the Beck Depression Inventory are not, even though reductions in clients' level of anxiety and depression are considered to be clinically salient as outcome criteria (Zink, 1990).

The question, of course, is this: What constitutes appropriate outcome criteria for this treatment? Conceptually, these are the tangible products of change occurring in clients' schematic processing structures and operations, that is, the products of a more elaborated and differentiated, and hence a more functional, perceptual-processing system. Thus, given the generic nature of this conceptualization, it may be argued that "change as outcome" may be experienced by the client in a variety of ways, across different domains of experience, and along a number of different dimensions (e.g., self-representations, perceptions of intra- and interpersonal experiences, beliefs, thoughts). In this sense, a battery of outcome measures that capture change across a cluster of these "products" or, alternatively, a multidimensional measure that provides a profile of these variables would be required for a more comprehensive assessment of client outcome in this method of therapy.

In conclusion, the main thrust of our empirical work described in this chapter has been the conviction that psychotherapy process research should be guided by an explicit conceptualization of client cognitive-affective functioning and that this framework should make use of relevant theory and research in the cognitive sciences. An equally important impetus for our work has been the belief that, if we are to advance our understanding of how clients change, process and outcome evaluations of psychotherapy should be based on sound assessment methods and procedures that adequately represent the theoretical constructs being studied. Our psychotherapy research program has attempted to address both issues in a preliminary way. The early returns from our research hold forth the promise that our efforts will be useful in the long run. We are aware of the fact, however, that there remains much room for theoretical and methodological refinement. The biggest challenge that lies ahead of us is to have the patience to face the enormity of the task and the willingness to expand and explore other ways of gaining insights that not only will further our research but will also be of maximum benefit to our clients.

Note

1. This conceptualization is consistent with Ingram and Kendall's (1986) suggestion that, when attempting to integrate an information processing perspective with clinical theory and research, it would be helpful to think of cognition in terms of "several interrelated but conceptually distinct components" or categories of cognitive constructs—categories such as structure, propositions, operations, and products.

References

Anderson, J. R. (1981). Concepts, propositions, and schemata: What are the cognitive units? *Nebraska Symposium on Motivation* (vol. 28, pp. 121-162). Lincoln: University of Nebraska Press.

Anderson, J. R., & Bower, G. H. (1973). *Human associative memory.* Hillsdale, NJ: Lawrence Erlbaum.

Angus, L. E. (1986). Metaphoric expressiveness within the psychotherapeutic relationship: A qualitative analysis. *Dissertation Abstracts International, 47,* 3507A.

Angus, L. E., & Rennie, D. L. (1988). Therapist participation in metaphor generation: Collaborative and non-collaborative styles. *Psychotherapy, 25,* 552-560.

Bargh, J. A. (1982). Attention and automacity in the processing of self-relevant information. *Journal of Personality and Social Psychology, 43,* 425-436.

Bargh, J. A., Bond, R. N., Lombardi, W. J., & Tote, M. E. (1986). The additive nature of chronic and temporary sources of construct accessibility. *Journal of Personality and Social Psychology, 50,* 869-878.

Beck, A. T. (1976). *Cognitive therapy and the emotional disorders.* New York: International University Press.

Blumenthal, A. L. (1977). *The process of cognition.* Englewood Cliffs, NJ: Prentice-Hall.

Broadbent, D. E. (1977). The hidden pre-attentive process. *American Psychologist, 32,* 109-118.

Bruner, J. S. (1964). The course of cognitive growth. *American Psychologist, 19,* 1-15.

Campbell, D. T., & Fiske, D. W. (1959). Convergent and discriminant validation by the multitrait-multimethod matrix. *Psychological Bulletin, 56,* 81-105.

Carver, C. S., & Scheier, M. F. (1986). Functional and dysfunctional responses to anxiety: The interaction between expectancies and self-focused attention. In R. Schwarzer (Ed.), *Self-related cognitions in anxiety and motivation* (pp. 111-141). Hillsdale, NJ: Lawrence Erlbaum.

Craik, F. I. M., & Lockhart, R. S. (1972). Levels of processing: A framework for memory research. *Journal of Verbal Learning and Verbal Behavior, 11,* 671-684.

Crockett, W. H. (1965). Cognitive complexity and impression formation. In B. A. Maher (Ed.), *Progress in experimental personality research* (pp. 47-90). New York: Academic Press.

Ellis, A. (1962). *Reason and emotion in psychotherapy.* New York: Lyle Stuart.

Fiske, S. T., & Dyer, L. M. (1985). Structure and development of social schemata: Evidence from positive and negative transfer effects. *Journal of Personality and Social Psychology, 48,* 839-852.

Fiske, S. T., & Taylor, S. E. (1984). *Social cognition.* New York: Random House.

Gibson, J. J. (1966). *The senses considered as perceptual systems.* Boston: Houghton Mifflin.

Goldfried, M. R., & Robins, C. J. (1983). Self-schema, cognitive bias, and the processing of therapeutic experiences. In P. C. Kendall (Ed.), *Advances in cognitive-behavioral research and therapy* (Vol. 2, pp. 33-80). New York: Academic Press.

Greenberg, L. S. (1984). A task analysis of interpersonal conflict resolution. In L. N. Rice & L. S. Greenberg (Eds.), *Patterns of change: Intensive analysis of psychotherapy process* (pp. 67-123). New York: Guilford.

Greenberg, L. S., & Safran, J. D. (1987). *Emotion in psychotherapy: Affect, cognition and the process of change.* New York: Guilford.

Guidano, V. (1984). A constructivist outline of cognitive processes. In M. A. Reda & M. J. Mahoney (Eds.), *Cognitive theory, research, and practice* (pp. 31-45). Cambridge, MA: Ballinger.

Guidano, V., & Liotti, G. (1983). *Cognitive processes and emotional disorders.* New York: Guilford.

Hayes-Roth, B. (1977). Evolution of cognitive structures and processes. *Psychological Review, 84,* 260-278.

Higgins, E. T., & King, G. (1981). Accessibility of social constructs: Information-processing consequences of individual and contextual variability. In N. Cantor & J. F. Kihlstrom (Eds.), *Personality, cognition, and social interaction* (pp. 69-121). Hillsdale, NJ: Lawrence Erlbaum.

Horvath, A. O. (1981). An exploratory study of the working alliance: Its measurement and relationship to therapy outcome. *Dissertation Abstracts International, 42,* 2503A.

Ingram, R. E., & Hollon, S. D. (1986). Cognitive therapy of depression from an information processing perspective. In R. E. Ingram (Ed.), *Information processing approaches to clinical psychology* (pp. 259-281). New York: Academic Press.

Ingram, R. E., & Kendall, P. C. (1986). Cognitive clinical psychology: Implications of an information processing perspective. In R. E. Ingram (Ed.), *Information processing approaches to clinical psychology* (pp. 3-21). New York: Academic Press.

Kagan, N. (1975). *Interpersonal process recall: A method of influencing human interaction.* (Available from N. Kagan, Educational Psychology Department, University of Houston, University Park, Houston, TX 77004.)

Kanfer, F. H., & Hagerman, S. (1981). The role of self-regulation. In L. P. Rehm (Ed.), *Behavior therapy for depression: Present status and future directions* (pp. 143-179). New York: Academic Press.

Kelly, G. (1955). *The psychology of personal constructs.* New York: Norton.

Leventhal, H. (1982). The integration of emotion and cognition: A view from the perceptual-motor theory of emotion. In M. S. Clark & S. T. Fiske (Eds.), *Affect and cognition: The 17th Annual Carnegie Symposium on Cognition.* Hillsdale, NJ: Lawrence Erlbaum.

Leventhal, H. (1984). A perceptual-motor theory of emotion. In L. Berkowitz (Ed.), *Advances in experimental social psychology.* (vol. 17, pp. 117-182). New York: Academic Press.

Linville, P. W. (1985). Self-complexity and affective extremity: Don't put all of your eggs in one cognitive basket. *Social Cognition, 3,* 94-120.

Mahoney, M. J. (1985). Psychotherapy and human change processes. In M. J. Mahoney & A. Freeman (Eds.), *Cognition and psychotherapy* (pp. 3-48). New York: Plenum.

Mahoney, M. J. (1988). The cognitive sciences and psychotherapy: Patterns in a developing relationship. In K. S. Dobson (Ed.), *Handbook of cognitive-behavioral therapies* (pp. 357-386). New York: Guilford.

Markus, H. (1977). Self-schemata and processing information about the self. *Journal of Personality and Social Psychology, 35,* 63-78.

Markus, H., & Kunda, Z. (1986). Stability and malleability of the self-concept. *Journal of Personality and Social Psychology, 51,* 858-866.

Markus, H., & Sentis, K. (1982). The self in social information processing. In J. Suls (Ed.), *Psychological perspectives on the self* (pp. 41-70). Hillsdale, NJ: Lawrence Erlbaum.

Neisser, U. (1967). *Cognitive psychology.* New York: Appleton-Century-Crofts.

Neisser, U. (1976). *Cognition and reality: Principles and implications of cognitive psychology.* San Francisco: Freeman.

Posner, M. I. (1978). *Chronometric explorations of mind.* Hillsdale, NJ: Lawrence Erlbaum.

Rice, L. N., & Greenberg, L. S. (Eds.). (1984). *Patterns of change: Intensive analysis of psychotherapy process.* New York: Guilford.

Rice, L. N., & Saperia, E. (1984). Task analysis of the resolution of problematic reactions. In L. N. Rice & L. S. Greenberg (Eds.), *Patterns of change: Intensive analysis of psychotherapy process* (pp. 29-66). New York: Guilford.

Rumelhart, D. E. (1984). Schemata and the cognitive system. In S. R. Wyer & T. K. Srull (Eds.), *Handbook of social cognition* (Vol. 1, pp. 161-168). Hillsdale, NJ: Lawrence Erlbaum.

Sander, H. D. (1990). The self-schemata of nondepressed and mildly depressed individuals: Induced changes in content and processing efficiency. *Dissertation Abstracts International, 51,* 1560B.

Schacter, F., & Singer, J. E. (1962). Cognitive social and physiological determinants of emotional states. *Psychological Review, 69,* 379-399.

Shiffrin, R. M., & Schneider, W. (1977). Controlled and automatic human information processing: II. Perceptual learning, automatic attending, and a general theory. *Psychological Review, 84,* 127-150.

Sinclair, L. M. (1990). Metaphor and client perceptual processing. *Dissertation Abstracts International, 51,* 4608B.

Taylor, S. E., & Crocker, J. (1981). Schematic bases of social information processing. In E. T. Higgins, C. P. Herman, & M. P. Zanna (Eds.), *Social cognition: The Ontario symposium on personality and social psychology* (Vol. 1, pp. 89-134). Hillsdale, NJ: Lawrence Erlbaum.

Toukmanian, S. G. (1983). *A perceptual-cognitive model for counselling and psychotherapy* (Tech. Rep. No. 138). North York, Ontario: York University, Department of Psychology.

Toukmanian, S. G. (1986). A measure of client perceptual processing. In L. S. Greenberg & W. M. Pinsof (Eds.), *The psychotherapeutic process: A research handbook* (pp. 107-130). New York: Guilford.

Toukmanian, S. G. (1988, June). The development and evaluation of self-schema change following short-term experiential therapy. In J. Martin (Chair), *The client's development of meaning structure: Cognitive and metacognitive considerations.* Symposium conducted at the 1st International Conference on Developmental Counseling Psychology, Porto, Portugal.

Toukmanian, S. G. (1990). A schema-based information processing perspective on client change in experiential psychotherapy. In G. Lietaer, J. Rombauts, & R. Van Balen (Eds.), *Client-centered and experiential psychotherapy in the nineties* (pp. 309-326). Leuven, Belgium: Leuven University Press.

Toukmanian, S. G., & Dunbar, C. A. (1991). *Client perceptual-processing in Gestalt two-chair resolution and non-resolution performances* (Tech. Rep. No. 193). North York, Ontario: York University, Department of Psychology.

Toukmanian, S. G., & Grech, T. (1991). *Changes in cognitive complexity in the context of perceptual-processing experiential therapy* (Tech. Rep. No. 194). North York, Ontario: York University, Department of Psychology.

Toukmanian, S. G., & Roese, R. (1989, June). *Self-schema change: Its assessment and relationship to therapeutic outcome.* Poster presentation at the annual meeting of the Canadian Psychological Association, Halifax, Nova Scotia.

Turk, D. C., & Spears, M. A. (1983). Cognitive schemata and cognitive processes in cognitive-behavioral interventions: Going beyond the information given. In P. C. Kendall (Ed.), *Advances in cognitive-behavioral research and therapy* (Vol. 2, pp. 1-32). New York: Academic Press.

Weimer, W. B. (1977). A conceptual framework for cognitive psychology: Motor theories of the mind. In R. Shaw & J. Bransford (Eds.), *Perceiving, acting and knowing: Toward an ecological psychology* (pp. 267-311). Hillsdale, NJ: Lawrence Erlbaum.

Wexler, D. A., & Rice, L. N. (1974). *Innovations in client-centered therapy.* New York: John Wiley.

Winfrey, L. L., & Goldfried, M. R. (1986). Information processing and the human change process. In R. E. Ingram (Ed.), *Information processing approaches to clinical psychology* (pp. 241-258). New York: Academic Press.

Zink, D. A. (1990). *Change in anxiety in the context of perceptual-processing experiential therapy: Process and outcome research.* Unpublished master's thesis, York University, North York, Ontario.

5

Cognitive-Mediational Research on Counseling and Psychotherapy

JACK MARTIN

Philosophers (e.g., Austin, 1961; Ryle, 1949; Wittgenstein, 1953), and most of us in our everyday experiences, know that the meaning and consequences of social acts are uncertain. This uncertainty arises because all acts in a social context lend themselves to multiple interpretations without full knowledge of specific situational factors and the unique experiential histories (and therefore beliefs and intentions) of the actors—knowledge that never is completely attainable.

Thus the client who interprets my therapeutic reflections as attempts to constrain her responses in predetermined, therapeutically acceptable ways, as opposed to recognizing and seizing opportunities to explore and elaborate her own experiences in a "safe" setting, is not behaving in an unusual or surprising fashion. At least her reactions in this context are no more surprising than my own expectations that she will respond to my reflective comments as my own personal knowledge of therapeutic discourse (gathered from a complex of theoretical and experiential inputs) indicates that she should.

As recently as 1986, Stiles, Shapiro, and Elliott (1986), in a well-argued, informative attempt to shed light upon the now familiar finding of relative equivalence in the therapeutic effects produced by credible but different

AUTHOR'S NOTE: Much of the conceptual and empirical work discussed in this chapter was supported by the Social Sciences and Humanities Research Council of Canada (Grant Nos. 410-84-0045, 410-86-0225, and 410-88-0022).

forms of psychotherapy,[1] failed to consider explicitly individual and situational uniqueness. They never once mentioned the simple idea that the unique ways in which different clients may respond to similar therapeutic interventions might help to explain why very different therapies produce similar results, and why very similar therapies sometimes produce very different results.

The basic question that has guided my research on counseling and psychotherapy is this: "Is it possible to conduct meaningful, scientific investigations into counseling and psychotherapeutic processes that recognize the uniqueness of individual clients and therapists?" In putting the question in this way, I wish to draw attention to what I see as the central dilemma that must be confronted when this question is asked. Psychological science assumes relatively stable individual response propensities across different people in similar situations and across time in the experiences of a single individual. Unfortunately, people often do not display such enduring propensities, tending often to respond more uniquely than the psychological assumption predicts. In an attempt to deal with this response uncertainty, psychologists generally have attempted to define situations or time frames more narrowly, developing more constrained theories. But this strategy simply moves the problem to a more "narrow gauge"; it does not resolve it. On the other hand, if one embraces individual uniqueness, what conceptual and methodological bases remain from which to construct a social science, in this case, a social science of psychotherapy?

The cognitive-mediational paradigm for research on counseling and psychotherapy has developed in the context of my attempt to contribute to the development of a social science of psychotherapy that does not overlook the uniqueness of individual clients and therapists.

Conceptual Model

Before a program of cognitive-mediational research could commence, it was necessary to develop a model of therapeutic interaction that highlighted the central role of clients' perceptions and cognitive operations. This conceptual move was based on my belief that uniqueness in human responding is primarily a consequence of the uniqueness of individual experiences and knowledge stored in highly personal theoretical and memory structures that underlie ongoing individual perceptual and cognitive processes. I have retained this basic assumption throughout my work.

Figure 5.1 (updated from Martin, 1987a, 1987b) is a schematic representation of the conceptual model that has guided my research on psychotherapy. This model reflects perspectives borrowed from theories of cognitive and social construction (e.g., Harré, 1984), cognitive information processing (Anderson, 1983; Martin, 1984, 1985a, 1985b), and cognitive-mediational models of teaching and learning (Winne & Marx, 1977, 1980). From a constructivist viewpoint, Figure 5.1 can be interpreted as a representation of the manner in which public, social (interpersonal) processes of information and knowledge construction during therapy interact with private, cognitive (intrapersonal) processes of information and knowledge construction.

In this model, intentions of participants in individual therapy are seen to arise from internal plans. These plans are constructed from complex combinations of processed information drawn from current situations and from tacit and explicit memory stores. The most important external information included in counselors' plans comes from their perceptions of the responses clients make in therapy. These perceptions are partially determined by therapists' personal knowledge in currently activated cognitive structures (memory stores). The internal knowledge represented in counselors' plans is highly personalized and includes the unique beliefs, attitudes, and symbolized experiences of individual therapists. Thus, during therapy, counselors perceive client responses, process this perceptual information in combination with personalized, experiential information existing in memory, formulate plans, and respond intentionally.

For their part, clients also are engaged in a continuously active process of perception, planning, and responding. Of particular importance is the way in which such cognitive activity on the part of the client results in the "internalization" (in a Vygotskian sense) of various elements from the co-constructed therapeutic discourse into the experiential memory stores of the client. Resultant changes to the experiential memory structures and personal theories of the client provide a basis for altered ways of being and behaving in the life circumstances that confront the client.

An example should help to make the processes depicted in Figure 5.1 more concrete. Let us assume that a counselor is working in a third session with a young man who is experiencing difficulty in interpersonal relationships. Toward the end of the second session, the counselor

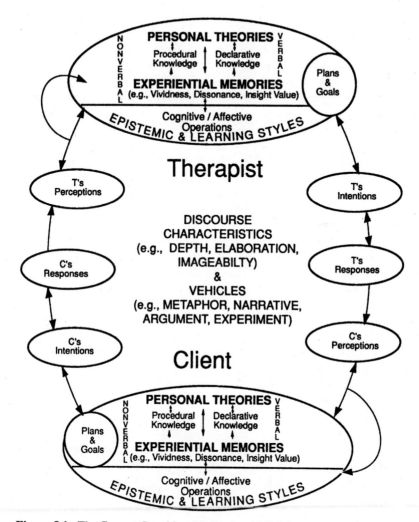

Figure 5.1. The Current Cognitive-Meditational Model
NOTE: Adapted from Martin, 1987a and Martin, 1987b.

and client discussed the possibility that the client's self-recognized difficulty in expressing his feelings to others, particularly his more "vulnerable" feelings, was an important element in his current difficulties. It was agreed that the client's communication of such "softer" feelings would be a major focus in the next (third) session.

As the third session begins, the counselor recalls the previously agreed focus for this session. She also knows that one way of approaching the client's difficulty in expressing emotions is to help him experience an in-depth exploration of his emotional reactions in the context of the therapeutic relationship. In fact, she has experienced success with this intervention strategy with past clients with similar difficulties. All of this information, in elaborate detail, is readily available in the counselor's internal cognitive structures (knowledge, memories, and symbolized experiences). As the client begins to talk about his views that expression of his "softer" emotions is both "unmanly" and dangerous (in the sense of increasing personal vulnerability), the therapist combines relevant memories with her current perceptions of the client's conversation and formulates a mini-intervention plan. The essence of this plan is that she will attempt to assist the client to express his vulnerability, and fears about displaying it, directly to her as part of the larger strategy of assisting the client to express his "softer" emotions. With the initial intention of helping the client deepen his experience of these feelings, she makes a reflective response that is grounded specifically in the contexts/situations the client currently is describing: "When you get this 'sinking' feeling, you briefly panic that you might break down completely and make a fool of yourself. This fear is so powerful that you ruthlessly squash it, and anger and resentment flood in to take the place of the panic."

The client perceives the counselor's reflective response and understands it in the context of information he possesses in his episodic, experiential memories of the previous therapy session and memories of a variety of specific situations in which he has reacted with the kind of panic, fear, and anger the counselor has described. After a brief (partially conscious and partially unconscious) consideration of the counselor's remark in the context of these memories and his own beliefs, he decides (again partially consciously and partially unconsciously) that his fears about disclosing personal vulnerability are often justifiable and plans to convince the therapist of this conclusion. With this intention, the client begins to describe a recent situation in which he believes he was wise not to reveal feelings of rejection and hurt.

In this way, the session continues. Both counselor and client perceive and comprehend the actions and words of each other through relevant portions of symbolized past experience, mnemonic information, personal beliefs, and knowledge. They then behave intentionally on the basis of ever-changing and ever-developing plans that they formulate on the basis of their ongoing perceptions and understandings (see Figure 5.1). Over time, this dynamic, ongoing process of interpersonal, social interaction and intrapersonal cognition can affect the content and organization of the client's personal cognitive/experiential structures and memories, thus creating a more adequate cognitive basis for novel and refined client behaviors in everyday life contexts that are more congruent with the personal therapeutic goals of the client.

From a cognitive-mediational perspective, the primary task of counseling or psychotherapy is to assist clients to acquire a level of cognitive functioning that will support their achievement of personal goals. Therefore the specific nature of client cognitive changes, thought ideally to result from the therapeutic processes modeled in Figure 5.1, deserves attention. At a structural level, these changes are thought to include (a) elaborations in the cognitive structures (schemata) of clients that contain information about their problems, (b) the acquisition and/or refinement of problem-solving structures that house information relevant to the possible resolution of client problems, and (c) the "empowerment" (strengthening, in the sense of creating a basis for effective personal action) of clients' self-schemata or self-theories (cognitive structures housing self-perceptions and self-knowledge) through the elaboration and integration of such self-structures with information from both problem-representation and problem-solving structures. (It is important to note, given the emphasis on human uniqueness that typifies the cognitive-mediational perspective, that all these underlying "deep-level" structural changes may be reflected in a wide variety of different "surface" contexts and client therapeutic responses.)

In our example of the client experiencing difficulty in expressing feelings of vulnerability in interpersonal relationships, successful therapy might promote a number of specific changes to the client's cognitive/experiential structures consistent with these three general types of therapeutic change. For example, this client might come to *understand* that the anger and avoidance that "cover" his fear of disclosing vulnerability produce social consequences that equal or exceed his worst fears. On the basis of this structural shift (elaboration of problem-relevant information), he may develop a "vulnerability-display" strategy that begins cautiously with something like, "I guess I'm not really certain how I feel about . . ." Finally, he may come to see himself as in control (empowerment of self-schema) of the extent to which he wishes, at any given time, to share his "softer" feelings with others (thereby reducing his fears about "completely breaking down"). Further, it is possible that experiential memories of specific events in therapy might "cue" the client to employ his new strategies and understandings appropriately in relevant, "real-life" contexts.

As a consequence of basic cognitive structural changes, clients in therapy also might be expected to experience increments in the efficiency and thoroughness with which they are able to process their personal experience, understanding, and awareness inside and outside of therapy. As clients acquire more elaborated and integrated information about themselves, their problems, and possible plans of action, they are better able to perceive, attend to, and operate cognitively on more and more aspects of their entire "problem space." Thus the "vulnerable" client in our example is better able to understand and use the therapist's interventions as he begins to experience the structural changes described above and as he begins to experiment with new understandings, strategies, and a sense of empowerment in his everyday personal experiences.

Much of the model building summarized schematically in Figure 5.1 has, of course, been conducted in the context of an ongoing program of research on counseling and psychotherapeutic processes. It is to this empirical work that I now wish to turn. Before doing so, however, I want to provide explicit definitions of what I mean by the terms process and therapeutic change in the context of my work on cognitive-mediational research on counseling and psychotherapy.

I use the term *process* in two distinct ways. On the one hand, I postulate therapeutic processes that occur at an *intrapersonal*, cognitive level. These include cognitive processes such as perception, encoding, comprehension, recall, self-monitoring, planning, and so forth. On the other hand, I talk about therapeutic processes that are *interpersonal* and social in nature. Examples of these latter processes include interactions between therapists and clients that foster desired therapeutic changes in the client.

Therapeutic change refers to any cognitive/affective and/or behavioral change experienced by the client that facilitates the client's movement toward desired personal goals, within acceptable moral and pragmatic constraints.

Research Methods, Strategies, and Findings

Researching social-cognitive construction and processing of information in counseling and psychotherapy proves to be a very tricky business, particularly if the researcher wishes to capture the unique character of individual intentions and actions. Research of this sort must be (a) ecologically valid (i.e., must examine real-life counseling processes), (b) phenomenological (i.e., must capture participants' self-reports of their subjective, internal experiences), and (c) still generate findings with credible levels of internal and external validity. (The third criterion is necessary, because, even if one abandons tightly positivistic, deterministic conceptions and methods, it is still necessary to demonstrate adherence to validity criteria appropriate to assessing the consistency and generalizability of the probabilistic results obtained.)

Research Methods

Three categories of research methods have been employed in cognitive-mediational research on counseling and psychotherapy: (a) thought report methods used to obtain data concerning therapist and client cognitive processes and memories, (b) free association and conceptual mapping methods used to obtain data on participants' cognitive structures, and (c) methods of content and protocol analysis employed to categorize, and explore characteristics of, verbal discourse from counseling interactions and from participants' subjective reports.

Thought report methods attempt to capture part of the ongoing stream of thinking that accompanies human action as it unfolds. In our research, methods of stimulated recall (Kagan, Krathwohl, & Miller, 1963; Martin, Martin, Meyer, & Slemon, 1986; Martin, Martin, & Slemon, 1987) or interpersonal process recall (Elliott, 1985; Kagan, 1973) have been employed most often. These methods involve playing back selected videotaped segments of a recently completed counseling session to participants in that session. Participants (interviewed separately) are asked to recall their thoughts as completely as possible during the videotaped segments observed but to refrain from reporting "new" thoughts (such as inferences, interpretations, or insights) that occur to them as they view the videotaped segments. Following the arguments advanced by Ericsson and Simon (1984), data obtained from such methods are likely to be incomplete because much human cognitive activity is not available for conscious verbal report. It is, however, unlikely that the data obtained in this way are invalid. People generally are able to describe their thoughts accurately but are not adept at explaining their thoughts or actions (see Ericsson & Simon, 1984). The thought report methods employed in cognitive-mediational research carefully avoid asking participants in counseling to attempt the latter activity.

A second form of thought report that has been employed more recently in our work is more memory than process oriented. In several recent studies (Martin, Paivio, & Labadie, 1990; Martin & Stelmaczonek, 1988), we simply have asked clients and therapists to recall "the most important thing (or things) that happened in the session just completed." We have developed systematic ways of locating the events that participants report in transcriptions of relevant sessions as well as locating "control" events from the same therapy sessions (immediately before or after the participant-recalled events). We then have employed a variety of 6-point scales to rate various aspects of the therapeutic discourse in these events that may render that discourse more or less memorable.

To obtain data about the cognitive structures of therapists and clients (i.e., the unique organizations of personal knowledge and experience available in individual memory stores), my colleagues and I have employed a third technique that combines free association with conceptual mapping methods. Immediately after engaging in counseling, clients or counselors are asked to free associate to key words associated with the client's problems or self-depictions. The actual key words employed usually are rather general words (such as "problems" or a particular participant's first name) or more specific words taken from the verbal exchanges that occurred during the counseling session just completed. Participants' free association responses are recorded by an interviewer on small gummed labels (one association per label). These labels then are returned to the person being interviewed together with a large sheet of thin, laminated bristol board, china marking pencils, and a supply of facial tissues. At this point, instructions such as the following are given to the interviewee:

> Arrange the stickers in a manner that indicates how, or if, the concepts they represent are related in your thoughts. If two concepts are related strongly, place their stickers close to each other; if they are related weakly, place their

stickers further apart. You may rearrange stickers until you are satisfied that what you have produced is a good representation of your understanding of these concepts and their relationships . . . (pause for participant response). Now use this marker to draw connecting lines between stickers that you feel are related. Use the tissues if you need to alter marker lines . . . (pause for participant response). Draw a circle around any clusters of concepts that seem to belong together. Label each circle you have drawn.

A number of indices have been developed for recording and analyzing various aspects of the conceptual maps produced (Martin, 1987a; Martin, Slemon, Hiebert, Hallberg, & Cummings, 1989). In addition, methods of qualitative analysis and descriptive statistical tools such as multidimensional scaling also have been employed.

The use of thought report and free association-conceptual mapping methods has provided a wealth of data that seems to capture some of the highly personalized meanings that clients and therapists construct and experience in therapeutic interactions.

In addition to these methods, we have employed and/or developed a variety of content and protocol analytic systems to summarize and categorize counselor and client intentions, behaviors, and cognitive operations as these appear in verbatim transcriptions of counseling discourse and participant self-reports. Coding systems developed by Clara Hill (Hill & O'Grady, 1985; Hill et al., 1981) have been used most often to supplement our own coding systems (Martin, Martin, & Slemon, 1989; Martin et al., 1990).

Research Strategies and Findings

To meet the three criteria of ecological, phenomenological, and scientific (internal/external) validity, cognitive-mediational research on counseling and psychotherapy typically involves intensive data collection across a small number (3 to 10) of therapeutic dyads at several points in the overall course of therapy. To facilitate a brief summary of the various research strategies employed and the general findings they have yielded, I have grouped the studies conducted to date into three broad types.

The first type of research has attempted to test the central tenet of the cognitive-mediational approach concerning the uniqueness of client response to therapist skills and interventions. This line of research has yielded descriptive information concerning the probabilities of various sequences of counselor intentions, counselor behaviors, and client cognitive responses to these therapeutic intentions and behaviors, both in the context of eclectic therapy (Martin et al., 1986; Martin et al., 1989) and in the context of person-centered and rational-emotive therapies (Martin et al., 1987).

The basic strategy employed in this first type of research has been to videotape real-life counseling sessions and to select at random a number of counselor behaviors from each of the videotaped sessions. Stimulated recall procedures, employing videotaped segments that include the selected counselor behaviors, have then been used to solicit counselor reports of the intentions that accompanied these behaviors and client reports of their cognitive responses to the counselor behaviors. Content analyses of the videotaped segments and the stimulated recall reports yield data that can be used to construct quantitative models of the probabilities with which various counselor behaviors and client cognitive operations are associated with particular counselor intentions.

Generally speaking, research of this first variety has shown that there exist reasonably stable, recognizable patterns of counselor behaviors and client cognitive operations that tend to be associated with specific counselor intentions. Figure 5.2 displays three examples of such sequential patterns. It is important to note the highly probabilistic character of these interactive therapeutic sequences. (The arrows in Figure 5.2 indicate the probabilities with which various components, in the sequence depicted, follow various other components.) The central tenet of the cognitive-mediational approach concerning the uniqueness of client responses to therapeutic interventions is reflected in these probabilistic models. While different clients, and the same clients at different times, appear to respond differently to the same counselor skills, there nonetheless exists a sensible, overall ordering of observed client responses to therapeutic actions and intentions. These patterns permit probabilistic predictions of certain kinds of client cognitive responses, given particular forms and patterns of counselor intentions and behaviors. Independent research undertaken by Hill and her colleagues (e.g., Hill & O'Grady, 1985) has replicated many of our findings in this area.

A second line of cognitive-mediational research has attempted to examine the nature of the cognitive, structural changes experienced by clients during and as a result of counseling. Free association and conceptual mapping methods have been employed to obtain graphic depictions of clients' knowledge structures related to their problems, their plans for problem resolution (or coping), and clients' self-knowledge. Both

COUNSELOR   COUNSELOR   CLIENT COGNITIVE
INTENTIONS   BEHAVIORS   OPERATIONS

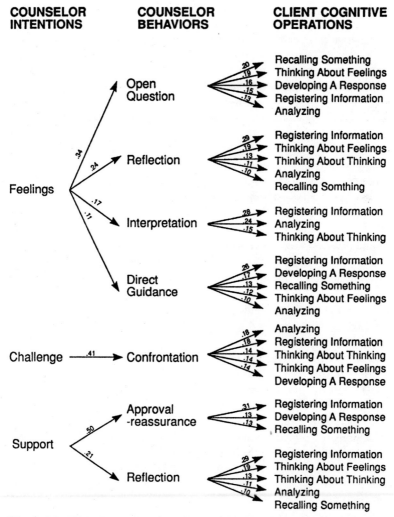

Figure 5.2. Three Examples of Probalistic Patterns of Relationships across
Counselor Intentions, Counselor Behaviors, and Client Cognitive Operations
NOTE: From Martin, Martin, and Slemon, 1988.

qualitative and quantitative methods (such as multidimensional scaling
and statistical analysis of standard numerical indices computed from

the raw data) have been employed to test for evidence of the kinds of structural changes predicted by our developing theory of client cognitive change (i.e., elaborations of problem schemata, acquisition/refinement of problem-solving structures, and empowered self-schemata).

Generally, research of the second type has confirmed the broad outlines of our theory of client cognitive change through therapy. In conceptual maps produced by several clients over time in counseling, we have been able to detect gradual increments in the complexity, comprehensiveness, orderliness, and integration of the self- and problem-related knowledge structures we have attempted to examine (Martin, 1987b; Martin & Reaume, 1988). We have, however, observed considerable individual variability in such patterns, with some clients showing little change in the conceptual maps they have produced and others producing such highly distinctive maps at different times that drawing comparison among them has been difficult due to an absence of common features. We believe that two factors are responsible for this pattern of results. First, it is likely that clients who experience little change through therapy will produce relatively static displays of their therapy-relevant knowledge. Second, the free association and conceptual mapping method we have used (like all projective methods) may be highly sensitive to temporal and situational factors other than those whose influences we are attempting to chart. This second factor is particularly noticeable when clients fail to maintain a consistent pattern of concerns across different counseling sessions.

A feature of our conceptual mapping results, which we believe is particularly important, is a general increase in the hierarchical organization of the therapy-relevant knowledge of many clients as counseling proceeds. Such increased organization is a common feature in the knowledge structures of effective, expert problem solvers in a variety of areas of human activity (see, e.g., Chi, Glaser, & Rees, 1982) and may reflect increased personal problem-solving expertise of clients as they advance through therapy. Once again, clients who meet with greater therapeutic success probably are more likely to display increments in the hierarchical organization of their problem-relevant knowledge than are clients for whom therapy is less successful.

Turning briefly to related research on therapists' cognitive structures, Hiebert (1987), using our method of free association and conceptual mapping, has reported analogous increments in the hierarchical organization of counseling interns' knowledge of therapeutic process over time in internship placements. Martin, Slemon, et al. (1989) recently have shown how such highly organized therapeutic knowledge allows experienced therapists to conceptualize specific client problems and intervention strategies more efficiently and parsimoniously than novice counselors who do not possess such organized knowledge.

The third line of cognitive-mediational research on counseling and therapy is of more recent origin (Martin & Stelmaczonek, 1988; Martin et al., 1990). In this work, we have attempted to increase our understanding of the mechanisms by which therapy produces long-term effects. As in the two lines of research summarized briefly above, we have pursued this objective through focusing on clients' cognitive processes and memory structures that mediate therapeutic experiences. Our primary assumption has been that, for therapy to produce lasting effects, clients must maintain information (insights, understandings, awarenesses) acquired during therapy in their long-term memories so that such information may be retrieved in their everyday lives as it is required.

We have asked clients, immediately following counseling sessions, to identify what they consider to be the most important events that occurred in these sessions. In stimulated recall interviews six months after the completion of therapy, we have tested clients' recall of the events they previously had identified as important. Our results indicate that clients are able to report accurately events that occurred during counseling, particularly when they considered these to be important (Martin & Stelmaczonek, 1988).

We also discovered that clients' identification of therapeutic events as important can be predicted from certain characteristics of the therapeutic discourse during these events. In particular, events that contain dialogue conducive to *deep, elaborative,* and *conclusion-oriented* information processing tend to be selected by clients as important. (With respect to the concern for individual uniqueness that typifies cognitive-mediational research, it should be noted that the actual content and surface characteristics of therapeutic dialogue may vary considerably across such client-identified important events. Only at a deeper level, revealed by the discourse characteristics examined in this study, are such therapeutic events similarly constructed.) These results seem to indicate that clients do retain therapeutic information in their long-term memories and that such retention may be enhanced if therapeutic interactions promote client thinking that is interpretive, critical, and analytic (i.e., is deep); that includes figurative language, images, and metaphors (i.e., is elaborative); and that includes hypotheses or interpretations (i.e., is conclusion oriented; Martin & Stelmaczonek, 1988). The study by Martin et al. (1990) builds on the work of Martin and Stelmaczonek (1988) and also offers some support for a more precisely theory-driven hypothesis based on A. Paivio's (1986) Dual Code theory of memory. In this study, scales demonstrating strong interrater reliability were used to score five "information processing" characteristics of 55 client-recalled important and 55 matched control events from actual therapeutic sessions of both cognitive and experiential psychotherapies. Results, consistent with those of Martin and Stelmaczonek (1988), indicated that scales scoring depth, elaborateness, and conclusion orientation of therapeutic dialogue during the events studied discriminated reliably and as predicted between client-recalled important and control events. Further, ratings of therapist talking turns during these events were largely responsible for the findings.

When the cognitive and experiential therapeutic events were considered separately, it was found that elaboration in the therapists' dialogue (i.e., use of experiential metaphors and visual images) during client-recalled important events differentiated these events from control events in the experiential but not in the cognitive therapies. This result seems consistent with the dual coding idea that verbal interactions elaborated through the use of concrete, imagery-laden language are more likely to be dually encoded (in both verbal and imaginal representational systems) and thus are more likely to be remembered and recalled by participants in those interactions.

Further support for the importance of elaboration as an important determinant of client recall of important events in experiential psychotherapy is supplied by S. Paivio (1989) in a case study of experiential therapy. In this research, Paivio showed that the outstanding characteristic of client-recalled important therapeutic events was extensive therapist use of visual imagery and metaphor.

Such results suggest possible links between our cognitive-mediational theorizing and more experiential theorizing about therapeutic construction by researchers such as Angus and Rennie (1988), Mahrer (1988), and Mahrer and Nadler (1986). This theoretical convergence is supported further by an analysis of client- and therapist-identified important events (Martin & Stelmaczonek, 1988) that coded such events using a slightly revised version of Mahrer and Nadler's (1986) system for identifying good moments in therapy. In this analysis, it was shown that the kinds of events identified as important by both clients and therapists in the Martin and Stelmaczonek (1988) study reported above were (a) experiencing a good therapeutic relationship, (b) experiencing and exploring of feelings, (c) attaining more elaborated personal meanings, (d) incorporating (internalizing) therapeutic processes, and (e) experimenting with and experiencing new ways of being and behaving. The fact that such therapeutic events tend to contain dialogue conducive to deep, elaborative, and conclusion-oriented information processing helps to explain how these experientially important classes of interpersonal therapeutic events penetrate the intrapersonal, cognitive, experiential structures of clients. In short, these data can be viewed as providing reasonably direct support for the cognitive-mediational view that therapy works when the social, public co-constructions of therapists and clients become internalized as bases for the cognitive, private constructions and reconstructions of clients.

In addition to the findings already summarized, the three lines of cognitive-mediational research that my colleagues and I have pursued have furnished a wealth of information concerning the nature of therapist and client subjective, cognitive experiences of therapy. Examples of such additional information include the observation that client cognitive work in therapy appears to be largely a matter of attempting to uncover and examine existing feelings and thinking patterns, and to supplement and restructure such cognitive and affective processes and structures with the aid of information provided by the therapist (Martin et al., 1986; Martin et al., 1987; Martin, Martin, et al., 1989). It is not surprising that therapist cognitive work in therapy appears to revolve around attempts to promote client self-exploration of feelings and thinking patterns and to provide information and guidance that helps clients to analyze and restructure these internal cognitions and emotions. Of course, the overarching goal of all this client and therapist work seems to be the social construction of plans that clients can internalize, refine, and use as a basis for action that helps resolve and/or cope with problems and assists them to achieve personal goals.

The foregoing summary of cognitive-mediational research on counseling and psychotherapy has been much abbreviated, with only major results mentioned and illustrated. Many additional models similar to those presented in Figure 5.2 are available in other sources (e.g., Martin et al., 1986; Martin, Martin, et al., 1989) as are detailed descriptions of all three lines of research. Nonetheless, I believe that the brief summary of this work presented here succeeds in providing an overall sense of the kinds of assumptions, questions, methods, and strategies that have come to typify the cognitive-mediational perspective.

I believe that cognitive-mediational research on counseling conducted to date demonstrates that clients do respond uniquely to therapist interventions based on their individual structures of knowledge and experience. At the same time, I think we are beginning to identify some general characteristics of therapeutic discourse (the social co-construction of therapists and clients) that increase the likelihood that such interactions and their content will be encoded, recalled, and perhaps used by clients.

Conceptual frameworks provided by contemporary theories of cognitive and social information processing and construction have permitted us to interpret a variety of rich data drawn from counseling interactions and the self-reports of counselors and clients, without removing individual differences from our total data set. Both the probabilistic character of our minimodels of therapeutic actions (see Figure 5.2) and the varied semantic and syntactic contents of the conceptual maps of individual knowledge that we have obtained attest to the existence of unique patterns of individual response to therapy.

Applications

Cognitive-mediational research on counseling and psychotherapy attempts to understand the interaction between social and cognitive information processing/construction that enables therapeutic talk between counselor and client to effect client change. By assuming client active agency (i.e., the possibility of unique client responses to therapeutic interventions), this research paradigm precludes drawing highly deterministic prescriptions for practice from its findings. Nonetheless, I believe that the broad outlines of the cognitive-mediational model portrayed in Figure 5.1 have been supported by the research we have conducted to date. Further, I believe both this model and its supporting research have a small number of important insights to offer practicing therapists, therapist educators, and researchers of psychotherapy.

For Therapists

From a cognitive-mediational perspective, it is clear that much of the combined excitement and frustration typically experienced by practicing counselors and psychotherapists stems from the ability of the counselor or therapist to influence but not control the therapeutic process. Therapy clearly is a two-way street. Therapists can assist clients to change, but they cannot change them in the absence of complementary change-directed activity on the part of clients themselves. Any attempt at change that does not directly engage the conscious agency of clients is unlikely to succeed in the long term.

While therapists cannot control how clients respond to therapy, they probably can, within probabilistic limits such as those illustrated in Figure 5.2, teach clients about therapy and therapeutic processes, thereby enhancing clients' abilities to benefit from their therapeutic experiences. Because clients actively process information during therapy, it makes good sense to assist them to comprehend both the rationale and the nature of therapeutic interventions. A major task for therapists is to form a working alliance with their clients so that they can go about the business of therapy as a joint, collaborative venture. Only by forming this kind of explicit therapeutic partnership is it possible to increase the likelihood that counselor and client activity during therapy will "mesh." I believe that therapists often spend too little time teaching clients about therapy per se. Consequently, clients often have greater difficulty adjusting their cognitive-perceptual activity to that of the counselor than is necessary.

The cognitive-mediational approach to the study of counseling and psychotherapy does not lead to the prescription of a specific model for the actual doing of therapy. The central tenets of human response uniqueness (active client agency) and the probabilistic nature of therapeutic interactions are assumed to hold for all types of psychotherapeutic interventions (cf. Rennie, this volume). Nonetheless, it seems logical to assume, as the immediately preceding discussion suggests, that effective therapy must somehow clarify client goals, establish a comfortable working alliance between counselor and client, help the client to understand therapeutic processes and interventions, and be structured to promote the kinds of cognitive changes described earlier. In our empirical and conceptual work, my colleagues and I have observed and described a number of basic therapeutic tasks and events that we believe are consistent with these process goals (Figure 5.3).

Although the therapeutic elements in Figure 5.3 have been ordered in what seems to me to be a logical sequence, we have observed many variations on this idealized sequence. At this time, we have little empirical evidence concerning the exact order, timing, or necessity

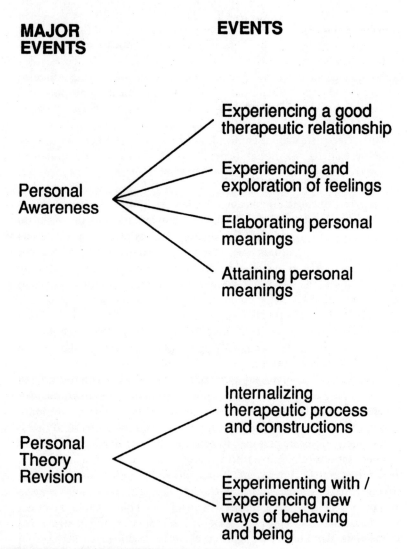

Figure 5.3. Therapeutic Tasks and Events.

of any of the elements in Figure 5.3. My only claims here are that the therapeutic elements summarized in the figure seem logically consistent with the implications for therapeutic practice that I have drawn from the cognitive-mediational perspective and that they can be observed frequently in therapeutic encounters with which both therapists and clients (in our studies) express satisfaction. I include Figure 5.3 so that readers might gain a more concrete impression of some of the specific therapeutic experiences reported by participants in our cognitive-mediational research program.

Building on the empirical work of Martin and Stelmaczonek (1988), Martin et al. (1990), and Mahrer (1988), I have attempted to group the six therapeutic events in Figure 5.3 (experiencing a good therapeutic relationship, experience and exploration of feelings, attaining more elaborated personal meanings, attaining personal insight, incorporating/internalizing therapeutic processes, and experimenting with and experiencing new ways of being or behaving) into two major tasks that I believe clients must accomplish to achieve significant change in psychotherapy (Martin, 1989). These two mega tasks are *personal awareness* and *personal theory revision.*

Personal awareness means recognition of one's own implicit theories about a concern or problem. It includes recognition of the ways in which these theories, and the thoughts, behaviors, and emotions associated with them, interact with one's experience of the concern or problem.

Personal theory revision begins with recognition of the inadequacies of current personal theories and associated patterns of thinking, feeling, and acting in relation to one's goals. Personal theory revision then entails subsequent initiation of serious, personally motivated attempts to alter one's personal theories (experiential, mnemonic, and knowledge structures) to promote one's goals more adequately.

The task of personal awareness is emphasized in many past and current approaches to psychodynamic, experiential, and cognitive therapy (e.g., those therapies developed by Adler, Beck, Ellis, Rogers, and their associates). The latter task of personal theory revision has historical associations primarily with the personal construct psychology of George Kelly (1955).

One more direct, practical (as opposed to indirect, conceptual) use that eventually might be made of our research concerns the manner in which therapists might employ types of language that could increase the likelihood that clients will perceive, encode, and recall therapeutic events as important. Obviously, our research (especially Martin et al., 1990; Martin & Stelmaczonek, 1988) suggests that therapist language rich in imagery, metaphor, timely interpretations, and attention to clients' personal meanings is more likely to be perceived, encoded, and recalled by clients.

For Therapist Educators

Much of what has been said concerning possible implications of the cognitive-mediational perspective for practicing therapists also may be applied to the education of therapists and counselors. Helping would-be therapists to comprehend realistic limitations to the role of therapist as change agent, and assisting them to gain comfort and skill in communicating information about therapeutic processes and interventions to clients, are perhaps the two most obvious examples. Both revolve around the central conceptualization of the therapist's role as involved, active, and collaborative as opposed to remote, passive, and authoritarian. Probably one of the best ways for therapist educators to provide student therapists with a meaningful understanding of this role is to model it themselves in their interactions with student therapists.

Because skills training is such a major component in the preparation of many counselors and therapists, I want to direct specific attention to this aspect of therapist education. In the past, many skills-training programs and courses have tended to emphasize the acquisition of counselor behaviors that constitute the skills being targeted for acquisition, with little explicit regard for the conditions and purposes associated with the use of therapeutic skills. I believe it is of fundamental importance to assist student counselors to acquire knowledge of the conditions (including therapeutic goals, client levels and styles of functioning, and current client responding) under which particular therapist skills might best be employed and to assist students to recognize these conditions as they arise during therapy. One of my long-term hopes is that detailed models of such conditional knowledge might eventually evolve from extensions and elaborations of the methods used to develop models such as those illustrated in Figure 5.2. (As an aside, I believe that much of the task-analytic, events paradigm research of Rice and Greenberg, 1984, and others provides excellent examples of research on psychotherapy that places therapist response operations in proper conditional context.)

In addition to emphasizing the acquisition of conditional knowledge in therapist skills training, I also believe it is important to emphasize the probabilistic nature of all counseling interactions. Student counselors need to know that clients' ever-present potential for unique responding means that even therapeutic skills that are well delivered under appropriate conditions may not always yield desired effects. Such occurrences themselves might be important to identify and perhaps to use as opportunities for initiating "in-therapy" discussions with clients concerning therapeutic processes and the nature of the therapist-client working alliance. Helping students of counseling and psychotherapy to acquire knowledge about, and comfort with, the probabilistic world of therapeutic interactions is an important part of therapist education. (Presumably, such comfort might free student counselors to be more spontaneous when faced with unexpected client behavior.) I believe that the cognitive-mediational perspective can be helpful to counselor educators for exactly these purposes.

For Researchers of Psychotherapy

It is, I think, fitting that this chapter ends with a discussion of applications of the cognitive-mediational research perspective to future research that attempts to increase our understanding of the processes and mechanisms by which psychotherapy assists clients to change. The entire cognitive-mediational enterprise has been devoted to increasing our understanding of these processes and mechanisms within a probabilistic framework that captures a fundamental truth about human action—which is that humans are capable of responding uniquely to any situation given their individual knowledge and experiential structures. The challenge of conducting social scientific research in the probabilistic world of human actions in counseling and psychotherapy has been both exhilarating and perplexing.

One of the real advantages gained by adopting a cognitive-mediational perspective on psychotherapy is the theoretical elucidation of therapeutic change mechanisms. In most extant theories of, and approaches to, counseling and psychotherapy, the exact manner in which therapy is thought to lead to client growth and change is not specified in sufficient detail to remove vestigial shrouds of mysticism that have enveloped many popular (and professional) conceptualizations of therapy. By denying human capacities for active agency (supported by individual knowledge and experiential structures developed through unique personal histories), many earlier, "scientific" theories of therapeutic change left a frustrating gap between change as promoted through therapeutic interactions and change as maintained and perpetuated in the everyday lives of clients. The cognitive-mediational theoretical key unlocks this riddle. It postulates (see Figure

5.1) that the construction of new perspectives, awarenesses, insights, understandings, and/or plans in the social conversation between client and therapist leads to the symbolic representation of these constructions in the minds of clients (e.g., elaborated problem schemata, newly acquired problem-solving structures, empowered self-schemata). Once they become part of clients' long-term memory and knowledge/theoretical structures, such structures can be activated when clients perceive problem stimuli in their everyday life experiences, thus providing clients with a cognitive basis for competent action that resolves or copes with these everyday situations. The perceived consequences of such client action further elaborate the now-expanding cognitive competence of clients, a competence that was initiated in the social construction and processing of information during counseling.

It should be made clear that the cognitive-mediational perspective also posits an analogous process of social-cognitive construction and information processing that affects counselors or therapists. Therapists also perceive, encode, and store information extracted from therapeutic interactions. Through this process, therapists gradually construct vast mnemonic stores of experiential knowledge that become integrated with their theoretical and personal knowledge to form the basis for unique personal theories of psychotherapy and therapeutic intervention (see Figure 5.1). Differences between novice and experienced therapists probably relate directly to differences in the experiential knowledge structures of therapists with differing levels of experience in therapy (cf. Martin, Slemon, et al., 1989).

For the researcher of psychotherapy, the major advantage gained from specifying a more precise theory of therapeutic change processes and mechanisms is the conceptual basis it provides for the conduct of research that tests, examines, elaborates, and eventually transforms the theory itself. My colleagues and I have found the cognitive-mediational perspective to be a powerful stimulus to the conduct of psychotherapy research.

While accessing and representing counselor and client cognitive processes and structures is fraught with difficulties, we have been assisted by much recent methodological and conceptual work in the fields of cognitive psychology and science (e.g., Ericsson & Simon, 1984; Merluzzi, Glass, & Genest, 1981). To date, we have been able to demonstrate in an initial way (a) that clients do respond in unique ways (particularly at the level of cognitive processing and construction) to therapeutic interventions (see Martin, Martin, et al., 1989, in particular), (b) that predictable changes in clients' cognitive structures related to their problems/concerns do seem to accompany therapeutic interventions for many clients (see Martin, 1987b, in particular), and (c) that clients tend to retain in their memories important information from certain identifiable kinds of therapeutic interactions long after therapy has ended (see Martin & Stelmaczonek, 1988, in particular).

I am optimistic that future research on psychotherapy will support an expanded view of the centrality of cognitive-mediational processes to both therapeutic change and therapist expertise. With respect to therapeutic change, such cognitive operations help to understand how the social, public, co-constructions of therapists and clients can become internalized in the cognitive, private constructions and reconstructions of clients (cf. Martin, 1989). With respect to therapist expertise, it seems clear that the cognitive operations and structures of therapists enable therapists of differing levels of experience and expertise to conceptualize client problems and therapeutic interventions more or less efficiently, thoroughly, and parsimoniously (cf. Martin, Slemon, et al., 1989).

Whatever the eventual course of research on psychotherapy, however, I believe that future generations of psychotherapists and psychotherapy researchers will continue to be challenged by the related realities of human response uniqueness, probabilistic therapeutic interactions, and the necessity for conditional therapeutic responding with which others and I have grappled in our therapeutic research and practice. I think, and I hope, that research on counseling and therapy that emphasizes these matters can provide important insights not only for psychotherapists and students of psychotherapy but for applied social scientists in general.

Note

1. Throughout this chapter, the terms *counseling, psychotherapy,* and *therapy* (as well as the related terms *counselor, psychotherapist,* and *therapist*) are used interchangeably with no intended differences in meaning. As used here, all these terms reference the enhancement of individuals' psychological and social functioning in the absence of severe behavioral, cognitive, and/or emotional impediments to such functioning.

References

Anderson, J. R. (1983). *The architecture of cognition.* Cambridge, MA: Harvard University Press.
Angus, L. E., & Rennie, D. L. (1988). Therapist participation in metaphor generation: Collaborative and non-collaborative styles. *Psychotherapy, 25,* 552-560.
Austin, J. L. (1961). *Philosophical papers.* London: Oxford University Press.
Chi, M., Glaser, R., & Rees, E. (1982). Expertise in problem solving. In R. Sternberg (Ed.), *Advances in the psychology of intelligence* (Vol. 1, pp. 7-75). Hillsdale, NJ: Lawrence Erlbaum.
Elliott, R. (1985). Helpful and non-helpful events in brief counseling interviews: An empirical taxonomy. *Journal of Counseling Psychology, 32,* 307-322.
Ericsson, K. A., & Simon, H. A. (1984). *Protocol analysis.* Cambridge: MIT Press.
Harré, R. (1984). *Personal being.* Cambridge, MA: Harvard University Press.
Hiebert, B. (1987). Exploring changes in cognitive structure of counselling practicum students. *Alberta Psychology, 17,* 3-7.
Hill, C. E., Greenwald, C., Reed, K. G., Charles, D., O'Farrell, M. K., & Carter, J. A. (1981). *Manual for counselor and client verbal response category systems.* Columbus, OH: Marathon Consulting & Press.
Hill, C. E., & O'Grady, K. E. (1985). List of therapist intentions illustrated in a case study and with therapists of varying theoretical orientations. *Journal of Counseling Psychology, 32,* 3-22.
Kagan, N. (1973). *Influencing human interaction: Eleven years of IPR (Interpersonal Process Recall).* Paper presented at the annual meeting of the American Educational Research Association, New Orleans.
Kagan, N., Krathwohl, D. R., & Miller, R. L. (1963). Stimulated recall in therapy using videotape: A case study. *Journal of Counseling Psychology, 10,* 237-243.
Kelly, G. (1955). *The psychology of personal constructs.* New York: Norton.
Mahrer, A. R. (1988). Research and clinical applications of "good moments" in psychotherapy. *Journal of Integrative and Eclectic Psychotherapy, 7,* 81-93.
Mahrer, A. R., & Nadler, W. P. (1986). Good moments in psychotherapy: A preliminary review, a list, and some promising research avenues. *Journal of Consulting and Clinical Psychology, 54,* 10-16.
Martin, J. (1984). The cognitive mediational paradigm for research on counseling. *Journal of Counseling Psychology, 31,* 558-571.
Martin, J. (1985a). Toward an information-processing theory of client change in counseling. *Counselor Education and Supervision, 25,* 107-121.
Martin, J. (1985b). Measuring clients' cognitive competence in research on counseling. *Journal of Counseling and Development, 63,* 556-560.
Martin, J. (1987a). Cognitive change in clients: Cognitive-mediational models. *Counselor Education and Supervision, 26,* 192-203.
Martin, J. (1987b). *Cognitive-instructional counseling.* London, Ontario: University of Western Ontario's Althouse Press.

Martin, J. (1989, June). *A theory of social-cognitive construction in therapy*. Paper presented at the annual meeting of the Society for Psychotherapy Research, Toronto.

Martin, J., Martin, W., Meyer, M., & Slemon, A. (1986). An empirical investigation of the cognitive mediational paradigm for research on counseling. *Journal of Counseling Psychology, 33*, 115-123.

Martin, J., Martin, W., & Slemon, A. G. (1987). Cognitive mediation in person-centered and rational-emotive therapy. *Journal of Counseling Psychology, 34*, 251-260.

Martin, J., Martin, W., & Slemon, A. G. (1989). Cognitive-mediational models of action-act sequences in counseling. *Journal of Counseling Psychology, 36*, 8-16.

Martin, J., Paivio, S. C., & Labadie, D. (1990). Memory-enhancing characteristics of client-recalled important events in cognitive and experiential therapy: Integrating cognitive experimental and therapeutic psychology. *Counselling Psychology Quarterly, 3*, 239-256.

Martin, J., & Reaume, D. (1988). [Cognitive structures of clients and counselors over time in therapy]. Unpublished research data.

Martin, J., Slemon, A. G., Hiebert, B., Hallberg, E. T., & Cummings, A. L. (1989). Conceptualizations of novice and experienced counselors. *Journal of Counseling Psychology, 36*, 395-400.

Martin, J., & Stelmaczonek, K. (1988). Participant identification and recall of important events in counseling. *Journal of Counseling Psychology, 35*, 385-390.

Merluzzi, T. V., Glass, C. R., & Genest, M. (Eds.). (1981). *Cognitive assessment*. New York: Guilford.

Paivio, A. (1986). *Mental representations: A dual coding approach*. New York: Oxford University Press.

Paivio, S. (1989). *Action-act sequences in important therapeutic events: A case study of experiential psychotherapy*. Unpublished master's thesis, University of Western Ontario, London, Ontario.

Rice, L. N., & Greenberg, L. S. (Eds.). (1984). *Patterns of change: Intensive analysis of psychotherapy process*. New York: Guilford.

Ryle, G. (1949). *The concept of mind*. London: Hutchinson.

Stiles, W. B., Shapiro, D. A., & Elliott, R. (1986). Are all psychotherapies equivalent? *American Psychologist, 41*, 165-180.

Winne, P. H., & Marx, R. W. (1977). Reconceptualizing research on teaching. *Journal of Educational Psychology, 69*, 668-678.

Winne, P. H., & Marx, R. W. (1980). Matching students' cognitive responses to teaching skills. *Journal of Educational Psychology, 72*, 257-264.

Wittgenstein, L. (1953). *Philosophical investigations*. Oxford, UK: Blackwell.

6

Helping and Hindering Processes in Client-Centered/Experiential Psychotherapy

A Content Analysis of Client and Therapist Postsession Perceptions

GERMAIN LIETAER

This chapter deals with the helping and hindering processes in client-centered/experiential therapy as perceived by clients and therapists. In client-centered therapy (Gendlin, 1970; Rogers, 1961), the basic attitudes of the therapist—acceptance, empathy, and genuineness—together with intense experiential exploration on the part of the client, are seen as the essential factors in constructive personality change.The question remains, however, as to what extent the client-centered theory of change coincides with what actually happens in practice. As has been shown by many psychotherapy process studies (Lambert, Shapiro, & Bergin, 1986; Orlinsky & Howard, 1986), there is still a gap between the theory and what goes on during therapy. In other words, the "com-

AUTHOR'S NOTE: This study was undertaken as a part of Research Project No. 3.0045.77, which was financed by the Belgian Research Fund of Medical Sciences (FGWO): Professor J. Rombauts and Professor G. Lietaer. We wish to thank Mrs. Marleen Neirinck for her important contribution to the research project.

mon ingredients" may prove to be more impactful than the specific factors advocated by the theory.

It was this gap that stimulated the members of my research team and me to carry out a study in which a large sample of Flemish clients and therapists were asked to write down their perceptions and experiences of what was helpful and hindering during a number of therapy sessions. We chose to use an open-ended question method so as not to inhibit the respondents but to allow them to formulate the helping and hindering processes in their own words. We also hoped that, in this way, we would be able to obtain more detailed and lively information than could be expected from the use of rating scales.

The study to be reported in this chapter was designed to shed some light on the following questions: (a) What processes do clients and therapists experience as being either helpful or hindering? (b) What is the proportion of each of the factors mentioned? (c) Are there differences arising from the vantage points of clients and therapists? (d) What processes most discriminate between "very good" and "rather poor" sessions? Finally, (e) to what extent do the research findings on the change process confirm the basic tenets of client-centered theory? The chapter is a revision and synthesis of two earlier reports (Lietaer & Neirinck, 1985, 1986).

Method

Procedure

Members of the Flemish Society for Client-Centered Therapy were asked to participate in a research project on "factors which play a role in the degree to which clients and therapists are satisfied with their sessions." Those who were interested in participating received a more concrete explanation about the course of the research project. They were requested to identify two clients who would be willing to cooperate. The clients were then contacted by the researcher, who offered them the possibility of discussing the project with her. Clients and therapists were remunerated for their cooperation.

A total of 25 therapists entered the project, of whom 16 participated with 2 clients and 9 with 1 client. Thus 41 clients were involved in the research. During the course of therapy, both the client and the therapist were asked to fill in a postsession questionnaire after every other session, for a maximum of 10 sessions. By using this procedure, we hoped not to overburden the client and therapist and to allow the evaluation of the different sessions to run as independently as possible. The anonymity of the research participants was emphasized. Both clients and therapists were asked to complete the questionnaire as quickly as possible following the session and to send it directly to the researcher.

There was a total of 349 sessions for which at least one of the participants had filled in the postsession questionnaire. The analysis was based on 325 sessions that were evaluated by both client and therapist, although in a few cases the questionnaire was only partially completed.

The postsession questionnaire consisted of the following components:

1. A global evaluation of the session on a scale ranging from "not good at all" (rating = 1) to "very good" (rating = 7).
2. Four open-ended questions, which were formulated for the client as follows:
   (a) What feelings and expectations did you have when coming to this session?
   (b) What was mostly discussed in this session?
   (c) Did things happen in this session that you feel were really helpful to you?
   (d) Did things occur in this session that you feel were not helpful at all (perhaps even the opposite)?
3. A rating scale of 76 items referring to different relational and task-oriented aspects of the therapeutic process consisted of items derived from a number of existing scales (Barrett & Lennard, 1981; Orlinsky & Howard, 1975; Snyder & Snyder, 1961; Strupp, Chassan, & Ewing, 1966) as well as items formulated on the basis of our own pilot study (Neirink, Lietaer, & Rombauts, 1981).

Only the analyses of the data concerning the perception of the helping and hindering processes (Questions 2c and 2d above) will be reported in this chapter. Data relevant to Questions 2b and 3 have been published elsewhere (Lietaer, 1989; Lietaer, Dierick, & Neirinck, 1985). In the near future, we also hope to publish the findings regarding clients' expectations (Question 2a).

Respondents

The therapists (mainly psychologists and a few psychiatrists) had been trained at the Counseling Centrum of the University of Leuven.

The postgraduate program they pursued is a two-year, half-time program in which practice, supervision, theory, and (group) personal therapy are integrated in a balanced way. The views of Rogers (1961), Gendlin (1970), Rice (1980), and Yalom (1975, 1980) form the foundations of the approach, which may best be characterized as "client-centered/experiential/existential" in nature. Almost all of the clients participating in the study were outpatients. The therapists were asked to briefly identify the nature of their clients' problems. Most of the disturbances were described as being neurotic in nature. In five cases, psychotic or borderline elements were also mentioned. The demographic characteristics of the therapists and the clients, and the frequencies of contact among them, have been presented elsewhere (Lietaer & Neirinck, 1986).

All phases of therapy were represented by the therapeutic dyads participating in this research. More than half of the sessions examined stemmed from relatively long-term therapies. The global evaluations of these sessions were fairly positive, although more from the clients' than from the therapists' point of view. Of the 311 sessions that were evaluated quantitatively by both clients and therapists, 63% ($n = 196$) of the therapists rated the session as 5 or higher on the 7-point scale, whereas 78% ($n = 243$) of the clients rated the session as 5 or higher. The ranges on the global evaluation were truncated and the correlation between client and therapist evaluation was low and nonsignificant ($r = .18$). The reader is referred to Lietaer and Neirinck (1986) for further details.

The lack of convergence between clients' and therapists' perceptions of session helpfulness has been found in many studies and has been interpreted (Lietaer, 1983) to be the function of moderate scale reliabilities, differences in response tendency and authenticity, idiosyncratic norms and expectations as a frame of reference for evaluation, multidimensionality of the therapy process (e.g., Barrett-Lennard, 1981), lack of explicit feedback (especially during the first phase of therapy), and lack of variability in the samples studied.

To investigate which of the helping processes differentiated best between "very good" and "rather poor" sessions, we selected from the total sample of sessions a high and a low group of 40 sessions, based on the global session evaluations. We did this for clients and therapists separately, given the low correlation between their ratings. Consequently, sessions that were evaluated by only one of the participants were also taken into consideration. Extreme scores were used to identify high and low sessions. A minimum difference score of 3 between high and low sessions was used as a criterion when both types of session were selected from the same dyad. To the extent that it was feasible, we also took into consideration the response tendencies of the participants. Special attention was paid to having the highest possible representation of clients and therapists. Thus, in each extreme group, no more than two sessions were selected from the same dyad. On the basis of this selection procedure, we obtained two extreme groups of 40 sessions each, whereby the 40 sessions stemmed from either 27 or 30 dyads, depending upon whether the sessions pertained to the high or the low group.

Content Analysis

A content analysis was used to evaluate clients' responses to the open question concerning the helping processes (Question 2c). In carrying out the procedure, the chief researcher, in cooperation with a second judge, set up a preliminary category system that was based on an analysis of a representative third of the research material. Because we wanted to assign each unit of analysis to a single category, we divided the responses of all of the sessions into the largest possible number of meaningful segments. We stayed close to the manifest content, taking into consideration the emphases that the participants themselves placed on their responses. This version of the taxonomy was discussed with the other staff members of the Counseling Center, who in turn scored a number of "exercise segments," assessed the meaningfulness and distinctiveness of the categories, and further refined the category system. In a final preparatory phase, the two judges worked on one fifth of the material and discussed their divergent categorizations. This gave rise to further amplification and refinement of the categories. The consistency of judgments with respect to the final form of this category system was tested on another fifth of the material. The segmenting of the material into meaningful segments was extremely reliable. The interjudge agreement regarding the categorizations during the content analysis was acceptable, yielding 83% agreement in the case of the client material and 78% agreement with respect to the therapist material.

The content analysis of the material pertaining to hindering processes was carried out in a similar way. Initial inspection of the raw data clearly revealed that clients and therapists differed vastly in their description of hindering processes. So as not to obscure this distinction, we decided to build two separate category systems. The interjudge agreement of each taxonomy proved to be high: 89% agreement for the client material and 82% for the therapist material.

It should be clear from the above description of our method that we were only minimally theory driven in establishing our category systems. We simply sorted the session answer segments into arrays according to their apparently similar meaning and then created a label to describe that meaning, which at the same time became the name of the category. We also worked, as indicated previously, with mutually exclusive judgments; every segment was assigned to only one category. It also should be mentioned that a given category was counted only once in cases where it occurred several times in one session answer. To provide the reader with a concrete illustration of the material and its coding, we present below a few session answers pertaining to perceived helping processes, together with the segmenting and coding that we performed. (For a summary of the meanings of these codes, see Table 6.1.)

Session 106: Client protocol. "I felt the warmth [A1: warmth and interest], the empathy and understanding [A3: empathic depth] of the therapist for my experience and feelings. Simultaneously, I felt a strong appeal to my energy and potential [A5: acceptance, respect, and patience] in order not to let myself slide into a depressive position. I felt somewhat relieved [C13: feeling relieved] after this session and had again courage to continue living and fighting [C14: positive experience of self]. I no longer felt my life to be meaningless [C14]."

Session 298: Client protocol. "After gaining insight into the fact that I am afraid of close contact [C9: self-insight], I started crying [C7: experiencing fully], something which I had given up because I always had negative experiences with it (was not allowed, was weak, etc.). This time, however, it was a positive experience [C14: positive experience of self]. I had the feeling that the therapist accepted me more [A4: acceptance, respect, and patience]. He was very kind [A1: warmth and interest] and understanding toward me [A3: empathic depth], which opened the way to different relationships [C15: experiencing progress]. I have thus learned that I can have a valuable contact when I show my feelings instead of hiding them [C11: insight into new possibilities], as I did previously."

Session 238: Therapist protocol. "I think that it was very important for my client to be able to express clearly that she wanted to stop with her relationship [C12: intentions and plans]."

"I think that she regained courage to fight for herself [C14: positive experience of self] through the attention she received from me [A1: warmth and interest]."

Session 347: Therapist protocol. "She was able to put into words what troubles her now in contact with her father [C3: deep exploration of experience], by means of focusing [B2: offering specific procedures]. This relieved her somewhat [C13: feeling relieved]. She also could express her feelings toward her sisters, with whom she is now again increasingly confronted [C7: experiencing fully]."

Findings and Comments

The system of categories depicting the helping processes has been reported earlier (Lietaer & Neirinck, 1986) and is summarized in Table 6.1. As indicated above, the clients' and therapists' differing views on hindering processes necessitated two separate taxonomies. The three category systems may be seen as the major result of our study. The categories give a concrete picture of the helping and hindering processes as they were remembered in response to open-ended questions by both clients and therapists either immediately or shortly after ending the therapeutic session. The different categories are defined on the basis of all response segments within each category. The different facets of content mentioned in each category description provide a rich source of information in terms of constructing items for a rating scale on helping and hindering processes, which could be used in further research.

In presenting the data, I have taken a macroscopic approach. Therefore I shall provide a global survey of the number and the percentage of segments in each category, without taking into account the differences among individuals. These differences were sometimes considerable. Some respondents gave numerous blank answers or were brief in their reactions, while others had a tendency to give lengthy answers comprising several response segments.

(Text continues on p. 144)

Table 6.1 Therapy Session Content Analysis of Helping Process

Sector A Categories	Full Sample (N = 325 sessions) Percentage Frequency				High and Low groups (N = 40 for each) Frequency: Client		Frequency: Therapist	
	Client	Therapist	Client	Therapist	High	Low	High	Low
1. Warmth and interest of therapist	21	6	3.9	1.2	4	2	2	1
2. Involvement and availability of therapist	11	—	2.0	—	2	—	—	2
3. Deep empathy of therapist	20	10	3.7	1.9	3	—	1	2
4. Acceptance, respect, patience of therapist	19	13	3.5	2.5	2	—	2	1
5. Therapist confirming and valuing the personhood of client	11	10	2.0	1.9	1	—	2	—
6. Good, relaxed contact	11	—	2.0	—	2	—	—	-|
7. Inner comfort and openness of therapist	—	7	—	1.4	—	—	—	—
8. Authenticity and personal presence of therapist	9	—	1.7	—	2	—	—	—
9. Personal, more mutual contact	7	—	1.3	—	2	1	—	—
10. Informal contact	3	3	0.6	0.6	—	1	—	—
Total A	112	49	20.9	9.5	18	4	7	4

Continued

141

Table 6.1 Continued

| Sector B Categories | Full Sample (N = 325 sessions) Percentage Frequency | | | | High and Low groups (N = 40 for each) | | | |
| | Client | Therapist | Client | Therapist | Frequency: Client | | Frequency: Therapist | |
					High	Low	High	Low
1. Stimulation and deepening of self-exploration	22	25	4.1	4.8	2	3	4	2
2. Offering specific procedures	9	14	1.7	2.7	3	1	3	—
3. Therapist self-disclosure	—	12	—	2.3	—	—	2	1
4. Confrontation and here-and-now feedback	29	26	5.4	5.0	5	4	9	1
5. Interpretation, cognitive restructuring	12	19	2.2	3.7	—	2	3	2
6. Giving advice	15	5	2.8	1.0	2	1	—	1
7. Reinforcing ideas, feelings, plans, behaviors	12	15	2.2	2.9	3	—	1	1
8. Confirming a positive evolution, instilling hope	11	3	2.0	0.6	2	—	1	—
Total B	110	119	20.5	23.1	17	11	23	8

Table 6.1 Continued

| Sector C Categories | Full Sample (N = 325 sessions) | | | | High and Low groups (N = 40 for each) | | | |
| | Percentage Frequency | | | | Frequency: Client | | Frequency: Therapist | |
	Client	Therapist	Client	Therapist	High	Low	High	Low
1. Having the opportunity to talk	23	16	4.3	3.1	1	—	—	2
2. Taking the risk to talk very personally	5	25	0.9	4.8	2	—	6	2
3. Exploring personal experiences more deeply	33	70	6.1	13.6	3	1	15	2
4. Fruitful self-exploration process	—	24	—	4.6	—	—	2	1
5. Touching the core issue	—	11	—	2.1	—	—	1	—
6. Exploration of the therapeutic relationship	15	16	2.8	3.1	4	2	—	1
7. Living through and experiencing fully	31	62	5.8	12.0	8	4	14	3
8. Self-acceptance	—	15	—	2.9	—	—	4	—
9. Insight: general; into oneself	78	47	14.5	9.1	7	7	8	2
10. Insight: into situations and others	14	5	2.6	1.0	2	1	1	—
11. Insight into new possibilities	15	12	2.8	2.3	3	1	1	—
12. Intentions and plans	27	5	5.0	1.0	6	1	1	—
13. Feeling relieved	20	13	3.7	2.5	4	2	3	1
14. A momentary positive experiencing of self	22	14	4.1	2.7	3		2	1
15. Experiencing progress	32	13	6.0	2.5	9	1	2	—
Total C	315	348	58.7	67.4	52	20	60	15
Total: All categories	537	516	100	100	87	35	90	27
Blank answers (out of 325)	46	76	14.1	23.4	1	15	1	22
Nonclassifiable answers	1	—	—	—	—	1	—	—
Unclear or ambivalent answers	17	23	—	—	2	4	1	6

Helping Processes

Main findings. On the basis of our data, which consisted of 1,053 response segments (537 client and 516 therapist segments) pertaining to the 325 sessions from 41 dyads, a reasonably accurate assessment was made of what was generally experienced as helpful in client-centered/experiential therapy. It can be seen from Table 6.1 that we could group these experiences into three main categories: (a) aspects of the relational climate (Sector A), whereby the participants referred to the basic attitudes of the therapist and to general characteristics of their mutual contact; (b) specific therapist interventions (Sector B); and (c) process aspects concerning the client (Sector C). Clients (21%), more than therapists (10%), seemed to perceive the relational climate (Sector A) as helpful, especially in discriminating "high" ($n = 18$) and "low" ($n = 4$) sessions. The client process sector (Sector C) contains the highest number of response segments, comprising 59% of all the client responses and 67% of all the therapist responses.

Table 6.2 groups the results in a more abstract manner. In other words, all subcategories with the same nuclear meaning were combined into broader categories, thus making it easier to highlight the central findings of the research. Because the study was exploratory and descriptive in nature, we did not use statistical tests. Only the salient findings are reported and commented upon here.

Category A contains all subcategories that point to empathy and acceptance. These basic relationship attitudes were clearly emphasized as helping factors more often by clients than by therapists (17% versus 8%). It is also apparent that this category tends to discriminate between high and low sessions for clients but not for therapists.

Category B colligates several subcategories pertaining to authenticity and transparency. It is confined to 3% to 4% of the answers. This limitation suggests that "encounter" and "mutualness" appeared only sporadically as helping factors in the process of individual client-centered therapy.

Category C contains all subcategories referring to self-exploration and its facilitation and forms the most frequent given class of responses. This is the case in the client material (20%) and is twice as evident in the therapist material (39%).

Category D points to the intensive living through of feelings and acknowledgment of painful aspects of self. This category received much more emphasis from the therapists than the clients (15% versus

Table 6.2 Content Analysis of Helping Processes in Therapy Sessions: Combined Categories

Combined Categories	Code Subcategories	Full sample (N = 325 sessions) Percentage		High and Low Groups (N = 40 for each)			
		Client	Therapist	Frequency: Client High	Low	Frequency: Therapist High	Low
A. Involved, empathic, accepting therapist; good contact	A1-A6	17.3	7.6	14	2	7	4
B. Personal contact with an authentic therapist	A7-A10/B3	3.6	4.3	4	2	2	1
C. Self-exploration; facilitation by therapist	B1-B2/C1-C6	19.9	38.9	15	7	31	10
D. Experiencing feelings fully; self-acceptance	C7-C8	5.8	14.9	8	4	18	3
E. Confrontation and feedback	B4	5.4	5.0	5	4	9	1
F. Insight into oneself and situations; interpretation by therapist	B5/C9-C10	19.4	13.8	9	10	12	4
G. Advice; reinforcement of feelings, plans, behaviors	B6-B7	5.0	3.9	5	1	1	2
H. Insight into new possibilities; intentions and plans	C11-C12	7.8	3.3	9	2	2	0
I. Momentary relief; experiencing progress; confirmation by therapist	B8/C13-C15	15.8	8.3	18	3	8	2
Totals		100.0	100.0	87	35	90	27

6%). It is also striking that, with respect to the therapist material, this category appears to discriminate very strongly between high and low sessions.

Category E involves the B4 category in the original taxonomy: confrontation and feedback. It accounts for 5% of all responses in the client material as well as in the therapist material. This percentage suggests the possibility that client-centered therapists may have become, during the course of therapy, a bit more directive than expected and may have brought more of their own reactions into the therapeutic relationship. With respect to the therapist material, the data suggest that this factor differentiates clearly between the high and low sessions. It does not seem to discriminate well for clients, however. Nevertheless, a closer analysis of clients' answers indicates that the confrontations in the low group were received with relatively more confusion and ambivalence. On the other hand, in the high group, the confrontations were experienced as welcome learning experiences.

Category F combines three subcategories pertaining to insight from interpretation by the therapist. Although a relatively frequent ingredient of client-centered therapy, this factor does not seem to discriminate between high and low sessions for the clients, but it does so for the therapists. A closer look at the specific content of the clients' answers shows that, in the low group, insight was formulated as being more hypothetical or as being purely cognitive, whereas, in the high group, it was described by adjectives such as "profound," "deeply felt," "new," "very important," and "for the first time."

Category G, giving advice and reinforcing feelings and behavior, appears occasionally. Again, these therapeutic operations went against the grain of client-centered theory.

Category H represents insight into new possibilities, intentions, and plans. Clients, more often than therapists, reported these aspects as being helpful.

Category I reflects clients' momentary relief, their experiencing of progress as well as confirmation by the therapist. Although this factor received more emphasis from clients than therapists (16% to 8%), it appeared to differentiate high from low sessions for both therapists and clients.

In summary, the difference between the two vantage points (clients and therapists) may be viewed as follows: Clients referred more frequently to aspects of the relational context of the session and to the immediate outcome aspects of the process. Therapists, on the other hand, referred more frequently to the process of deep and cathartic like self-explorations.

Helping ingredients in client-centered therapy. Is there a gap between theory and practice? Our general impression is that, to a large extent, the data support the theoretical position of client-centered therapy on change-producing factors. Although there were some differences in emphasis, both the clients and the therapists perceived self-exploration and experiential insight as the salient ingredients of their therapy sessions. Clients seemed to indicate—more strongly than therapists— that this was more likely achieved in a safe relationship with an accepting and empathic therapist.

Because all fruitful therapy must lead to mastery and experiences of success (Frank, 1971; Korchin, 1983; Murray & Jacobson, 1971; Strupp, 1973), one may speculate about the kinds of corrective experiences clients go through in client-centered therapy. In this respect, the data lead us to draw the following picture: Clients find comfort and support in having a trustful relationship with an involved therapist. Self-esteem is nourished by the therapist's acceptance and confirmation. Through exploring their own inner world with the empathic facilitation of their therapists, clients come to face, accept, and integrate hitherto denied aspects of their experience. This process of self-exploration, along with the feedback and reactions of the therapist, fosters clients' insight into feelings, relational patterns, and troublesome life situations. Gaining insight helps them to feel powerful and more in control. It also opens new possibilities and encourages them to behave in new ways, which may be reinforced by their therapists. When some of these processes occur, clients experience some progress or relief that strengthens their hope for further improvement and their motivation to continue their efforts.

Specific therapist interventions. In this study, clients and therapists referred to specific therapist interventions as helpful moments in 21% and 23% of their response segments, respectively (see Table 6.1, categories B1 to B8). These interventions seem to be only partially in line with the "classic image" of client-centered therapy of the Chicago period. A closer look at the data reveals that exploratory questions, restatement of content, and reflection of feeling (category B1) represent only about one fifth of all therapist interventions mentioned. Although, infrequently, other kinds of interventions seem to emerge: At times, these client-centered therapists offered specific procedures to stimulate the experiential process; they revealed personal aspects of themselves;

they confronted, interpreted, gave feedback, reinforced, and sometimes made suggestions or gave advice. This is in sharp contrast with earlier studies by Strupp (1955, 1957, 1958), in which about 70% of all interventions fell under the category "reflection of feeling."

This wider range of interventions may reflect some changes in client-centered therapists in the direction of a broadly conceived experiential psychotherapy in which therapists do not stay within the client's frame of reference on a continuous basis but at times intervene from their own frame of reference. The question remains, however, whether or not these "non-classic" response patterns are really inconsistent with the client-centered theory's fundamental premise that the only proper source of authority about the person's life is the person. We think that they are not. Our view is that it depends on *how* the interventions are made. These "more intrusive" interventions can be made in a client-centered/experiential way, if the therapist respects the pace of the client and if the client's immediate experience remains the continuous touchstone with regard to anything brought in by the therapist.

I wish to emphasize, however, that such inferences are derived from the group of therapists' under study, a sample of Flemish therapists who were trained in a two-year postgraduate program characterized by an integration of Rogerian and Gendlinian concepts. A comparison with other groups of client-centered therapists would be very helpful and interesting.

Hindering Processes

Psychotherapists do not seem to talk or write easily about their failures, about impasses in psychotherapy, or about the things that go wrong in their work. There is not much literature on failure cases or on hindering processes. Yet we all know from practice and from research that psychotherapy is not always rosy in its process or outcome. We can refer here to such well-known facts as high dropout rates, the 25% of clients who do not make any progress at all (even when staying in therapy for a fairly long time), and the phenomenon of deterioration (Lambert, Bergin, & Collins, 1977; Lambert et al., 1986; Strupp, Hadley, & Gomes-Schwartz, 1977). Such outcomes are sufficient reason to direct our attention to negatively acting processes. The qualitative description (Tables 6.3 and 6.4) of the categories and the quantitative data of our study (Tables 6.5 and 6.6) regarding this phenomenon reveal the following.

Table 6.3   Client Category System for Hindering Processes

A. Attitudes and interventions of the therapist

A1 *Lack of warmth, involvement, understanding.* T is not there for C during the conversation.

A2 *The therapist is too passive, confronts too little.* C wants T to be a bit more confronting, which would have helped.

A3 *T is too active. T constantly tries to go further into how C feels towards people whom C ignores.* This is dragging; C does not get ahead.

A4 *Disapproval and undervaluing by T.* Example: "The therapist briefly considered letting me use a technique but he himself thought that I, with my character, would perhaps not be able to do it well."

A5 *T gives advice and suggestions that are painful and leave the client not understood.* Example: "It hurt me deeply when the therapist asked whether I had never wondered if the absence of my child would not be better."

A6 *T gives suggestions of interpretations which the client finds inadequate or inaccurate.* Example: "At a certain moment, T told me that it was better to talk about how I felt now, how I viewed it now. He told me that I anticipated a lot. At that moment, I stopped talking about the past, even if I did not feel like it."

A7 *T is too intrusive.* T tries to bring C to a deeper level of experiencing or to direct C to more intimate material, causing C to block or withdraw/comes too close to C as a person/gives feedback (especially about double messages) that makes C confused or insecure/gives evaluations (positive or negative) of the therapy that provoke anxiety in C/proposes something (i.e., to go into group therapy) for which C is not ready.

B. The client's process

B1 *C hinders the conversation by waiting, remaining silent, not cooperating.* Example: "My long periods of silence during the conversation are, in my opinion, excuses in order not to have to say anything."

B2 *C prevents deepening of the conversation.* C talks/narrates too much or talks about superficial issues; C changes the subject too often.

B3 *C cannot talk, or does not dare to talk about certain issues.* Example: "I had hoped to talk about all the problems which I had written down on paper. However I was not able to, which gave me a negative impression about the session."

Continued

Table 6.3   Continued

B4 *The conversation does not bring anything new.* C repeats things about him/herself which C already knows, or keeps repeating the same things.

B5 *The session leaves behind a feeling of confusion and uncertainty.* C doubts the relevance of what s/he discussed/ does not see the link between whatever was discussed/ feels uncertain of the therapist's opinion about him/her.

B6 *The session was too confronting or too heavy.* C faces things which s/he would prefer to avoid, causing reticence; C is afraid of reliving a traumatic experience.

B7 *C is discouraged by the lack of progress or hope.* C doubts whether change is possible/runs repeatedly into the same problems/advances too slowly/acquires insight but this does not change anything yet.

B8 *C feels left to his/her fate at the end of the session.* Example: "Towards the end, a profound sadness appeared in me. Then I have to go home and cope with it alone. It can sometimes last a whole day."

C. External or structural factors

Example: "The fact that my husband was present, and that he can muster little or no understanding for inner feelings (with which I am now stuck), made the session unhelpful for me."

Frequency and nature of the hindering processes. We found that, when we asked the participants to comment on hindering processes, no comment was given 60% of the time by the therapists and 75% of the time by the clients. Even in the low groups, the number of blank answers was fairly high. This is in sharp contrast to the proportion of blank answers (23% for therapists and 14% for clients) on the question about helping processes. This large number of blank answers should not surprise us. The majority of the sessions examined were drawn from long-term therapies that were, in their totality, experienced as positive. Thus it would probably be more accurate to speak about "nonhelping" or "rather disturbing" factors. Negative processes leading to serious impasses or to termination of therapy occurred only sporadically in this study. Instead, the clients' and therapists' descriptions often had the flavor of "a missed opportunity"; also, the nonhelping was sometimes described as a short episode in an otherwise positive session ("at a certain moment," "towards the end"). It was also striking to see that a

Table 6.4   Therapist Category System for Hindering Processes

A. Attitudes and interventions of the therapist

A1 *T perceives himself/herself as too passive,* as contributing too little, letting C talk too much about himself in an unproductive way (i.e., C is too theoretical/little in touch with himself/focused on others or unimportant subjects/lengthy/engaged in narrative); T feels that s/he leaves C too free in certain decisions concerning the therapy.

A2 *T does not become emotionally attuned to C's experiential world,* cannot sufficiently concentrate on it; s/he feels far away, lacking empathy.

A3 *T simply does not understand C.* T often can barely follow impenetrable way of speaking; it also happens that T cannot recall what was discussed in the previous session.

A4 *T focuses too little on the personal meaning of C's message.* T does not succeed in reaching the deeper feeling level.

A5 *T's interventions are beside C's experiential track.* T makes irrelevant/non-impactful interventions/focuses unilaterally and sometimes for too long on aspects that are important from his/her own frame of reference/brings up personal comments and experiences that distract the client or draw too much attention to himself/herself.

A6 *T does not focus on what is going on in the here-and-now relationship.* Negative feelings in T or in C/disturbances in the contact/remain untouched.

A7 *T interprets too little.* T pays too little attention to exposing certain connections/behavior patterns/latent meanings.

A8 *T interventions are too rational.* T too focused on analyzing/explaining; T gets seduced into discussion.

A9 *T interprets too quickly/too deeply.* T sometimes continues to "push"; this is threatening or confusing for C.

A10 *T is too concerned with direct help.* Out of "furor sanandi"/ impatience, T starts being too active/suggests solutions which are perhaps simplistic or not to the point/tries to encourage C.

A11 *T reacts inadequately because of counter-transferential feelings.* T's own needs/unresolved problems/fear of certain feelings/depreciation of C's values or way of being/ irritation and tenseness about C's reaction towards the therapist lead to inability to go serenely into C's feelings/occasional—sometimes covert—aggressive reactions and confrontations/manipulation of the client or inability to let him or her be as he or she is.

A12 *T feels powerless.* T is discouraged by the lack of progress.

Continued

Table 6.4   Therapist Category System for Hindering Processes

B. The client's process

   B1 *C is blocked, anxious, even defensive.* The conversation proceeds with difficulty and C does not, or does not fully succeed in expressing feelings/what really preoccupies him/ her.

   B2 *C talks too superficially.* C talks too little about self, too much about facts/others; C narrates too much, is too uninvolved.

   B3 *C does not go far enough in making self-exploration specific or concrete.* Example: Suicidal idea, discussed briefly, without going deeper into its meaning.

   B4 *C moves too much on a rational, explicative, abstract level.* Example: "During the last fifteen minutes, he exposed a whole theory."

   B5 *C's talk is too chaotic.* C is too busy/quick/abundant; hard to disentangle, jumping from one topic to the next.

C. External and structural factors

   The conversation is disturbed by interruption or noise. T finds the session too short or the interval between sessions too long. T finds individual therapy unsuitable for C.

considerable number of these answers either conveyed a note of uncertainty ("perhaps") or referred to something that was "difficult at the time" without perhaps being negative in the long run. The latter characterization occurred especially in the client categories B5 (session leaves a feeling of confusion or uncertainty) to B8 (client left to his or her fate at end of session), all of which refer to the intermediate outcome aspects of the sessions. We touch here upon the problem of distinguishing between "deterioration" and "therapeutic disintegration" (Rogers & Kinget, 1959, p. 134). A temporary upset sometimes may be just a "growing pain," which has a constructive meaning when viewed in the context of the therapy as a whole. No doubt, a portion of the answers belong to this category. Nevertheless, we believe that the processes were in essence of low or of antitherapeutic value.

The quantitative data revealed that the clients experienced their sessions as less negative than did the therapists. The clients gave a markedly higher number of blank answers, more than double those of

(Text continues on p. 157)

Table 6.5 Content Analysis of Hindering Processes From the Client's Perspective: Number and Percentage of Segments in Each Category

Categories	Full Sample (325 sessions) Answer Segments		High and Low Groups (N = 40) Frequency	
	Frequency	Percentage	High	Low
Cluster A: Therapist's Attitudes and Interventions				
1. Lack of warmth, involvement, understanding	5	5.5	—	5
2. T is too passive, confronts too little	6	6.6	1	2
3. T is too active	2	2.2	1	1
4. C feels disapproved of or undervalued by T	3	3.3	1	1
5. T's suggestions are painful to C	4	4.4	3	—
6. T's suggestions do not feel "right" to C	7	7.7	—	—
7. T is too intrusive (e.g., too intimate, too confrontational)	7	7.7	—	3
Total A	34	37.4	6	12

Continued

153

Table 6.5 Continued

Categories	Full Sample (325 sessions) Answer Segments		High and Low Groups (N = 40) Frequency	
	Frequency	Percentage	High	Low
Cluster B: The Client's Process				
1. C does not cooperate: by waiting, silence	4	4.4	—	1
2. C does not cooperate: by talking superficially	5	5.5	—	1
3. C does not dare to talk about certain things	8	8.8	—	—
4. The session doesn't bring anything new	5	5.5	—	1
5. The session is confusing	10	11.0	1	4
6. The session is too confrontational, too heavy	7	7.7	—	1
7. C is disappointed about the lack of progress	14	15.3	1	3
8. C feels left to his fate at the end of the session	3	3.3	1	2
Total B	56	61.5	3	13
External or structural factors	1	1.1	—	1
Total	91	100	9	26
Blank answers	245	75.4	31	20

43% Session Outcome

Table 6.6 Content Analysis of Hindering Processes From the Therapist's Perspective: Number and Percentage of Segments in Each Category

Categories	Full Sample (325 sessions) Answer Segments		High and Low Groups (N = 40) Frequency	
	Frequency	Percentage	High	Low
Cluster A: Therapist's Attitudes and Interventions				
1. Perceives himself as too passive	18	9.0	—	5
2. Doesn't get emotionally attuned to the client's experiential world	14	7.0	—	4
3. Doesn't understand the client; T cannot follow C	6	3.0	1	1
4. Focuses too little on the personal meaning of the client's message	22	11.0	2	3
5. Interventions are beside the client's experiential track	19	9.5	—	3
6. Does not focus on what is going on in the here-and-now relationship	9	4.5	—	5
7. Interprets too little	5	2.5	—	1
8. Interventions are too rational	12	6.0	1	4
9. Interprets or confronts too early or too deeply	16	8.0	4	3
10. Is too much concerned with "direct help"	12	6.0	—	4
11. Reacts inadequately out of his or her own incongruent feelings (countertransference)	13	6.5	—	2
12. Feels powerless, discouraged	6	3.0	1	3
Total A	152	76.0	9	38

(Items 3 and 4 bracketed: 30% Poor Emp.)

Continued

155

Table 6.6 Continued

Categories	Full Sample (325 sessions) Answer Segments Frequency Percentage		High and Low Groups (N = 40) Frequency High	Low
Cluster B: The Client's Process				
1. Is blocked, anxious, defensive	11	5.5	—	2
2. Talks too superficially (about nonself)	11	5.5	—	1
3. Doesn't go far enough in making his or her self-exploration specific, concrete, to the point	8	4.0	1	1
4. Explores himself or herself too much on a rational level	6	3.0	—	3
5. Talk is too chaotic	6	3.0	—	2
Total B	42	21.0	2	9

the therapists (200 versus 91). They were thus more lenient in their judgment. One may, however, wonder whether clients dared to write about the negative. We tried to eliminate this problem by reassuring them that their comments would not come into the hands of their therapists. Rennie's (1985, 1990) finding that clients are reluctant to criticize their therapist, however, suggests that intrapsychic barriers might have played a role here.

Main sectors. Responses to Question 2d ("Did things occur in this session that you feel you were not helpful at all?") were divisible into two main sectors, the therapist's attitudes and interventions, on the one hand, and the client's process, on the other. I would like to emphasize that, in the first sector, it proved impossible to separate aspects of the relational climate (i.e., the therapist's basic attitudes or the general aspects of interpersonal contact) from those specific to therapist interventions. We did not have this difficulty, however, when coding the helping processes. Negative processes are thus, with a few exceptions (see C-A1: lack of warmth and so on; T-A1: therapist too passive; T-A2: therapist not emotionally attuned), described as specific, concrete moments of interaction in which, in the majority of cases, the response content revealed an intermingling of underlying relational attitudes and interventions, of "person and technique."

At this level of analysis, it was remarkable to find that both parties tended to attribute the negative to themselves. We found that 76% of the therapists' negative responses were categorized in the intervention sector, whereas 61% of the clients' negative responses were categorized in the process sector. Comparing this finding to the parallel division of response segments in the helping processes, the difference is most obvious with respect to the therapists. They referred to their own influence on positive events in only one third of their answers, whereas clients referred mainly to their own process here as well. It would seem therefore that, although clients tended to see the positive as well as the negative coming mainly from themselves, therapists tended to present an intrapunitive reaction; that is, the helpful was mainly attributed to the client, the harmful to their own defective interventions. This should perhaps be viewed as a sign of humility befitting a therapist. As professionals, these therapists perhaps had learned to look at themselves when something did not turn out right in therapy, somewhat analogous to what motivated clients do.

Content categories. A detailed inspection of the various content categories revealed the following: With respect to the attitudes of the therapists, both groups of participants perceived the opposite of empathy and acceptance. There were the same intervention categories as in the helping processes, but these were dispensed in the "wrong dosage." The therapist was either too passive or too active (in word and deed), too confronting or not confronting enough, too interpretive or insufficiently interpretive. Thus the art and know-how of therapy would seem to be a matter of "dosage" and "timing."

When we directed our attention to *client-therapist differences* within the intervention sector, we discovered that 30% of all therapists' responses were categorizable directly and explicitly as lacking in empathy (A2 to A5). We also found that they paid more attention to "transference and countertransference," that is, avoidance of what happened in the here and now of the relationship and lack of congruence (A6 and A11). Finally, they mentioned explicitly "flight into rationality" as a hindering process in themselves (A8) as well as in the client (B4).

With respect to process factors, therapists mentioned various forms of useless self-exploration, such as can be found in the lower levels of the Experiencing Scale (Klein, Mathieu, Gendlin, & Kiesler, 1970). Clients did this as well but emphasized more explicitly their own resistance. Similar to client responses in the helping processes, the higher percentage of client responses in this sector was due to the fact that clients referred more often to the immediate outcome of the sessions. They indicated that too much or too little happened or that they did not have an opinion on what had happened (B4 to B8): 43% of all their answers fell into these categories. The therapists, on the other hand, did not pay much attention to the temporary outcome of sessions, except when feeling powerless (A12).

Comparison between high and low groups. For clients and therapists alike, the number of hindering processes was significantly higher in the low group than in the high group. Even in the high group, or "very good" sessions, however, a number of negative experiences were mentioned. An unusual and surprising finding here was the frequency of responses in client category A5 (painful advice and suggestions). There were three responses in the high group and none in the low group, a finding for which we have no explanation. In any event, it demonstrates that sessions containing painful interventions could still be experienced as positive in their totality.

Little can be said with certainty about the degree to which the content categories differentiated between the high and low sessions because the frequencies are too small to be reliable. Nevertheless, we would like to highlight the most obvious differences, albeit with due reservation. Those content categories that refer to aspects of the relational climate discriminated the most. For clients, we found all five response segments of category A1 (therapist too passive) to be in the low group; for therapists, there were nine response segments from categories A1 (therapist too passive) and A2 (therapist not emotionally attuned) in the low group, and none in the high group. These refer to general negative attitudes, which, more than concrete interventions, undermined the experience of the whole session. Intrusive or confronting interventions discriminated well between the clients' evaluations of high and low sessions (A7: therapist is too intrusive) but not at all between the therapists' appraisals (A9: therapist interprets too quickly). These client-centered therapists thus appear to have adopted an ambivalent attitude toward deep confrontation and interpretation. They mentioned these interventions as hindering, yet we found these same interventions in sessions valued as high as well as in sessions valued as low. In addition, we found that the B5 category (client feels confused and uncertain) differentiated fairly well between high and low sessions as perceived by clients and that the A6 category (not focusing on the here-and-now interaction) was differentiating in the view of the therapists.

Implications for supervision. This array of hindering processes and missed opportunities provides a wealth of information that is useful for supervision. It indicates where "the shoe pinches" and where supervision could be helpful. The content categories suggest that supervision has to address two interrelated levels: the process of self-exploration and the relationship (Rice, 1980). With respect to the former, the therapist supervisee can learn a great deal from listening to episodes of therapy and from receiving feedback about possible interventions that may enliven and deepen the client's narration. This is the technical-didactic approach that Rogers emphasized especially in the initial period in the history of client-centered therapy. As he remarked, "I cannot exaggerate the excitement of our learnings as we clustered about the machine that enabled us to listen to ourselves, playing over and over some puzzling point at which the interview clearly went wrong, or those comments in which the client moved significantly forward" (Rogers, 1975, p. 3).

Apart from this (although not independent of it), however, the difficulties experienced by therapists may lie largely on a more personal level. The therapists' attitudes and feelings toward therapy, themselves, and the client in question should not be underestimated as factors interfering with therapeutic work. The importance of this aspect appears clearly in the response categories that refer to the inadequate handling of what happens in the "here and now" of the relationship (T-A6 and T-A11). In addition, other categories betray underlying problems that may have something to do with the person of the therapist such as retreating into passivity, not being attuned emotionally to the client, being too intrusive, and wanting too much to "rescue" the client.

Together with Rice (1980), I feel that a subtle balance between these two aspects of supervisory work should be attempted. I also would like to align with Lambert (1980) and Martens (1984) in pointing out the importance of the quality of the relationship in supervision. Only when supervisees feel sufficiently secure will they take the risk of examining more closely and exploring more deeply the personal and interpersonal aspects of their therapeutic work. It thus seems obvious that supervision will remain wanting if the focus is too exclusively on the client's psychodynamics at the expense of what happens within the therapist. This means that Carkhuff's (1972) short-term training programs are insufficient. This type of training aims only at teaching elementary therapeutic techniques, emphasizing perhaps too directly the concrete verbal-communicative aspects of the intervention and neglecting vulnerable spots and personal difficulties that can occur in the relationship between client and therapist in the framework of long-term therapy.

References

Barrett-Lennard, G. T. (1981). The empathy cycle: Refinement of a nuclear concept. *Journal of Counseling Psychology, 28*, 91-100.

Carkhuff, R. R. (1972). Toward a technology for human and community resource development. *The Counseling Psychologist, 3*(3), 12-30 (Comments, pp. 31-87).

Frank, J. D. (1971). Therapeutic factors in psychotherapy. *American Journal of Psychotherapy, 25*, 350-361.

Gendlin, E. T. (1970). A theory of personality change. In J. T. Hart & T. M. Tomlinson (Eds.), *New directions in client-centered therapy* (pp. 129-174). Boston: Houghton Mifflin.

Klein, M. H., Mathieu, P. L., Gendlin, E., & Kiesler, D. J. (1970). *The Experiencing Scale: A research and training manual* (vol. 1). Madison: University of Wisconsin. Extension Bureau of Audiovisual Instruction.

Korchin, S. J. (1983). Nonspecific factors in psychotherapy. In W. R. Minsel & W. Herff (Eds.), *Methodology in psychotherapy research* (Vol. 1, pp. 1-30). Frankfurt am Main, Germany: Peter Lang.

Lambert, M. J. (1980). Research and the supervisory process. In A. Hess (Ed.), *Psychotherapy supervision: Theory and practice* (pp. 423-450). New York: John Wiley.

Lambert, M. J., Bergin, A. E., & Collins, J. L. (1977). Therapist-induced deterioration in psychotherapy. In A. S. Gurman & A. M. Razin (Eds.), *Effective psychotherapy: A handbook of research* (pp. 452-481). New York: Pergamon.

Lambert, M. J., Shapiro, D. A., & Bergin, A. E. (1986). The effectiveness of psychotherapy. In S. Garfield & A. E. Bergin (Eds.), *Handbook of psychotherapy and behavior change* (pp. 157-211). New York: John Wiley.

Lietaer, G. (1983). On the lack of convergence between client and therapist perception of therapeutic conditions: Methodological and clinical reflections. In W. R. Minsel & W. Herff (Eds.), *Research on psychotherapeutic approaches* (Proceedings of the First European Conference on Psychotherapy Research [Trier, 1981]; Vol. 2, pp. 125-135). Frankfurt am Main, Germany: Peter Lang.

Lietaer, G. (1989). De werkrelatie in client-centered psychotherapie. Bedenkingen bij bevindingen uit een vragenlijstonderzoek. In H. Vertommen, G. Cluckers, & G. Lietaer (Eds), *De Relatie in Therapie* (pp. 207-236). Leuven, Belgium: Leuven University Press.

Lietaer, G., Dierick, P., & Neirinck, M. (1985). Inhoud en proces in experiëntiële psychotherapie. Een empirische exploratie. *Psychologica Belgica, 25,* 127-147.

Lietaer, G., & Neirinck, M. (1985). Niet-helpende en storende processen in experiëntiële psychotherapie. Een analyse van postsessie-commentaren. *Tijdschrift voor Psychiatrie, 27,* 253-271.

Lietaer, G., & Neirinck, M. (1986). Client and therapist perception of helping processes in client-centered/experiential psychotherapy. *Person-Centered Review, 1,* 436-455.

Martens, J. (1984). Helpende en storende factoren in groepssupervisie van client-centered therapeuten. Een empirische studie. In G. Lietaer, P. H. van Praag, & J. C. A. G. Swildens (Eds.), *Client-centered Psychotherapie in Beweging. Naar een procesgerichte benadering* (pp. 254-272). Leuven, Belgium: Acco.

Murray, E. J., & Jacobson, L. I. (1971). The nature of learning in traditional and behavioral psychotherapy: Conclusions and implications. In A. E. Bergin & S. L. Garfield, *Handbook of psychotherapy and behavior change* (pp. 734-741). New York: John Wiley.

Neirinck, M., Lietaer, G., & Rombauts, J. (1981). Empirisch onderzoek over goede en slechte therapeutische sessies. *Gedrag. Tijdschrift voor Psychologie, 9,* 288-306.

Orlinsky, D. E., & Howard, K. I. (1975). *Varieties of psychotherapeutic experience.* New York: Teachers College Press.

Orlinsky, D. E., & Howard, K. I. (1986). Process and outcome in psychotherapy. In S. Garfield & A. E. Bergin (Eds.), *Handbook of psychotherapy and behavior change* (pp. 311-381). New York: John Wiley.

Rennie, D. L. (1985, June). Client deference in the psychotherapy relationship. In D. Rennie (Chair), *The client's phenomenological experience of psychotherapy.* Symposium conducted at the annual meeting of the Society for Psychotherapy Research, Evanston, IL.

Rennie, D. L. (1990). Toward a representation of the client's experience of the psychotherapy hour. In G. Lietaer, J. Rombauts, & R. Van Balen (Eds.), *Client-centered and experiential psychotherapy in the nineties* (pp. 155-172). Leuven, Belgium: Leuven University Press.

Rice, L. N. (1980). A client-centered approach to the supervision of psychotherapy. In A. Hess (Ed.), *Psychotherapy supervision: Theory research and practice* (pp. 136-147). New York: John Wiley.

Rogers, C. R. (1961). *On becoming a person*. Boston: Houghton Mifflin.

Rogers, C. R. (1975). Empathic: An unappreciated way of being. *The Counseling Psychologist, 5*, 2-9.

Rogers, C. R., & Kinget, G. M. (1959). *Psychotherapie en Menselijke Verhoudingen. Theorie en Praktijk van de Non-directieve Therapie.* Utrecht/Antwerpen: Spectrum/Standaard.

Snyder, W. J., & Snyder, B. J. (1961). *The psychotherapy relationship.* New York: Macmillan.

Strupp, H. H. (1955). An objective comparison of Rogerian and psychoanalytic techniques. *Journal of Consulting Psychology, 19*, 1-7.

Strupp, H. H. (1957). Multidimensional comparison of therapist activity in analytic and client-centered therapy. *Journal of Consulting Psychology, 21*, 301-308.

Strupp, H. H. (1958). Performance on psychoanalytic and client-centered therapists in an initial interview. *Journal of Consulting Psychology, 41*, 265-274.

Strupp, H. H. (1973). On the basic ingredients of psychotherapy. *Journal of Consulting Psychology, 41*, 1-8.

Strupp, H. H., Chassan, L. B., & Ewing, J. A. (1966). Toward the longitudinal study of the therapeutic process. In L. A. Gottschalk & A. H. Auerbach (Eds.), *Methods of research in psychotherapy* (pp. 361-400). New York: Appleton-Century-Crofts.

Strupp, H. H., Hadley, S. W., & Gomes-Schwartz, B. (1977). *Psychotherapy for better or worse: An analysis of the problem of negative effects.* New York: Jason Aronson.

Yalom, I. D. (1975). *The theory and practice of group psychotherapy.* New York: Basic Books.

Yalom, I. D. (1980). *Existential psychotherapy.* New York: Basic Books.

7

Client and Therapist as Analysts of Significant Events

ROBERT ELLIOTT
DAVID A. SHAPIRO

In this chapter, we describe how client and therapist can be enlisted as collaborators in the analysis of their own significant therapy events. We will illustrate how this can be done and what can be learned about the varying perspectives of client, therapist, and observer, using an event from a first session of an interpersonal-dynamic therapy. We will close with clinical commentary by the therapist.

The work that we will present is an extension of earlier work on significant therapy events, work that may be unfamiliar to many. Therefore, to accomplish our goal, we will first summarize the assumptions and methods of this earlier work. In particular, we will lay out the rationale for studying significant therapy events in the way that we do as well as the methods we use for identifying, describing, and analyzing events.

AUTHORS' NOTE: An earlier version of this chapter was presented at meeting of the Society for Psychotherapy Research, Toronto, June 1989. The significant event described in this chapter was collected while Elliott was on sabbatical at the Social and Applied Psychology Unit at the University of Sheffield. We thank the client who identified the event, the students in the first author's Interpersonal Process Analysis class (Spring 1988), and Claudia Clark for their contributions.

Background

Significant Events

Significant therapy events are portions of therapy sessions (generally 4-8 minutes in length) in which clients experience a meaningful degree of help or change (Elliott & Shapiro, 1988). We see significant events as a windows into the process of change in psychotherapy. From our point of view, studying significant events is a sampling strategy: Instead of taking random samples from therapy sessions, we look where the "action" is most likely to be. We assume that the change processes that we see operating in significant events will be present elsewhere in therapy but that they will be more prevalent in such events. In other words, we hold that significant events represent important general therapeutic factors but in more concentrated form (Elliott, 1983, 1985; Elliott, James, Reimschuessel, Cislo, & Sack, 1985).

The concept of a significant event has taken various meanings in the literature and in our work (e.g., Elliott, 1983, 1984; Elliott & Shapiro, 1988; Mahrer & Nadler, 1986; Rice & Greenberg, 1984). In this chapter, however, we specifically define a *significant event* as that part of a given therapy session experienced by the client as most helpful or important.

Comprehensive Process Analysis: A Qualitative Approach to Significant Events

Psychotherapy research has been dominated by premature quantitative, hypothesis testing approaches at the expense of qualitative, discovery-oriented research (see Elliott, 1989; Mahrer, 1988; Rennie, Phillips, & Quartaro, 1988). While quantitative measures of therapy process and outcome have their place, we contend that therapy researchers generally do not yet know enough about therapeutic change processes to specify what to look for in advance. Therapy researchers have been particularly guilty of ignoring the role of context in understanding change processes. Careful, open-ended description of significant events is one way of generating knowledge about therapeutic change processes.

The Comprehensive Process Analysis method (CPA; Elliott, 1989) is a systematic, qualitative research procedure for analyzing significant events. In it, we seek to understand (a) the *context* out of which significant events arise (e.g., client coping style, therapeutic alliance),

(b) the important features of the *event* itself (e.g., therapist interpretation, client expression of interpersonal fears), and (c) the *impacts* of the event (e.g., insight, decreased depression).

In Comprehensive Process Analysis, qualitative judges systematically apply a framework of potentially important factors to develop models of the change process in particular significant therapy events. Methodological safeguards are an important aspect of this method and include the use of multiple judges and confirming the clinical significance of events by means of quantitative data (session ratings, outcome measures). In this chapter, we propose a variant of the use of multiple qualitative judges, namely, employing clients and therapists as judges of their own events.

There are two main types of CPA work, the analysis of individual events and the analysis of themes across events. The overall goal of CPA is to develop general models of particular kinds of significant events, models that can be used to improve the practice of psychotherapy. This chapter focuses on the first type of CPA work, the analysis of individual events.

Importance of Client and Therapist Perspectives

In applying the Comprehensive Process Analysis method to significant events, we give the views of client and therapist primary, but not exclusive, importance. Clients and therapists have "privileged access" to a large store of personal and shared background information. In addition, they have access to something that is often unavailable even on videotape—their own momentary private experiences. Furthermore, comparisons between client, therapist, and observer perspectives have often turned up striking discrepancies (e.g., Caskey, Barker, & Elliott, 1984; Orlinsky & Howard, 1975; Parry, Shapiro, & Firth, 1986; Rennie, 1985).

Traditional measurement theory is based on an epistemological position of "realism" (Hill, 1961) in that it assumes the existence of specific "true scores" (Wiggins, 1973). From this point of view, discrepancies between different perspectives are seen as "error," unreliability, or invalidity. In contrast, in this chapter, we take the relativistic view favored by phenomenological or hermeneutical psychologists (e.g., Packer & Addison, 1989; Rennie et al., 1988) and, indeed, by the modern psychometric theory of generalizability (Cronbach, Gleser, Nanda, & Najaratnam, 1972). Differences between client, therapist, and observer perspectives are interesting in their own right and need to be understood and integrated into a larger perspective.

Therapy researchers have long used clients and therapists as sources of data about therapy (see reviews by Elliott, 1986; Elliott & James, 1989; Orlinsky & Howard, 1986). In this chapter, however, we propose to go a step further in taking client and therapist perspectives seriously. Here we will describe how client and therapist can be enlisted as collaborators in the analysis of significant events. (We chose the client perspective for identifying significant events because it is likely to be most informative to us as researcher-therapists; we will balance this by allowing the therapist to have the "last word.")

Brief Structured Recall: Collecting and Describing Significant Events

To identify significant events more efficiently and to obtain rich descriptions of these events by client and therapist, we developed Brief Structured Recall (Elliott & Shapiro, 1988). This procedure is a form of tape-assisted recall, also known as Interpersonal Process Recall (Kagan, 1975; see Elliott, 1986), in which the tape of a session is played back for the participants immediately afterward to obtain descriptions of their experiences at particular moments. The power of the method is that it helps clients and therapists to recapture momentary experiences in a way that links them directly to observable events in the session. Earlier recall methods (Elliott, 1986; Hill, Helms, Spiegel, & Tichenor, 1988) had clients and therapists review entire sessions, giving ratings on a narrow range of variables. This was a very lengthy process and did not produce data of the depth and range needed for Comprehensive Process Analysis.

The Brief Structured Recall procedure (BSR; Elliott & Shapiro, 1988) differs from earlier ones in several ways: First, it is event focused; instead of reviewing entire sessions or sampling predetermined parts of sessions, the client begins by identifying the most helpful event in the session. The client (and later the therapist) then provides a wide range of information about the identified significant event, information designed for use in CPA (Elliott & Shapiro, 1988). To assess delayed effects, client and therapist review the event later (two months later for the event described in this chapter). Brief Structured Recall uses a blend of quantitative rating scales and qualitative description; psychometric data for the quantitative portions are generally good (Elliott et al., 1988).

Method: Using Client and Therapist as Analysts of Their Own Events

Now we will show how we enlisted the aid of client and therapist in the analysis of a significant event. In doing this, we will at the same time introduce our illustrative event. We will organize this section into three subsections: data collection, analysis by observers, and organization and combination of client and therapist data into the CPA framework.

Data Collection

Client and therapist. The client was a 32-year-old clergyman, who presented with depression and career concerns. He was seen by the second author, a research clinical psychologist with 14 years' postdoctoral clinical experience and thorough training in both cognitive-behavioral and relationship-oriented therapies. The client was treated according to the protocol for the First Sheffield Psychotherapy Project (Shapiro & Firth, 1987), receiving eight sessions of Exploratory Therapy (an interpersonal-dynamic treatment), followed by eight sessions of Prescriptive Therapy (a cognitive-behavioral treatment).

Event. The client identified the most helpful event from each of his 16 sessions. We selected the event to be presented here on the basis of two criteria: *significance* and *typicality*. First, it (along with one other event) received the highest combined helpfulness ratings from client and therapist. Second, according to client and therapist ratings, it exemplified the most common impact in the treatment, namely, insight. The event to be presented comes from the first session of therapy and thus represented an initial session of Exploratory Therapy.

Immediately after the session, the client and therapist each completed postsession questionnaires. Among other things, the client was asked to describe the most helpful event in the session on the Helpful Aspects of Therapy (HAT) Questionnaire (Llewelyn, Elliott, Shapiro, Firth, & Hardy, 1988). He wrote the following:

Dr. Shapiro picked up an aspect of "I'm not a minister while I'm here," i.e., that I was saying something other than that I was simply "off duty." Ministers are not "supposed" to denigrate the ministry, but are "supposed" to revel in its "brotherhood," "privilege," etc. It was good to face a reality that it's usually safer to avoid, and thereby get a sense of relief. (Helpfulness: 8 = "greatly helpful")

The first author then played portions of the tape of the session until the event was located; after that, the client indicated the exact beginning and end of the event. The event occurred about 25 minutes into the session; a detailed transcript is given in Table 7.1. The researcher then asked the client to describe the context of the event (its meaning and what led up to it), the event itself (especially what the therapist did or said), and its impact (its effect on the client and which specific impacts, from a list, applied).

In a separate interview, the researcher played the identified event for the therapist and asked him to describe the event's context, his intentions during the event, and its impact on the client.

Analysis of Event by Observers

Three years later, the first author selected this event (using the criteria given earlier) as a class demonstration for an advanced undergraduate course on Comprehensive Process Analysis. Prior to reviewing the earlier recall data, and in collaboration with this class, he analyzed the event following the CPA framework given in Table 7.2. Each part of the analysis either was carried out in class or was done outside of class and then gone over and agreed to by the class. The CPA framework consists of four main sections: Expansion, Context, Event, and Impact. The following description of the observers' analysis will be illustrated by examples from each main section.

Following the procedure described in Elliott (1989) and Labov and Fanshel (1977), the observers started by expanding the key or peak responses in the event. This event centered on a single key therapist response, which followed a remark by the client (C2.4 in Table 7.1) to the effect that he was no longer a minister while he was in the therapy session:

T3: You're no longer a minister while you're here. That's k- quite a strong statement.

In developing an expansion for this key response, the observers spelled out the implied meanings carried by the response in its context, as follows:

1. I don't know if you heard yourself, so I want to direct your attention to what you just said.

Table 7.1   Transcript of Event 121-1: "You're no longer a minister while you're here."

T1: (8.7) I wondered how important it is to you:, the question of, how what we do here relates to:, religious, questions, just-, it just flashed through my mind when you said about, 'h ( ) (uh) people who are not Christians saying things about the church which might turn out to be true='h. mm- Maybe there was:, 'h some room for you somewhere to ask yourself, "Well what am *I* going to say about the Church?=What do I believe or feel about the Church." (2.0) I was wondering (whether) that might affect, our work together. (7.5)

C1: I don't think I follow you (2.0)

T2.1:[*T410*]: 'h (Well) that I just picked up a *hint* in what you said about other people, 'h that are not Christians saying things, against the Church, (C: Hmm) 'h and that somehow for you presenting a challenge, so (that), perhaps maybe sometimes things that you would like to be able to refute might turn out to be true, (1.0)

[Event begins here:]

T2.2: [T420]: As to whether that could be linked with a, 'h with a concern about what I might feel about the Church and where- 'h what I (C: 'HH Ohh) can do with you, would relate to, your work in the Church (<.5)

C2: [C2.1:] 'HH No, u:m h (2.8) [C2.2:] 'H Wh- Whether you are or are not attached to the Church i-is, irrelevant, as far as, I'm concerned, because 'hh, whether on a Sunday you go to Church, is, entirely separate, to me, (uh) for me, to you sitting in this room, as Dr. Shapiro doing this piece of work, 'h (2.1) [C2.3:] Just as for me, u:m I changed out of me collar because I am not on *duty.* [C2.4:] I am, (T: Hmm) no(he) lo(he)nger a minister, 'HH while I'm here. (1.0)

*T3: [T433: Therapist Peak; Helpfulness=7.5]: [T3.1:] You're no longer a minister while you're here. (.7) (C: Hh-Ye:hs Uh-heh=) [T3.2:] That's k- quite a strong (C: e) statement (<.5)

C3: [C3.1:] U:m (.8) [C3.2:] Ye(he)s °I suppose°, 'hh yes, [C3.3:] I don't-I, I didn't think I'd said that, but maybe I// did.

T4: You *did]* say that, didn't (C: Uh Yes) you? (2.0) I think that's a big issue for you (C: 'h), (1.3) to what extent are you a minister, (C: H-Hh) all your life. (.6)

Continued

Table 7.1   Continued

C4: Ye:s Wh- What I *thought* I was saying was that I- I am a- a- an individual human being (T: Mmm), with, with a different identity (T: Mm) when I'm //here, but 'h Mm

T5: [*T442*]: Mm, Mm, Sure] (1.6) Maybe it's quite hard for you to keep that sense, 'h that your identity, is intact, when you're wearing the collar *and* when you're not, that it's the same you (C: Mm), somehow it feels, a bit oppressive, (1.3) the collar. (20.3) 'HH [*Event ends*]

NOTE: Transcription symbols (from Sacks, Schegloff & Jefferson, 1974) are as follows: "H", "h", out-breaths; "'Hh", "'h", in-breaths; ":" prolongation of sound; "°" softer than expected; "(T: Mhm)" backchannel utterances; "( )" or e.g., "(house)", inaudible or unclear; "=" absence of expected pause ("latching"); "(he)", "(h)", laughter within a word; "//", "]", beginning and end of interruption; "t", tongue click; numbers in parentheses are timings of internal and interresponse pauses.

 2. You said you perceive yourself as not a minister while here in the therapy room with me. (= key proposition)
 3. However, I suspect that what you just said is a much stronger (broader, more intense) statement than its specific, literal meaning.

(Space limitations preclude the presentation of the expansion of the client's description of the event, given above.)

The observers next analyzed the important features of the key therapist response more broadly, using the four headings of Content, Action, Style/State, and Quality, as indicated under the heading Event Factors in the CPA framework (see Table 7.2). For each heading, observers described qualitatively any aspects of the therapist's response that they thought might have helped to make the event significant for the client. Their descriptions for the Action and Style sections were as follows:

Action:
 a. *response modes:* reflection (quote*, implication); (implied process advisement) (*key mode)
 b. *tasks:* Confront client with (get C to look at, be aware of) what he just said ("slip").

Style/state: quiet, musing, gentle, but emphatic, brief interresponse latency

After analyzing the key response, the observers moved on to the context of the event, describing factors that seemed to have led up to the event. For example, *Background,* defined as "relevant features of

Table 7.2   Framework for Comprehensive Process Analysis (1986)

I. *Expansion of implicit and explicit propositions in event* (What is said "between the lines," in the event and the client's description of it.)

II. *Contextual Factors:* (What leads up to and gives meaning to the event.)

    A. *Background* (Relevant features of client and therapist which preceded and were brought to treatment.)

    B. *Presession Context* (Important events that have occurred since treatment began.)

    C. *Session Context* (Important aspects of the session in which the significant event occurs.)

    D. *Episode Context*[a] (Important features or events within the episode that contains the significant event.)

III. *Event Factors:* (Here, important characteristics of the key therapist response.)

    A. *Action* (What the therapist is doing or trying to do in the peak(s); therapist tasks and response modes.)

    B. *Content* (What therapist is talking *about* that is relevant to the impact.)

    C. *Style/State* (How the therapist is talking or acting.)

    D. *Quality* (Degree of therapist skillfulness in peak.)

IV. *Impact on Client:* (The effects of the event.)

    A. *Process Impact Pathway* (The sequence of observable client actions which display the immediate impact of the event.)

    B. *Client Experience Pathway* (The sequence of client experiences in the event.)

    C. *Delayed Impact of Event* (Subsequent therapeutic impacts and changes in client apparently due to event.)

    D. *Effectiveness of Event* (Quantitative measures: within- and postsession impact, treatment outcome.)

[a]An episode is indicated by a marked shift in topic or task. Sometimes the event contains the entire episode; in that case this section is combined with Event Factors.

client and therapist which preceded and were brought to treatment," consisted of five areas. The observers' analysis of the first two of these areas, *Client Conflicts* and *Client Style/Symptoms,* was as follows:

Client conflicts:

    a. Wants to be free to be an individual human being, fears being trapped in his role as a minister, by others' expectations

  b. Wants to be understood and supported by others; fears having his needs disregarded

Client style/symptoms:

  a. Burned out, depressed
  b. Intellectual: expresses ideas well but has trouble expressing self in a personal way
  c. Has trouble asking for help; withdraws instead

Finally, the observers described the impact of the event, including the sequence of actions and experiences following the key therapist response and data on the effectiveness of the event as a whole. For example, the client's behavior following the key response (*Process Impact*) was described as a sequence of four steps:

  1. C avoids, backs away from statement, while reluctantly agreeing.
  2. T confronts C with his version of event.
  3. C shifts to intellectualizing.
  4. C later refers to event in context of expressing relief.

Development of Client and Therapist Versions and Comparison of Versions

Once the observers had completed their analysis, the client and therapist data were transformed into a usable format. To do this, the first author transcribed the client recall session data (the therapist data had been taken down verbatim during recall), then arranged client and therapist material into the CPA framework. This resulted in three different analyses of the event, from the perspectives of observers, client, and therapist.

Collating the three versions left us with a complex set of information requiring further analysis and synthesis. To complete this process, we carried out three analyses: First, we identified the types of similarities and differences between perspectives, using a grounded theory (Rennie et al., 1988) approach to develop a scale describing relationships between versions. Second, we selected the areas of greatest discrepancy for further analysis using a reflective-empirical method like that developed by the Duquesne school of phenomenological researchers (e.g., Giorgi, 1975; Wertz, 1985). Third, we used the results of the first two analyses to develop a consensus version of the event. For all three analyses, an iterative, cyclical process was used in which the first author developed a draft analysis, which was then corrected and added to by the second author (the therapist), which served as the basis for a revised analysis by the first author, and so on until consensus was achieved.

Results: Comparison and Integration of Versions

Analysis of Relationships Between Versions

The first thing we discovered was that the versions contained many points of similarity and difference. For each heading in the analysis, the three versions were arranged so that similar descriptions were juxtaposed, for example:

Client conflicts:

a. **Observer:** Wants to be free to be an individual human being, fears being trapped in his role as a minister, by others' expectations

Client: I spend most my life feeling trapped. . . . On all occasions I feel a sense of entrapment . . .; on the vast majority of . . . occasions I find it destructive.

Therapist: [There is] a profound dilemma at the heart of C's presenting problem. Being a minister is in conflict with being a person, a core part of him. There is a contradiction between being a minister and being himself.

b. **Observer:** Wants to be understood and supported by others; fears having his needs disregarded

For each possible comparison between perspectives, we identified the type of relationship. Thus, in the example above, three similar descriptions were grouped together under heading "a" on the basis of the following relationships: First, complete correspondence exists between the observer and the client versions of the client's fear, in that the *same word* is used ("trapped"). Second, we judged the observer's specification of the client as wanting to be free as the *same content* as the therapist's description of the client as wanting to be a person but differing in language used. Third, while the client did not describe wanting to be free or a person, as both observer and therapist did, this is quite *complementary* with his reported fear of being trapped.

On the other hand, observer description "b" given in the example is an aspect ignored by the other perspectives but at the same time is *not inconsistent* with them.

Proceeding in this manner through the analyses of the event, we found that the similarities and differences between versions fell into a set of categories, naturally ordered on a continuum ranging from virtual identity to moderate inconsistency, with many points in between. These categories, along with examples, are given in Table 7.3.

The result of this analysis was that, for this event, perspectives generally agreed, sometimes precisely (Category 1 in Table 7.3), but most often described the same thing in different language (Category 2) or provided complementary but nondiscrepant information (Categories 3 and 4). There were only four instances of moderate discrepancies (Category 5, all presented in Table 7.3) and no cases of sharp, clear discrepancies (Category 6, added to anchor the top end of the scale). Thus the sources of the three perspectives were all clearly discussing the same event, and what they had to say about it was generally consistent or complementary.

Analysis of Discrepancies

From a phenomenological point of view, differences in how different people see events can yield useful clues about how they see the world more generally, revealing their interpretive "fore-structures" (Addison, 1989) or taken-for-granted assumptions.

Most commonly, as the current event illustrates, the differences between versions take the form of different language and emphasis, revealing the varying experiences and tasks of client, therapist, and observers. Thus, on reflection, observers' descriptions here can be seen to be general, to use jargon, and to be grounded in the research literature (e.g., "professional identity," "general role demands of minister"). The client's descriptions were more specific and vividly grounded in his lived situation, including the problems that had brought him to therapy (e.g., "I am a guide or supposedly a guide to a lot of people"; "I spend most of my life feeling trapped"). The therapist's descriptions were grounded in his lived professional situation and his understanding of the theory of Exploratory Therapy (e.g., "feelings and defenses that gave rise to that statement," "testing to see what would happen: Can C use it?").

Table 7.3   Types of Relationships Between Perspectives, With Examples Taken From Event 121-1

1. *Complete correspondence between perspectives:*
   a. Client Conflicts (Background):

   Observer: C fears being trapped in his role as a minister.

   Client: I spend most of my life feeling trapped.

   b. Therapist Response Modes (Event Action):

   Observer: Reflection (implied process advisement)

   Therapist: *Reflection in service of advisement*

2. Content same, but language differs:
   a. Therapist Event Content:

   Observer: C's professional identity

   Therapist: *What it means to be a minister*

   b. Client Situation (Background):

   Observer: General role demands of minister: helping professional, moral example and judge . . .

   Client: I am a guide or supposedly a guide to a lot of people . . . I am expected to be judgmental as to whether a person is a Christian or Nonchristian.

3. *Content related, but different aspects are picked up, complementing one another:*
   a. Client Conflicts (Background):

   Client: I spend most of my life feeling trapped . . .

   Therapist: *Being a minister is in conflict with being a person . . . There is a contradiction between being a minister and being himself.*

   b. Therapist Event Content:

   Observer: C's communication (local cue)

   Therapist: *Feelings and defenses that gave rise to that statement*

4. *Aspect described by one is ignored by another, but is not inconsistent:*
   a. Therapist Personal Characteristics (Background):

Continued

Table 7.3   Continued

> *Observer:*   T working in exploratory mode of therapy
>
> *Therapist: C may know Shapiro is a Jewish name. This might be an issue between us; C might be constrained by [differences] in religious beliefs.*
>
> *Client:* No data

   b. Therapist Event Tasks:

> *Therapist:*   Testing to see what would happen: can C take it? Can he use it? . . . , a pacing issue.
>
> *Observer:*   Confront C (get C to look at, be aware of) what he just said ("slip")

   c. Predominant Immediate Impact on Client:

> *Client:*   Relief
>
> *Therapist: Personal Insight*

5. *Aspects described are different and somewhat inconsistent* (Every instance from present event):

   a. Therapist Episode Tasks (Episode Level of Context):

> *Therapist: Trying to get C to be more reflective; get C off barroom talk to more personal exploration*
>
> *Observer:*   Explore and confront C's professional identity issues; build therapeutic relationship by exploring C feelings about being in therapy

   b. Relevant Episode Events (Episode Level of Context):

> *Observer:*   C tries to reassure T that therapy's being separated from the religious context is not a potential problem, but is in fact an advantage in C's view.
>
> *Therapist: Then, C says, "No, I'm off duty" and expresses his view of the symmetry about our roles. He responded without being personal.*

   c. Local Cue (Episode Level of Context):

> *Therapist: C is denying anxiety and talking in a smooth, chatty manner.*
>
> *Client: My statement about [not] being a minister [in therapy].*

Table 7.3   Continued

d. Client Experience Step 1 (Impact):

Therapist: The newness is there. C realizes it is not possible to say I'm human without having to deny being a minister . . . Personal Insight, Awareness

Client: Aware of T's understanding. I was getting [i.e., feeling] vulnerable because he had been astute.

6. *Sharp and clear discrepancy in views:* (No examples in present event; example from a different case)

   a. Therapist Event Task:

      Client: T was expressing deepest empathy

      Therapist: Trying to change the subject, to get C to talk about something else

NOTE: With the exception for categories 5 and 6, examples are taken from Background Context and Event sections of the analysis of event 121-1. For category 5, *all* instances in present event are listed. No instances of sharp discrepancy (category 6) occurred in this event, so an example from a different event (Elliott, 1983) is used.

Given the high degree of consistency, we decided to focus on the exceptions. We did so because we found that these discrepancies (a) are central to understanding the event, (b) are theoretically interesting, and (c) present problems for integrating the different versions. The following are our reflections on the four instances of moderate discrepancy.

Episode context: Client working versus avoiding. Three of the four discrepancies occurred in the Episode Context of the event and revolved around a single issue, which we will discuss first: The therapist had been perceiving the client as responding in an impersonal, smooth, and chatty "barroom" manner, denying anxiety, while the observer and the client perceived the client as working at trying to clear up a potential relationship problem raised in T1 (Table 7.1) regarding potential client-therapist differences in religious beliefs. In short, the therapist saw the client as avoiding, while the client and observer saw the client as working. (This discrepancy was not classified as sharp and clear—Category 6—because the client is not characterized as clearly or strongly working versus avoiding.)

The working versus avoiding discrepancy is central to the event, because it is the therapist's view of the client as avoiding that motivated his key response; as the therapist said, he hoped to "catch him out," to get the client to be more personal. While we might argue about whether the client was "really" avoiding in the speaking turn leading up to the event, it is clear that the therapist saw the client as avoiding, and that is what led him to respond as he did.

The role of such a discrepancy in generating a significantly helpful event is also important theoretically and methodologically. In traditional realist epistemologies, discrepancies between perspectives are evidence of the fallibility of measurement, that is, of "error" or invalidity. From a phenomenological point of view, however, what is important is that client and therapist saw what they saw and were influenced by their perceptions. The analysis must therefore encompass the discrepancy instead of trying to eliminate it through selecting a single "true" version or by "averaging" versions.

The belief that such inconsistencies are problematic is part of the assumptive world of most therapists. The current event comes from Exploratory Therapy (Hobson, 1985). This method combines elements of dynamic and experiential approaches, which typically place a high value on accurate therapist empathy and shared frame of reference, often defined as a "resonance" or "consonance" between client and therapist perceptions (Barrett-Lennard, 1981). Within such therapies, discrepancies between client and therapist perceptions are recognized as being inevitable but generally undesirable, to be avoided in that they indicate that the therapist is out of the client's frame. The dilemma for therapies that place a high value on therapist empathy is that, in this event, the "error" has proved helpful for the client.

A major source of differences in perspectives is the differential *privileged access* possessed by client and therapist. For example, in explaining the event, the client tells how, when the therapist raised the issue that potential religious differences might be a problem for the therapy, he reacted negatively:

[I had] a slight feeling of "Oh, not again!, someone expects certain things of me, expects me to slot into a mold, and therefore have certain stances on certain subjects?" A sort of teeth-gritting bit. I mean I don't want to make it sound as though I was preparing to throw the phone at him, but it was a kind of watershed that had to be got over.

The Local Cue for the event clearly derives from this experience, but there is no direct evidence of the client's annoyance and dread in his actual words:

C2:   No, whether you are or are not attached to the Church is irrelevant, as far as, I'm concerned. . . . Just as for me, I changed out of me collar because I am not on *duty*. I am, no longer a minister, while I'm here.

Similarly, the therapist gave no direct evidence that he thought the client was either avoiding or being superficial.

Finally, the discrepancy over whether the client was avoiding or working immediately prior to the key therapist response can be understood by making use of the concept of a psychological or phenomenological "baseline" or set of expectations. The therapist's baseline appears to be a schema of ideal client behavior specified in the treatment model: Clients should be open, personal, and express feelings. On the other hand, the client's baseline is the model of himself as a helper and "guide" to others, a role in which he is not permitted (or does not see himself as permitted) to be open, personal, or vulnerable.

It is interesting that both client and therapist agree the client's talk resembles that often engaged in by intellectuals in English pubs but reveals the varying social meanings that this sort of interaction has. At the end of the session, the client wistfully describes:

Passing a pub after a long meeting, and thinking, "God, what I wouldn't do for a pint!" You know, just to prop up the pub for an evening instead of propping up committees, wouldn't that be lovely? Doing something normal.

For the therapist, however, "barroom" talk has a superficial, intellectualizing connotation and is to be avoided in therapy.

Impact of event: Insight versus feeling understood. The other moderate discrepancy present in the event is rather different in nature, in that it turns on "matters of fact" about the client's experience rather than judgments about the quality of the client's preevent performance. In describing how he initially responded to the key therapist intervention, the client described feeling understood and vulnerable, while the therapist described the client as obtaining an insight into his main problem. The client's description is based on privileged access, as described earlier, and must be taken seriously for that reason. The therapist's attribution of insight, however, is based firmly on the text of the event, which displays the client's obvious surprise in reaction to the key therapist response:

C3:   U:m (.8) Ye(he)s °I suppose°, yes, I don't- I, I didn't think I'd said that, but maybe I did.

This response has several features of a typical "insight marker" (Elliott, 1984), including pondering ("um"), agreement ("yes"), and nonverbal cues of surprise (the laugh, the look of surprise noted by the therapist). Furthermore, the "I didn't think I'd said that" is similar to the "I never saw that before" of clear insight events (Elliott, 1984). The client is clearly surprised, but what is he surprised *about*? Is he surprised at being astutely "caught out" in a "slip" (the client's version), or does he see something new about himself here (the therapist's version), or are both valid?

From a "realist" point of view, it seems that the therapist has "misattributed" later insight/awareness to earlier surprise. When shown the event two months later, the client also reported insight to be central. Again, the discrepancy makes sense when related to more general differences in how client and therapist view their shared situation. The client is nervous about his first session and concerned about how the therapist will view him and whether the therapist will be able to understand him. For him, the initial salient meaning of the event is an interpersonal one of feeling first vulnerable and then relieved at having been understood in such a dramatic way. In contrast, the therapist views the event in the context of his anticipation of what is to come in the therapy. This anticipation is later lived out by therapist and client, so that the client comes to share the therapist's view that the event is an initial insight foreshadowing extensive further exploration of the client's dilemma of feeling trapped between his role as a minister and his personal needs for support.

A complementary view is that the discrepancy emerges out of relatively minor differences in language and perceived time sequence. In recall, the client describes his experience of the impact of the event as following this sequence:

1. Feels T *understands;* vulnerable to T
2. *Relief* at having talked about something held inside

. *Aware* in a rational way (trapped by the therapist versus being trapped elsewhere in his life)
4. Wonders how he can find other situations in which feeling trapped isn't destructive (i.e., problem clarification)

Although it is useful conceptually to draw a distinction between insight and awareness (Elliott et al., 1987), in fact they often overlap, and the client and therapist here do not appear to distinguish between them. Thus the combination of the client's sense of being vulnerably understood (step 1 above) and his slightly delayed "rational awareness" (step 3) correspond to the "newness" reported by the therapist as the client's initial reaction. It seems likely that the client covertly experienced the first three reported impacts in rapid succession, and that these impacts may have been simultaneously manifested nonverbally, leading the therapist to perceive them as a single experienced impact—insight.

Suggested guidelines for developing consensus versions of events. After analyzing the instances of moderate discrepancy in the event, it was easy to develop a consensus version of the event. (Unfortunately, space limitations preclude our presenting this consensus version.) Each type of relationship described among perspectives (see Table 7.3) suggests a guideline for developing a consensus:

1. Complete correspondence: Combine versions with minor editing only.
2. Same content, language differs: Select clearest, best articulated version or merge versions.
3. Related content, complementary aspects: Merge versions, editing for smoothness.
4. Different aspects, but not inconsistent: Evaluate relevance of aspect for explaining event; if relevant, retain.
5. & 6. Different aspects, somewhat or clearly inconsistent: (a) Analyze discrepancy; (b) depending upon results of analysis, integrate as differing perceptions (e.g., the avoiding versus working discrepancy); merge and edit (e.g., insight versus understanding discrepancy); or drop (if data appear to be artifactual; no examples in this event).

These guidelines appear to have general utility for developing consensus versions in CPA research and have been used in a subsequent study (Clark, 1990).

Discussion and Clinical Commentary

Research Implications

The research implications of this approach can be summarized as follows: First, it is both possible and useful to enlist clients and therapists as analysts of their own significant events. Second, doing this requires the use of intensive, qualitative research methods. Third, the traditional view of differences in perspectives as error variance is not useful and results in the loss of important information about the nature of the different perspectives on therapy process. Fourth, further discovery-oriented research on the origins of discrepancies in client, therapist, and observer perspectives is required.

Clinical Commentary and Implications

The clinical implications of this analysis were apparent to the therapist, who, after reviewing the analysis, provided the following clinical commentary:

(1) The difficulties of treatment model adherence. The therapist's view in the central discrepancy (avoiding versus working) comes from a set of idealized demands of the therapy model for intensification and client openness. The therapist is reluctant to take at face value the client's acceptance of separation between therapy and religious context (Table 7.1, C2.2), because this runs counter to the therapist's model that requires links to be made between domains. This rigorous following of the model, however, has the disadvantage of blinding the therapist to some of the client's concerns.

Furthermore, the therapist's view of the client as not working leads him to set goals that may be inappropriately demanding for the first session, at times leading to client anxiety high enough to obstruct the exploratory process. If both client and observer see the client as working, then maybe a gentler approach would be more productive. For example, the therapist's push for insight in the first session may be too ambitious. Such considerations need to be contained in treatment manuals.

(2) The usefulness of echoic reflection for confrontation. On the other hand, various features of the key therapist response enable it to transcend the limitations of the therapist's view of the client at the time. Specifically, the echoic content confronts the client with what he has just said and leads him to explore its implications but without prejudging their nature or

requiring the therapist to provide a rationale for the response. (Had such a rationale been presented, it might have led to an understandable denial by the client of the therapist's inaccurate construction.)

In a way, this is a kind of "conjuring trick" in that the client may believe that the therapist really understands, whereas all the therapist needs to know is that the statement echoed is important in some way or other. The therapist can then follow the lead of the client's efforts to give meaning to the statement that was echoed. This intervention may be most useful in early sessions, where there is not enough information for accurate interpretation. At the same time, of course, it takes a "good" client to use such an event productively by (a) being ready to accept the implication that the echoed statement has hidden meanings and (b) being able to work on these. Less secure clients might well decline to engage in this task. Thus, in first sessions, such interventions also have the quality of trial interventions, to find out how well the client can work.

(3) The value of misunderstandings in exploratory therapy. Going beyond the problematic nature of discrepancies between client and therapist perceptions discussed earlier in this chapter, the event raises the point that, in the Exploratory Therapy model, misunderstandings and their resolution can play an important role:

> Understanding is achieved . . . by an imaginative exploration in different but related languages between persons who are at once alone and together. Learning how to correct misunderstandings is one (and perhaps the) most important therapeutic factor. (Hobson, 1985, p. 16)

Resolution of alliance breakdowns such as misunderstanding is an important component of the therapy process (see Bordin, 1980; Harper, 1988). Provided the therapist's style (e.g., negotiating) sustains the alliance, the model functions in spite of limitations in the therapist's powers of observation, empathic resonance, or ability to articulate. In fact, such breakdowns can provide therapeutic opportunities.

(4) The potential of therapy research as supervision. From the point of view of the interface between research and clinical practice, this analysis of contrasting perspectives can be highly educational for the therapist. The data allow for the corroboration and revision of therapist views and illustrate the multiple-perspectival nature of the therapy process (cf. Parry et al., 1986). In addition, the exercise provides the therapist with training in building and testing models of the entire process, encompassing all three points of view.

In effect, taking part in this research was for the therapist like receiving supervision from the client and research colleagues. The therapist was required to make explicit his rationales and purposes and to have these checked out against the experiences of the client and sense made of the process by observers. Like all good supervision, this process is often challenging and stressful but can be very useful for continued learning, particularly if the validity of the therapist perspective is recognized and respected.

(5) Specific learnings. The event described here offers several examples of such learnings: First, if the therapist can recognize typical patterns of discrepancy between his or her and the client's experiences, he or she can begin to evolve strategies for making use of these to build the alliance. Second, the discrepancies highlight the simultaneous importance and limitations of therapeutic role induction (Hoen-Saric et al., 1964), or the need to educate clients about therapy process and goals. Especially in early sessions, clients often are too preoccupied with basic alliance-formation issues to attend to the treatment model. Finally, identifying commonalities of perspectives can be reassuring in that they show that the therapist is not totally out of touch, thus sustaining sufficient confidence to continue the difficult business of doing therapy!

References

Addison, R. B. (1989). Grounded interpretive research: An investigation of physician socialization. In M. J. Packer & R. B. Addison (Eds.), *Entering the circle: Hermeneutic investigation in psychology* (pp. 39-57). Albany: SUNY Press.

Barrett-Lennard, G. T. (1981). The empathy cycle: Refinement of a nuclear concept. *Journal of Counseling Psychology, 28,* 91-100.

Bordin, E. S. (1980, June). *Of human bonds that bind or free.* Presidential address presented at the meetings of the Society for Psychotherapy Research, Pacific Grove, CA.

Caskey, N., Barker, C., & Elliott, R. (1984). Dual perspectives: Clients' and therapists' perceptions of therapist responses. *British Journal of Clinical Psychology, 23,* 281-290.

Clark, C. A. (1990). A comprehensive process analysis of focusing events in experiential therapy. *Disertation Abstracts International, 51, 6098B.*

Cronbach, L. J., Gleser, G. C., Nanda, H., & Najaratnam, N. (1972). *The dependability of behavioral measurements: Theory of generalizability for scores and profiles.* New York: John Wiley.

Elliott, R. (1983). "That in your hands. . . ": A comprehensive process analysis of a significant event in psychotherapy. *Psychiatry, 46,* 113-129.

Elliott, R. (1984). A discovery-oriented approach to significant events in psychotherapy: Interpersonal Process Recall and Comprehensive Process Analysis. In L. Rice & L. Greenberg (Eds.), *Patterns of change* (pp. 249-286). New York: Guilford.

Elliott, R. (1985). Helpful and nonhelpful events in brief counseling interviews: An empirical taxonomy. *Journal of Counseling Psychology, 32,* 307-322.

Elliott, R. (1986). Interpersonal Process Recall (IPR) as a process research method. In L. Greenberg & W. Pinsof (Eds.), *The psychotherapeutic process* (pp. 503-527). New York: Guilford.

Elliott, R. (1989). Comprehensive Process Analysis: Understanding the change process in significant therapy events. In M. Packer & R. B. Addison (Eds.), *Entering the circle: Hermeneutic investigation in psychology* (pp. 165-184). Albany: SUNY Press.

Elliott, R., Clark, C., Kemeny, V., Wexler, M. M., Mack, C., & Brinkerhoff, J. (June, 1988). *Brief Structured Recall of significant therapy events in experiential therapy of depression.* Paper presented at the meetings of the Society for Psychotherapy Research, Santa Fe, NM.

Elliott, R., & James, E. (1989). Varieties of client experience in psychotherapy: An analysis of the literature. *Clinical Psychology Review, 9,* 443-467.

Elliott, R., James, E., Reimschuessel, C., Cislo, D., & Sack, N. (1985). Significant events and the analysis of immediate therapeutic impacts. *Psychotherapy, 22,* 620-630.

Elliott, R., & Shapiro, D. A. (1988). Brief Structured Recall: A more efficient method for identifying and describing significant therapy events. *British Journal of Medical Psychology, 61,* 141-153.

Elliott, R., Shapiro, D. A., Firth-Cozens, J., Stiles, W. B., Hardy, G., Llewelyn, S. P., & Margison, F. (1987). Insight events in prescriptive and exploratory therapies: A comprehensive process analysis. In R. Elliott, *Comprehensive process analysis.* (book in preparation)

Giorgi, A. (1975). An application of phenomenological method in psychology. In A. Giorgi, C. Fischer, & E. Murray (Eds.), *Duquesne studies in phenomenological psychology* (Vol. 2). Pittsburgh, PA: Duquesne University Press.

Harper, H. (1988, June). *When the alliance is under challenge.* Paper presented at the meetings of the Society for Psychotherapy Research, Santa Fe, NM.

Hill, C. E., Helms, J. E., Spiegel, S. B., & Tichenor, V. (1988). Development of a system for assessing client reactions to therapist interventions. *Journal of Counseling Psychology, 35,* 27-36.

Hill, T. E. (1961). *Contemporary theories of knowledge.* New York: Ronald Press.

Hobson, R. F. (1985). *Forms of feeling: The heart of psychotherapy.* New York: Tavistock.

Hoen-Saric, R., Frank, J. D., Imber, S. D., Nash, E. H., Stone, A. R., & Battle, C. C. (1964). Systematic preparation of patients for psychotherapy: 1. Effects on therapy behavior and outcome. *Journal of Psychiatric Research, 2,* 267-281.

Kagan, N. (1975). *Interpersonal Process Recall: A method of influencing human interaction.* (Available from N. Kagan, Educational Psychology Department, University of Houston, University Park, Houston, TX 77004.)

Labov, W., & Fanshel, D. (1977). *Therapeutic discourse.* New York: Academic Press.

Llewelyn, S. P., Elliott, R., Shapiro, D. A., Firth, J., & Hardy, G. (1988). Client perceptions of significant events in prescriptive and exploratory periods of individual therapy. *British Journal of Clinical Psychology, 27,* 105-114.

Luborsky, L. (1984). *Principles of psychoanalytic psychotherapy: A manual for supportive-expressive treatment.* New York: Basic Books.

Mahrer, A. R. (1988). Discovery-oriented psychotherapy research: Rationale, aims, and methods. *American Psychologist, 43,* 694-702.

Mahrer, A. R., & Nadler, W. P. (1986). Good moments in psychotherapy: A preliminary review, a list, and some promising research avenues. *Journal of Consulting and Clinical Psychology, 54,* 10-16.

Orlinsky, D. E., & Howard, K. I. (1975). *Varieties of psychotherapeutic experience.* New York: Teachers College Press.

Orlinsky, D. E., & Howard, K. I. (1986). The psychological interior of psychotherapy: Explorations with the Therapy Session Reports. In L. Greenberg & W. Pinsof (Eds.), *The psychotherapeutic process.* New York: Guilford.

Packer, M. J., & Addison, R. B. (Eds.). (1989). *Entering the circle: Hermeneutic investigation in psychology.* Albany: SUNY Press.

Parry, G., Shapiro, D. A., & Firth, J. (1986). The case of the anxious executive: A study from the research clinic. *British Journal of Medical Psychology, 59,* 221-233.

Rennie, D. L. (1985, June). *Client deference in the psychotherapy relationship.* Paper presented at the meeting of the Society for Psychotherapy Research, Evanston, IL.

Rennie, D. L., Phillips, J. R., & Quartaro, G. K. (1988). Grounded theory: A promising approach to conceptualization in psychology? *Canadian Psychology, 29,* 139-150.

Rice, L. N., & Greenberg, L. (Eds.). (1984). *Patterns of change.* New York: Guilford.

Sacks, H., Schegloff, E. A., & Jefferson, G. (1974). A simplest systematics for the organization of turn-taking in conversation. *Language, 50,* 696-735.

Shapiro, D. A., & Firth, J. (1987). Prescriptive vs. exploratory psychotherapy: Outcomes of the Sheffield Psychotherapy Project. *British Journal of Psychiatry, 151,* 790-799.

Wertz, F. J. (1985). Methods and findings in the study of a complex life event: Being criminally victimized. In A. Giorgi (Ed.), *Phenomenology and psychological research.* Pittsburgh, PA: Duquesne University Press.

Wiggins, J. S. (1973). *Personality and prediction: Principles of personality assessment.* Reading, MA: Addison-Wesley.

8

Metaphor and the Communication Interaction in Psychotherapy

A Multimethodological Approach

LYNNE E. ANGUS

The following chapter is an overview of a series of investigations that have emerged from an initial qualitative study of metaphor in psychotherapy. Following a discussion of the core findings from this project, a series of quantitative studies, designed to explore correlates identified in the qualitative analyses, are described. Accordingly, the overall approach may be characterized as one of methodological pluralism. With this approach, an attempt is made to explicate phenomena and to test hypotheses back and forth between quantitative and qualitative research methods and designs. Findings emerging from the contrasting contexts of field and laboratory research paradigms are juxtaposed to synthesize the research results into a cohesive model. New avenues for further inquiry follow from this integrated perspective.

Metaphor in Psychotherapy: A Qualitative Analysis

In an initial qualitative study, 11 metaphor episodes selected from four therapy dyads were examined from the perspective of the client, the therapist, and the researcher. The latter was an external observer of the therapeutic interaction. Four pairs of therapists and clients were recruited for the study. One therapist was a psychoanalyst, another was a Gestalt/experiential therapist, and the remaining two were eclectics working within a person-centered and psychodynamic framework. Two therapists had more than 25 years of experience in the field, one had 15 years of experience, and the fourth had been practicing for 5 years. All of the therapists were men. The four clients who participated in the study had been in therapy for at least 12 sessions. Three of these clients were women attending postsecondary institutions while the fourth client was employed as a salesman.

The study was limited to a single audiorecorded therapy session of each of the four dyads. When selecting metaphor episodes from the therapy session tapes, the expanded definition of metaphor as advanced by Lakoff and Johnson (1980) was used as a general guideline. According to this definition, *metaphor* is a form of verbal expression and cognitive structuring that invokes a transaction between different contexts of meaning and construct systems. A concrete example might be helpful to make this definition clear. Paivio (1979) suggests that we understand a figurative expression such as "metaphor is a solar eclipse" by filtering our conceptual system of metaphor through the imagery-laden context of a solar eclipse. This integration of two differing contexts of meaning (i.e., metaphor versus a solar eclipse) results in a reconceptualization of metaphor where, like a solar eclipse, it may now be construed as both obscuring and revealing phenomena. The 11 metaphor episodes selected for intensive analysis in this study were judged to have met this definition.

Separate inquiry interviews with the client and therapist of each dyad were conducted within 24 hours of the therapy session. During the inquiry, the selected instances of metaphoric interchanges were replayed a few words at a time. A variation of Kagan's (1975) Interpersonal Process Recall procedure was carried out. The respondents were asked to recall thoughts, images, emotions, and feelings that they were experiencing at the moment in the session represented in the tape segment just played. Care was taken to have the participants attempt to discriminate between actual recall of their experiences and construction of what they were likely experiencing in the light of their reflection on it during the inquiry. Each inquiry interview was audiotaped and transcribed.

The procedures involved in the analysis of the inquiry interviews may be viewed as a blend of empirical phenomenology (Giorgi, 1970) as practiced by Fessler (1978) and grounded theory (Glaser, 1978; Glaser & Strauss, 1967) as practiced by Rennie, Phillips, and Quartaro (1988). Each metaphoric interchange was summarized in terms of the participant's recalled experience of it during the session as well as his or her understanding of it upon reflection, having heard it a second time in the inquiry interview. A third vantage point was provided by observations of the interviewer/researcher. These summaries provided a moment-by-moment comparison of each client's and therapist's experiences as they moved through the metaphoric sequences during the therapy session.

A category system was developed simultaneously with and directly from these summaries. Initially, each characteristic or property of metaphor that was either displayed by the participants or conceptualized by the researcher was entered as a heading on an index card, assigned a number, and dated. A total of 676 cards resulted from this analysis. After the analysis of the inquiry transcripts of the first two dyads, the index cards were sorted in terms of conceptualized, unifying themes. Subsequently, as the analyses of the remaining transcripts were completed, the components of the category system were resorted to better reflect the themes.

As the number of themes increased, two global categories emerged that represented perceived relationships among the themes. One global category was titled the Associated Meaning Context (Angus & Rennie, 1989), the components of which represented the participant's initial experience of either saying or hearing the metaphor in the session. The other global category to emerge was titled the Metaphoric Communication Interaction (Angus & Rennie, 1988), wherein the dyadic style of communication was related to the development of either shared understanding or misunderstanding between client and therapist.

The following presentation of my current research program is organized into three sections. The first two sections deal with the Associated Meaning Context and the Communication Interaction, respectively, and describe the quantitative studies that were designed to validate the patterns that emerged from the qualitative analysis. The third and final section details the implications of these findings for future process research studies and for psychotherapy practice.

The Associated Meaning Context

The Associated Meaning Context category represents the initial impact of hearing or speaking the metaphor in the session and is characterized as a juncture point in the communication interaction. This category has three main properties: (a) metaphor as associative link, (b) metaphor as self-identity, and (c) metaphor as role relationship pattern.

The participants' intrasubjective experiences at these juncture points often involved an initial awareness of kinesthetic sensations and/or emotional responses. To give meaning to their experiences, the participants then proceeded to embed their felt experiencing within an associated context or network of thematically linked memories and visual images. It became apparent that one of the major organizing principles of the Associated Meaning Context was the particular set of role relationship patterns that underscored the network of visual images and recollected memories related to the metaphor spoken in the session. It was in this way that certain metaphors came to be understood by both members of the therapy dyad as symbolic representations of the client's beliefs about self and others.

In most instances, the client's reflection upon the metaphor in the session led to the elaboration of specific memories or images related to an inner experience. Furthermore, in the inquiry interview, these memories led to additional elaboration of important themes. For example, the metaphor sequence titled "all covered up" began with the client making connections between her daughter's relationship with her eldest child and her own experiences of having been the oldest child in a family. As she put it, "having had to be a 'good' baby somehow makes me feel angry." In the inquiry interview, the client recalled that, as she spoke in the therapy session, an image came to mind:

> I was recalling how I must have felt as a baby. I had an image of myself when I was about a year old and I was dressed in this little white dress and I had little stockings on that are white and go all the way down, and I just feel all covered up. I was having the sensation, as a baby, of being distanced from myself by my clothes (pause) all covered up or closed in. At the beginning of the sequence I think I was feeling this sort of veil or whatever and it distanced me from my own feelings and the photograph of myself as a baby just popped into my mind (pause) I suppose, looking like how I was feeling then.

In the session, the client had then described this vivid image to the therapist, again noting that she had felt all covered up as she had visualized the photograph in her mind's eye.

In the inquiry, the therapist recalled that, at this moment in the session,

> When she said, "I had a picture" and then said "covered up," I saw a crib and I saw the—even the face of the baby was covered up—I don't know if that was her (image) and I didn't bother to check it out but I did have that picture throughout (pause) this child in a crib and a kind of white woolly blanket totally covering her, almost like she were dead in a sense.

He stated further that he understood the client's description of herself in the photograph as being like a "giant metaphor" for how she viewed herself interacting with others in the world. He went on to say,

> It seems like she is saying there has always been, or "I've always felt covered up, there has always been something between me and others, which they couldn't touch me or I couldn't be touched;" it's one of the ways she has felt herself to be in the world all her life.

His request to the client in the session—to describe how it felt to be "covered up"—reflected his hope that the client would "stay with the awareness of her subjective experiencing" and explore further the feelings evoked by the imaged photograph.

In response to the therapist's question, the client said: "It makes me feel the way I feel now, itchy (pause) as if my skin were saying 'touch me.' It really is; when you itch you want to rub and things like that. My skin is saying 'touch me.' " With this description, she had linked the experience, which she had felt in relation to imaging herself as a baby "all covered up," with her current feelings as an adult in relation to significant others. The metaphoric context of a baby unable to physically touch its own body or be touched by others vividly articulated her current sense of being "out of touch" with herself and emotionally cutoff from others. The meaning conveyed by the metaphor appears to have evolved out of an interpretive process whereby the client had achieved a synthesis of her current bodily experiencing within the metaphoric context of a baby "all covered up."

In summary, the foregoing metaphor sequence exemplifies the three properties of the Associated Meaning Context in the following ways: (a) The metaphor "all covered up" functioned as an associative link that thematically integrated an emotional state and an associated visual image with her current sense of feeling disconnected from others; (b) the imaginal representation of a baby covered in woolly clothing came to articulate one aspect of this client's sense of self; and (c) the scope of the metaphor was extended by both the client and her therapist to include the client's sense of self in her current relationship with others (the felt inability to touch or be touched emotionally by another). In general, this co-constructive process of meaning transformation, in which bodily feeling states and imaginal associations are articulated within the framework of a verbal metaphor, was evident in the accounts given by therapists and clients engaged in collaborative interactions (Angus & Rennie, 1988).

The following study emerged out of consideration of the category titled the Associated Meaning Context. This project was undertaken to understand more fully the relationship between awareness of private, subjective sensory and visual images—as was characterized by clients and therapists in the collaborative metaphor sequences—and the elaboration of metaphors.

Metaphor and Referential Activity

My goals for this project were twofold. First, given that psychotherapy is only one context of many in which metaphor generation has been associated with achieving a new insight or understanding, more general models of cognitive and perceptual processing should inform the investigation of modes of symbolic processing in therapy. Drawing on extant theories of cognitive processing would also guide the selection of assessment measures for inclusion in the study. The second aim of this project was to select assessment measures of metaphor ability and of experiential processing that would be adaptable to the assessment of individual differences in clients and therapists in future psychotherapy process studies.

For this study, Paivio's (1986) Dual Code model of cognitive functioning was selected as the theoretical framework in which the relationship between visual imagery and verbal metaphor would be conceptualized. In his theory, Paivio (1986) suggests that there are two functionally and structurally distinct representational systems. The verbal code is specialized for the representation and processing of language. The information is organized according to abstract properties and hierarchical orderings of a given category. An example of this mode of representation would be the following: A pine is a type of evergreen, which is a kind of tree, which is a form of vegetation, which is a part of the natural ecosystem.

The nonverbal code is involved in processing sensory experiences and imagery and is specialized for representing concrete properties of things. Drawing on the pine tree again, an example of this mode of representation would be the following: A pine feels prickly like a porcupine's quill; its smell and color remind me of the grassy meadow behind my cottage, after a summer rainstorm. The schemata of the nonverbal systems are built on experience and reflect shared perceptual properties of things, or sequences of events as they occur. Representations of things are connected because they occur in the same place at the same time, because they play interacting roles in the same event(s), or because they look, feel, or taste alike wherein one image evokes another through such connections. Ice and glass are associated because they are perceptually similar; that is, they are both shiny and clear. Bucci (1985), who has also drawn on the Dual Code model in her research, views emotional schemata as structures in the nonverbal system that are made up of elements of that code: visual and sensory images, representations of movement, and representations of visceral, bodily experience.

Paivio uses the term *referential processing* to depict the activation of one system by units in the other system. Evidence for referential processing is shown clearly in acts of reference such as providing names for objects and identifying objects by pointing to them. The ability to conjure up mental images to words is another example. Paivio has demonstrated empirically that these referential linkages are most direct for concrete words and their nonverbal representations.

In their research, Bucci and her colleagues have focused exclusively on the referential processing aspect of the dual coding model. They use the term *referential activity* (RA) to denote the degree to which the system of referential connections is involved in verbal and nonverbal representations. In a series of studies, Bucci (1985) examined individual differences in the activity of the system of referential connections and developed an externally rated performance measure of referential ability. Findings from these investigations suggest a correlation between high levels of RA and the use of vivid, metaphoric language.

Bucci and Freedman (1978) found that high-RA subjects—defined as those individuals who on the Stroop color-naming task (Stroop, 1935) gave the lowest reaction-time difference scores corrected for word reading time—exhibited more concrete, specific, and definite language in their 5-minute monologues. It was also noted that high-RA subjects were more likely to use vivid, metaphoric language in their descriptions of their personal experiences. The Referential Activity Scale (Bucci, 1987) is a rating system that was designed to evaluate written or spoken text on those dimensions found to characterize the monologues of high-RA subjects. Accordingly, each text or rated unit is evaluated on the basis of four 10-point scales (concreteness, specificity, clarity, and imagery), and an overall RA score is generated by summing across the four scales.

In more recent studies, researchers have examined the relationship between the Referential Activity Scale and other conceptually related variables. Ellenhorn (1986) found a significant positive correlation between RA language style in a 5-minute monologue and subjective experience of imagery based on a self-report measure of vividness of mental imagery. In a related study, Eichan and Ellenhorn (1988) found a positive relationship between focused voice quality (Rice & Kerr, 1986) and referential activity (Bucci, 1985). They suggest that the inward deployment of attention in focusing relates to the process of accessing nonverbal material and representing it verbally.

Bucci (1987) speculates that the Dual Code model might be an appropriate theoretical framework for explaining deep structural change in psychodynamic therapy and psychoanalysis. In essence, she suggests that high-RA clients have greater facility for entering into an experiential mode such that they are able to focus attention on and verbally articulate sensory and visual images. Accordingly, metaphor, which effects a transaction between differing contexts or representational systems, may be viewed as a type of referential processing. Bucci hypothesizes that, where referential linkage is sparse or inactive, the verbal and nonverbal systems retain the modes of organization intrinsic to their own schemata. Where referential linkage is active, on the other hand, the schemata of the two systems will interact. It is in the context of this referential process, in which visual images and emotional schemata are articulated within the context of the verbal code, that metaphor is thought to play a vital role in therapy.

Accordingly, to examine empirically the relationship between individual differences in RA ability, metaphor ability, visual imagery, and styles of experiential attunement, a two-part laboratory study was undertaken with undergraduates as participants. To date, we have collected data from 75 subjects (56 women, 19 men) and are at the point of organizing and transcribing our research protocols for further rating and analysis. As this exploratory study was part of a larger collaborative project, only those measures that pertained to my focal interests will be indicated here.

The first testing session entailed the completion, in a group format, of a variety of paper and pencil measures to evaluate the participants on a range of cognitive and perceptual style dimensions. Awareness of experiential processes and sensory images was assessed by two self-report measures: the Openness to Experience Scale (McCrae & Costa, 1985) and the Vividness of Visual Imagery Questionnaire (Marks, 1972). Attentional style was assessed by means of the Tellegen Absorption Scale (Tellegen & Atkinson, 1974). Metaphor ability was evaluated using the Symbolic Equivalences Test (Barron, 1969), which measures an individual's capacity to generate original metaphors in relation to five stimulus images. The Advanced Vocabulary Test (French, Estrom, & Price, 1963) was also given to assess whether or not differences in word knowledge correlated with adequacy of metaphor productions.

In the second and final session, each participant met individually with a same-sex research assistant and was requested to complete two tasks. The first task was a modified version of a metaphor production test, originally developed by Hunt and Popham (1987). An adaptation of the *I Ching* (Wing, 1979), this task requires the integration of two disparate metaphor phrases to form an integrated whole. The participants were requested to think aloud as they completed the task, and all performances were audiotaped for future analyses. A qualitative rating manual (Grant, Hunt, & Angus, 1990), based on the original work of Hunt and Popham, was used to analyze the research protocols.

Referential activity was assessed on the basis of three, 5-minute, audiotaped monologues in which the participant was asked to describe a vivid, or memorable, relationship event with a parent, a friend, and another significant relationship. The monologues were transcribed and assessed for RA using Bucci's (1987) Referential Activity Scale. Training in the use of this rating system is under way, and a comprehensive training manual for the four RA scales has been completed. Using monologues rated by Bucci and her colleagues as a criterion, one judge in our training program has demonstrated good levels of reliability for all four scales: concreteness (Pearson $r = .93$), specificity ($r = .87$), clarity ($r = .93$), and imagery ($r = .93$). The next step is to develop adequate levels of interrater agreement between this rater and others in our training program.

In summary, there is empirical evidence to suggest that absorption and openness to inner experience appear to be elements of a cognitive style of attending to the experience in a focused manner. This attentional ability and the creation of a cognitive space, where one can focus on visual images and internal experiencing, may relate positively to vividness of visual imagery, referential processing, and metaphor generation. Once we have completed data collection, a correlational analysis will be undertaken to explore the extent of the interrelationship between these cognitive style factors and metaphor-generation ability.

The Metaphoric Communication Interaction

The second core category that emerged from the qualitative analysis, described earlier, was titled the Metaphoric Communication Interaction. This category represented the dyadic style of communication and was based on the occurrence of either conjunction or disjunction in the client's and therapist's joint understanding of a given moment in therapy (hereafter referred to as "meaning conjunction" or "meaning disjunction"). Whether the members of a dyad produced a meaning conjunction or disjunction seemed to depend on whether or not a discovery-oriented, collaborative style of engagement had been established in the relationship. An atmosphere of collaboration and discovery stimulated both participants to share their personally held meanings regarding the metaphor, which in turn facilitated the development of a mutually constructed understanding of the phrase, ie., meaning conjunction. Conversely, the absence of a collaborative mode mitigated a sharing of personal associations to the metaphor and potentiated a meaning disjunction. The following metaphor episode exemplifies the properties associated with collaborative interactions.

The metaphor sequence titled "like a little child" began when a therapist asked his client, "Why are you so touchy about the subject of the neglected kid?" In the inquiry interview, when the therapist reflected upon why he had asked the question, he recalled, "I want her to come up with it, [not] impose it upon her; [to have her] try to understand what of her past experience may be contributing to her current perceptions and reactions." He further recalled that he had anticipated that the client probably would not make the connection between her current outrage about a known instance of child neglect and her own past as an abused child. As he said, "I think eventually I had to tell her anyway; I don't think she put it together herself." It was with great surprise that he learned, during the tape replay in the inquiry, that the client did in fact answer his question in the session. She had stated, "Because I know what it's like to be a neglected child." Upon hearing this response, the therapist remarked, "Isn't that interesting; I didn't think she got it on her own; I thought I had to tell her." He then recalled that this connection between her having been a neglected child and her current feelings about mother-child relationships had been discussed before, but that it had been "more intellectual; it wasn't nearly as arousing in the therapy as this was."

From the client's perspective, the therapist's question had been "expectable" and even anticipated during the session.

> I knew he was going to ask me the question (pause). You see, I didn't tell him that 'cause I didn't want to spoil it for him (pause). I had the feeling like, I know the next question he's going to ask me is "How come you feel this way about neglected kids?" I knew it; I could feel it.

For her, the therapist's ensuing confirmation of the correctness of her answer ("Darn right that's the reason") had been an important sign. As she said in the inquiry interview, "It made me feel like I was right for once in my life; made me feel more confident that at least I've got brains."

During the inquiry, the therapist recalled that, at this moment in the session, he had begun to synthesize the general theme of the client as the neglected child with another theme. The second theme was the circumstance of the violent daydream that she had discussed earlier in the session. He had found himself thinking,

> "My God, I'm going to give her a very complex interpretation; a long, complex interpretation and I think she's going to understand it." I was kind of amazed as I was talking that I could be making such a complicated interpretation to this patient.

This juncture in the collaborative sequence marked the emergence of the metaphor. It began with the therapist reminding the client of a daydream that she had previous to the therapy session, in which she angrily destroyed the therapist's office. The therapist remarked: "You see, you had a daydream before you came here and in the daydream you come in here and act like a little child."

The client then interrupted the therapist and elaborated his remark with the comment: "And I took a temper tantrum." The therapist repeated this remark. The client then added, "And I started screaming and hollering at you; the thing is I wanted you to help me." The therapist then incorporated the client's co-elaboration of the "like a little child" analogy and extended the scope of the metaphoric transfer to the therapeutic relationship itself:

> And you act like a neglected child, and the question you are asking me in the daydream was, would I pay attention to a neglected child; would I pay attention to you; would I take you seriously or, if you're a pill or if you have a temper tantrum, whether I would neglect you the way you have been neglected in the past when you were a kid.

During the inquiry, the therapist was unable to recall exactly what he was thinking or feeling as he proceeded to "flesh out" his interpretation. He explained:

> When I make a complicated interpretation, I am almost in a dissociative state, and I'm kind of amazed myself sometimes the things that come out of my mouth, including puns, slips of the tongue, which have a big impact on me and the patient as they elaborate on what I'm trying to say.

In the inquiry, the client reported her reaction to the therapist's elaboration of the metaphoric implications of the daydream:

> It just made more sense than anything I could even think of, it just made more sense; I was just listening to him and I was recording it all in my head; it just fit where it should've fitted to begin with.

Furthermore, she stated that, as the therapist dwelt on the metaphor, she had experienced vivid, visual recollections of her experiences as an abused child. In addition, the therapist made a strong emotional impact on the client by focusing on her feelings about the therapeutic relationship:

> He gave me a feeling; in a way he showed me that I was wanted; I don't know if the word is "showing," "showed," or whatever; he was releasing a feeling of me being wanted. I don't know how to explain; he was describing me all over again. That's what he was doing; he was giving, showing me through him; he was wearing my shoes at that moment.

The client's experience regarding this metaphor was typical of her experience of other metaphors in the session. It was also representative of the experience of the second client in this study who engaged in a collaborative relationship with her therapist. Both clients described feeling as if the therapist understood them and experienced the therapist's or analyst's words as successfully "embodying" and reflecting back their feelings. Both felt that they shared with the therapist a fully developed context of meaning regarding the use of certain metaphors spoken in the dialogue and anticipated that the therapist knew what they intended to mean during the session.

Moreover, the creative "dissociative state" described by the therapist as contributing to the "like a little child" metaphor was also reported by both participants in the second collaborative dyad. The client in this dyad described articulating her inner world "one word at a time," with little sense of where she had been headed until she had expressed herself fully. Similarly, her therapist likened the discovery process to that of translating from Greek to English, where the full meaning of the statement remains unknown until the entire sentence is completely transcribed.

In the foregoing example, the interactive, transactional nature of the collaborative therapeutic relationship is evident. Both the therapist and the client co-elaborated and co-constructed each other's interpretive statements such that there appeared to be a sharing and transaction between the meanings they attributed to the metaphoric scenario of the "little child." In essence, each participant's understanding of a particular event was transformed by the contributions of the other. As such, the final product of this co-constructive process represents neither the therapist's meaning nor the client's meaning but rather a cohesive synthesis and reorganization of both perspectives.

What can occur in a noncollaborative therapeutic interaction is reflected in "the litany" metaphor sequence selected from the first dyad interviewed for this study. In the inquiry interview, the client recalled that, during the metaphor sequence, she had been monitoring a series of vivid memories as the therapist had spoken in the session. The topic under discussion in the sequence was the nature of her relationship with her future mother-in-law. She recalled in the inquiry that, during the session, she had been remembering a conversation that she recently had with her fiancé's mother. Specifically, she stated, "I was thinking about her face in the car." This recollection in turn had led to another memory in which her future mother-in-law had made some obscure critical comments about her weight. Here the client indicated that "she [i.e., her future mother-in-law] tried to make it seem affectionate but it really bothered me." She described her immersion in tracking these imaginal recollections as "blanking out" from the immediate interaction with the therapist during the session. As she had not described the inner visual images/memories to the therapist, he had remained unaware of their importance or meaning for her.

The therapist, on the other hand, indicated in the inquiry that, at that point in the metaphor sequence, the client had looked as if she had not understood what he had been talking about in the session. The therapist had then attempted to compensate for this perceived misunderstanding by repeating his statement.

From the perspective of the researcher, it would appear that many of the visual images and memories that the client had associated to the metaphors spoken in the session had been thematically linked to important relationship issues. In electing to withhold from her therapist the disclosure of these vivid recollections of images and memories, she had lost the opportunity to explore the full context of the meaning associated with this particular issue.

Perhaps more important, by not expressing the imaged memories, both the client and the therapist were denied the opportunity of co-constructing a new perspective on an old relationship problem. The articulation of her current experiencing/feelings in the therapy session within the imaged context of the recalled visual memories might have provided the opportunity for client and therapist alike to generate a shared, new understanding of a recurrent relationship problem.

I will now describe a research project that was developed to investigate empirically findings that emerged from the qualitative analyses of the Metaphor Communication Interaction.

Coding the Communication Interaction

A measure, titled the Interactional Coding System, emerged out of findings from the core category, the Metaphor Communication Interaction. The primary goal of this project was to develop a reliable method of identifying the occurrence of collaborative and noncollaborative interactions throughout a therapy session. A secondary aim of this study was to develop an external rating system such that both the client's and the therapist's statements and activities could be evaluated on the same criteria. One advantage of using a rating system for evaluating the therapeutic interaction is that it can be applied to transcripts of therapy sessions and does not require the arduous, in-depth analysis demanded by the qualitative approach. Additionally, judges can be trained in the use of the assessment measure to ascertain the reliability of their evaluations over time. A review of the extant research literature pertaining to the rating of clients' and therapists' activities/statements in sessions revealed that, in almost all instances, coding systems have been developed to characterize clients and therapists on dimensions/criteria thought to be of importance for a particular therapeutic orientation (e.g., transference interpretations, focused voice quality). Furthermore, with these rating systems, therapists and clients are assumed to be engaged in distinctly different kinds of activities during the therapy hour.

An example of this approach to evaluating the therapeutic interaction is a rating system titled the Sequential System for Coding Therapist Interventions and Client Responses (Marziali & Angus, 1986). This system was developed within a psychodynamic framework and drew upon the work by Malan (1980). It was designed specifically to target the relationship focus of the therapists' open-ended inquiries and interpretive statements. The system is summarized in Table 8.1.

It is evident that this rating system is based on the implicit assumption that the therapist's job is to provide direction and offer interventions in therapy while the client's job is to follow and respond. This assumption is challenged by the results of the qualitative study of the 11 metaphor episodes obtained from therapeutic orientations described earlier in this chapter. At different points in the verbal interaction, all clients and all therapists in this study were found to initiate topics, make interventions, and follow the lead of the other participant. Had the four sessions been rated with the Sequential Coding System, however, the activity and reflexivity (Rennie, 1990, this volume) of the clients would have been rendered invisible by the a priori decision to classify client statements as responses to therapists' interventions.

Accordingly, I set out to systematically revise the Sequential Coding System to delineate the interactive, co-constructive nature of the therapeutic dialogue. The current form of the Interactional Coding System (ICS; Angus, Slater, Paupst, & Marziali, 1990) represents a comprehensive measure whereby all client and therapist verbalizations are rated on the same criteria. More specifically, the system was developed to identify the kinds of activities that characterize patterns of client and therapist behaviors in collaborative and noncollaborative interactions, irrespective of therapeutic orientation. In the main, the categories address the level of speech acts in the immediate context of the therapy dialogue.

The 13 categories of the ICS represent three different types of codes. The first set of codes (1-4) focuses on types of actions initiated in the therapy session, ranging from giving advice and instructing the other

Table 8.1   A Sequential System for Coding Therapist Intervention and Client Responses (Marziali & Angus, 1986)

Therapist statements

T1   therapist statements that address the therapeutic relationship

T2   therapist statements that focus on the client's relationship with   significant others

T3   therapist statements that link patterns apparent in the therapeutic relationship with aspects of the client's relationship with significant others.

TSC   therapist statements that address aspects of the client's self-beliefs, self-concepts or self-experiences.

Client response to the therapist response

C0   client offers no response

C1   client agrees/accepts therapist statement

C2   client responds in an ambivalent manner, "yes, but . . . "

C3   client openly disagrees with therapist statement

CF   client changes focus of the discussion

Q   client questions therapist

C   client requests further clarification from therapist

---

participant to changing the topic of discussion and making summary statements:

1. Introduces shifts, or changes focus or topic
2. Reflects back statements or summarizes
3. Offers advice
4. Instructs other participant

The second set of codes (5-7) characterizes the participant's discussions of focal issues in terms of *point of view* (either focused outward on external events or inward on experiential states) and *level of analysis* (either descriptive or analytic and reflexive):

5. Descriptive elaboration of external events; personal/work relationships, episodes: focus on description of external events
6. Descriptive elaboration of subjective experience or point of view in response to an event or issue pertaining to self and relationship to others;

may include description of visual images, memories, points of view: focus on description of inner experiencing

7. Reflexive analysis or exploration regarding subjective state or relationship events with others: focus on achieving understanding/integration

The final set of codes (8-13) pertains to utterances that convey agreement or disagreement with the other participant's actions or points of view:

8. Expressed agreement with or acceptance of advice, instructions, and statement made by others

9. Expressed feelings of being heard or understood: "That's exactly what I was going through!"

10. Expressed partial agreement

11. Restatement of position or returning to previous topic of discussion

12. Rejection or disagreement with suggestions, interpretations, instructions, and so on

13. Expressed misunderstanding of feelings or being misunderstood or misrepresented/may request clarification from the other

In addition, the content of the relationship focus is coded separately for each statement made by the client or therapist in the following manner:

TH: statements that address the therapeutic relationships

SO: statements that focus on the client's relationship with significant others

SC: statements that address the client's self-concepts, self-beliefs, or self experiences

ST: statements that address the therapist's self-concepts, self-beliefs, or self-experiences

E: statements that describe external events or background material

The categories of the ICS require a low level of inference by the raters. Based on the rating of 210 meaning units from one psychotherapy session, an adequate level of interrater agreement (87%) was achieved after 30 hours of training. Application of an earlier version of the ICS to the four therapy sessions (Paupst, 1988), which formed the basis of my qualitative study of metaphor (Angus & Rennie, 1988, 1989), yielded some interesting results: 60% of all topics introduced in the session were initiated by the client; clients initiated and/or provided 20% of all interpretive statements and 25% of all restatements and summarizations.

In a more recent pilot project (Slater & Angus, 1990), the ICS was used to analyze transcripts of the "Gloria films" with Rogers, Ellis, and Perls (Shostrom, 1966). Preliminary results from this analysis suggest that the ICS differentiates among these three therapeutic encounters. The percentages reported represent the frequency of occurrence of a particular code in the context of the total number of responses coded for a particular therapy session.

In terms of the first set of ICS actions (codes 1-4), it is apparent that, true to form, Rogers offers by far the greatest percentage of reflection/summarization responses (21% versus 2.9% for Ellis and 6.2% for Perls) while Perls concentrates on instructing Gloria (20% versus 7.2% for Ellis and 2.4% for Rogers) during the session. Overall, Perls's responses are coded most frequently as representative of the action codes (32%) followed by Rogers (27%) and Ellis (14%).

Although highest with Rogers (11% versus Ellis, 3% and Perls, 5.1%), it appears that, in general, Gloria's responses in the sessions receive far fewer action codes than do the therapists' responses. Given the agential focus of these codes, this result suggests that Gloria felt relatively constrained in asserting a measure of control in the therapy session. Perhaps this finding is not so surprising given the knowledge that Gloria was well aware that she was meeting with three renowned psychotherapists. Deference to the authority of the therapist (Rennie, 1990) was to be expected in this context.

The second set of ICS codes categorizes responses in terms of whether they provide a narrative description of (a) external events (code 5), (b) subjective experiences (code 6), or (c) reflexive/analytic inquiry (code 7) about the meaning of external events and subjective experiences. Overall, the narrative categories are the most frequently occurring codes for all three therapists (Rogers, 59%; Ellis, 44%; Perls, 45%). Of the three narrative categories, the reflexive/analytic focus is the most frequently occurring subcode (Rogers, 42%; Ellis, 35%; Perls, 29%), irrespective of therapeutic approach. In contrast, irrespective of therapist, approximately half of Gloria's responses in the sessions were categorized as focusing on the description and elaboration of inner subjective experiences.

The third set of ICS codes embrace an evaluative dimension in which responses are characterized as indicating either agreement (codes 8, 9) or disagreement (codes 10, 11, 12, 13) with the viewpoints of the other participant. It is interesting that Rogers offers fewer positive evaluative remarks (agreement 9% and disagreement 4%) than does Ellis (agreement 20% and disagreement 20%) while Perls delivers more disagreement responses (17%) than agreement responses (5%) during his session with Gloria. Ellis in fact offers more positive and negative evaluative responses than either Rogers or Perls.

Gloria in turn is rated as having a higher percentage of disagreement ratings (20%) and agreement ratings (28%) with Ellis than any other therapist. Congruent with the therapists' ratings, she is coded as having a relatively higher percentage of agreement (23%) versus disagreement (18%) responses with Rogers while the inverse relationship holds with Perls (agreement 5% and disagreement 28%).

A comparison of the pattern of content codes for the three therapists and Gloria reveals a marked symmetry between client and therapist in terms of issues discussed in the sessions. It may be of interest to note that, irrespective of therapeutic orientation, all three therapists focused predominantly on issues pertaining to Gloria's self-concept and beliefs about self within the context of a reflexive/analytic mode of inquiry. Ellis's responses are coded as centering on the issue of Gloria's beliefs and attitudes toward self 91% of the time, while Gloria's statements in her session with him are coded as belonging to this category 95% of the time. Ellis's heavy concentration on this content category is of course consistent with his rational-emotive therapeutic orientation. In contrast, 35% of Perls's responses address issues pertaining to his relationship with Gloria and 61% of his responses focusing on issues pertaining to her self-concept and beliefs about self. The emphasis on the client's experience of the therapeutic relationship is consistent with the here-and-now focus of Gestalt therapy. Gloria's statements in her session with Perls parallel the content focus established by Perls: 35% of her responses are coded as focusing on the therapeutic relationship and 61% of her responses are coded as focusing on aspects of her own self-beliefs and self-concepts.

Rogers in turn blends a focus on aspects of relationships with significant others (24%) with a centering on Gloria's beliefs and feelings about herself (59%). In interaction with Rogers, Gloria concentrates on aspects of her relationship with others 32% of the time and deals with issues pertaining to her self-concept 60% of the time. From these data, it seems clear that, when interacting in the filmed sessions, Gloria was pulled into the unique therapeutic orbit of each of her three "star" therapists.

A fuller representation of the transactional, interactive nature of the therapeutic encounter would seem to be a promising direction for future research. The delineation of the narrative codes in particular may be of special interest for process researchers. In a recent study, Angus and Hardtke (1991) dealt exclusively with the narrative codes of the ICS and developed the Narrative Sequences Coding Manual. Using this manual, raters are able to subdivide and characterize a complete therapy session according to three narrative sequence codes (subjective/experiential description, description of external events, and reflexive analyses of current or past events). This coding system in turn allows researchers to unitize sessions according to narrative type irrespective of therapeutic modality. Accordingly, both the frequency of narrative codes as well as their patterns of occurrence within the sessions can be traced.

Utilizing sessions according to type of narrative sequence may also allow for a more precise, appropriate use of external rating systems that have been developed to measure different aspects of the therapy process. For instance, the Experiencing Scale (Klein, Mathieu-Coughlan, & Kiesler, 1986) could be used to rate the depth of experiencing for the internal narrative sequences while the Referential Activity Scale (Bucci, 1987) could be applied to evaluate the quality of verbal expression associated with the narrative sequences focusing on descriptions of external events. Such an approach to process research would not give primacy to either the experiential emphasis of the Experiencing Scale or the psychodynamic underpinnings of the Referential Activity Scale. Instead, it would allow the researcher to trace the contribution made by both types of description to the therapy discourse. In this regard, the Narrative Sequences Coding System may prove to be a useful tool for furthering our understanding of what is common to the therapy experience, irrespective of therapeutic techniques or modalities.

Summary and Conclusions

I have presented an overview of the development of my concurrent research interests in metaphor and the therapeutic communication interaction. The studies were undertaken to explore trends that emerged from the intensive, qualitative analysis of a limited number of metaphor sequences. With this multimethodological approach, I have attempted to draw on the strengths of both the qualitative and the quantitative research paradigms in furthering our understanding of the role metaphorical thinking plays in developing insight about our conceptions of self and others.

By understanding more fully the role that individual difference variables such as attunement to subjective experience, imagery awareness, and cognitive complexity play in the ability to generate metaphors and express oneself verbally, we may in turn be able to develop more precise training models for novice therapists. Additionally, we still know very little about how individual metaphor phrases come to symbolize shared contexts of meaning over the course of a complete therapy. The qualitative inquiry into selected metaphor events throughout the course of a short-term therapy relationship would in part address this gap.

Furthermore, it would seem that the construal of the psychotherapy interaction as a form of narrative expression holds special promise for psychotherapy practitioners and researchers alike. While there is currently much theoretical debate about narrative and the construction of meaning (Bruner, 1990; Sarbin, 1986; Spence, 1982; White & Epston, 1990) in psychotherapy, few empirical studies have tried to address systematically these issues in the context of psychotherapy process research. To this end, an investigation of the relationship between verbal expressiveness, metaphor use, and narrative types in productive therapy sessions might make an important contribution to an understanding of how our clients reconfigure their life stories.

In addition, based on the findings of the qualitative research program, some tentative recommendations for psychotherapy practice and process research can be put forward. In terms of understanding how clients and therapists generate metaphors, it is apparent that the experience of apprehending an initial, immediate flood of varied imagistic and emotional associations often precedes the act of conceptualizing meanings for metaphors. Furthermore, returns from the inquiry interview method suggest that the simple act of verbally describing privately experienced images, recollections, and feelings leads participants to a fuller awareness of felt emotions and implicit beliefs about self and others.

In another aspect, in the collaborative dyads, the metaphors generated by the clients and therapists resonate with their inner experiencing during the therapy sessions. It is during these moments that metaphoric communication most clearly resembles a spontaneous self-discovery process. In contrast to the psychotherapy research literature, however, which tends to focus on the client's creativity, it is both the clients and the therapists in the collaborative dyads who describe being engaged in a spontaneous process of creative self-discovery during the metaphor sequences. The therapist's role in this creative process is to model the highlighting and prizing of inner experiences as a way of fostering self-discovery. Accordingly, supervisors might be well advised to encourage novice therapists to be aware of their own experiential reactions during therapy sessions and to use this awareness as a vehicle for discovery about themselves as well as their clients. As suggested by one collaborative therapist in the study, the imaginal associations evoked in the listener by a spoken metaphor might best be understood as a co-construction of the descriptors contained in the phrase combined with idiosyncratic, private associations of the listener. In terms of psychotherapy, a stance of critical self-awareness may be the only safeguard a therapist has against the inappropriate and perhaps damaging expression of countertransferential responses to clients.

Even in response to hackneyed metaphors, therapists should never automatically assume that they share a common understanding or meaning of a phrase with their clients. It is striking how often therapists and clients have distinctly different private imaginal representations of the same metaphor spoken in a session. In fact, misunderstandings between clients and therapists typically occur in those metaphor sequences in which either one or both participants have incorrectly assumed that they are drawing upon a shared context of meaning (Angus & Rennie, 1988).

Finally, the participants' ready ability and willingness to collaborate with the researcher in the inquiry interviews, and to provide elaborations of their experiences evoked by the metaphors, would seem to provide a model for what potentially could take place within the therapeutic relationship itself. It is in this sense that the collaborative exploration of spontaneously generated metaphors would seem to provide a promising context for discovery that cuts across psychotherapeutic genres and treatment approaches.

References

Angus, L., & Hardtke, K. (1991). *A rating manual for the Narrative Sequences Coding System.* Unpublished manuscript. (Available from the Department of Psychology, York University, North York, Ontario, M3J 1P3)

Angus, L., & Rennie, D. (1988). Therapist participation in metaphor generation: Collaborative and non-collaborative styles. *Psychotherapy, 25,* 552-560.

Angus, L., & Rennie, D. (1989). Envisioning the representational world: The client's experience of metaphoric expression in psychotherapy. *Psychotherapy, 26,* 372-379.

Angus, L., Slater, S., Paupst, C., & Marziali, E. (1990). *A rating manual for the Interactional Coding System.* Unpublished manuscript. (Available from the Department of Psychology, York University, North York, Ontario, M3J 1P3)

Arlow, J. (1979). Metaphor and the psychoanalytic situation. *Psychoanalytic Quarterly, 48,* 363-385.

Barron, F. (1969). *Creative person and creative process.* New York: Holt, Rinehart & Winston.

Bruner, J. (1990). *Acts of meaning.* Cambridge, MA: Harvard University Press.

Bucci, W. (1985). Dual coding: A cognitive model for psychoanalytic research. *Journal of the American Psychoanalytic Association, 33*(3), 571-607.

Bucci, W. (1987). *A manual for the coding of referential activity.* Unpublished manuscript, Adelphi University, Garden City, NY.

Bucci, W., & Freedman, N. (1978). Language and hand: The dimension of referential competence. *Journal of Personality, 45,* 594-622.

Eichen, A., & Ellenhorn, T. (1988, June). *Vocal quality, personality style, and expressive language.* Paper presented at the meetings of the Society for Psychotherapy Research, Santa Fe, NM.

Ellenhorn, T. J. (1986, August). *Nonverbal correlates of language: Evidence for dual-coding.* Paper presented at the meetings of the American Psychological Association Convention, Washington, DC.

Fessler, R. (1978). A phenomenological investigation of psychotherapeutic interpretation. *Dissertation Abstracts International, 39*(6B), 2981-2982.

French, J., Estrom, R., & Price, L. (1963). *Manual for kit of reference tests for cognitive factors.* Princeton, NJ: Educational Testing Service.

Giorgi, A. (1970). *Psychology as a human science: A phenomenologically based approach.* New York: Harper & Row.

Glaser, B. G. (1978). *Theoretical sensitivity: Advances in the methodology of grounded theory.* Mill Valley, CA: Sociology Press.

Glaser, B. G., & Strauss, A. (1967). *The discovery of grounded theory: Strategies for qualitative research.* Chicago: Aldine.

Grant, K., Hunt, H., & Angus, L. (1990). *A manual for the I Ching Metaphor Production Task.* Unpublished manuscript. (Available from the Department of Psychology, York University, North York, Ontario, M3J 1P3)

Hunt, H., & Popham, C. (1987). Metaphor and states of consciousness: A preliminary correlational study of presentational thinking. *Journal of Mental Imagery, 11,* 83-100.

Kagan, N. (1975). *Interpersonal process recall: A method for influencing human interaction.* Unpublished manuscript. (Available from N. Kagan, Educational Psychology Department, University of Houston, University Park, Houston, TX, 77004)

Klein, M., Mathieu-Coughlan, P., & Kiesler, D. (1986). The Experiencing Scales. In W. Pinsof & L. Greenberg (Eds.), *The psychotherapeutic process: A research handbook* (pp. 21-72). New York: Guilford.

Lakoff, G., & Johnson, M. (1980). *Metaphors we live by*. Chicago: University of Chicago Press.

Malan, D. (1980). *Toward the validation of dynamic psychotherapy*. New York: Plenum.

Marks, D. (1972). Individual differences in the vividness of visual imagery and their effect on function. In P. W. Sheehan (Ed.), *The function and nature of imagery*. London: Academic Press.

Marziali, E., & Angus, L. (1986, June). *The development of a sequential system for coding therapist interventions and patient responses*. Presented at the meeting of the Society for Psychotherapy Research Conference, Ulm, Germany.

McCrae, R., & Costa, P. (1985). Openness to experience. *Personality, 1,* 145-172.

Paivio, A. (1979). Psychological processes in the comprehension of metaphor. In A. Ortony (Ed.), *Metaphor and thought* (pp. 150-171). London: Cambridge University Press.

Paivio, A. (1986). *Mental representations: A dual coding approach*. London: Oxford University Press.

Paupst, C. (1988). *The Interactional Coding System: Identifying meaning conjunction and meaning disjunction between psychotherapy participants*. Unpublished honours' thesis. (Available from the Department of Psychology, York University, North York, Ontario, M3J 1P3)

Rennie, D. (1990). Toward a representation of the client's experience of the psychotherapy hour. In G. Lietaer, J. Rombauts, & R. Van Balen (Eds.), *Client-centered and experiential therapy in the nineties*. (pp. 155-172). Leuven, Belgium: Leuven University Press.

Rennie, D., Phillips, J., & Quartaro, G. (1988). Grounded theory: A promising approach to conceptualization in psychology? *Canadian Psychology, 29,* 139-150.

Rice, L., & Kerr, G. (1986). Measures of client and therapist vocal quality. In L. S. Greenberg & W. M. Pinsof (Eds.), *The psychotherapeutic process: A research handbook* (pp. 73-105). New York: Guilford.

Sarbin, T. (1986). *Narrative psychology: The storied nature of human conduct*. New York: Praeger.

Shostrom, E. (1966). *Three approaches to psychotherapy* [Film]. Santa Ana, CA: Psychological Films.

Slater, S., & Angus, L. (1990, June). *Three faces of Gloria*. Presented at the annual meeting of the Canadian Psychological Association, Ottawa, Ontario.

Spence, D. (1982). *Narrative truth and historical truth: Meaning and interpretation in psychoanalysis*. New York: Norton.

Stroop, J. R. (1935). Studies of interference in social verbal reactions. *Journal of Experimental Psychology, 18,* 643-662.

Tellegen, A., & Atkinson, G. (1974). Openness to absorbing and self-altering experiences ("absorption"), a trait related to hypnotic susceptibility. *Journal of Abnormal Psychology, 83,* 268-277.

White, M., & Epston, D. (1990). *Narrative means to therapeutic ends*. New York: Norton.

Wing, R. (1979). *The I Ching work book*. Toronto: Bantam, Doubleday.

Yoos, G. (1971). A phenomenological look at metaphor. *Philosophy and Phenomenological Research, 32,* 78-88.

9

Qualitative Analysis of the Client's Experience of Psychotherapy

The Unfolding of Reflexivity

DAVID L. RENNIE

This chapter portrays a qualitative approach to psychotherapy process research. As an outgrowth of a study of variables associated with the acquisition of counseling skill (e.g., Rennie, Brewster, & Toukmanian, 1985; Toukmanian & Rennie, 1975), I became interested in the client's subjective experience of therapy. This change in focus began about a decade ago. At that time, most researchers were conceptualizing the psychotherapeutic process from the vantage point of the therapist (Phillips, 1984). The studies that did address the client's experience varied widely

AUTHOR'S NOTE: This chapter is derived from a paper on clients' reflexivity presented at the First International Conference in Developmental Counseling, Oporto, Portugal, July 1988, and from a related paper presented at the Twentieth Annual Meeting of the Society for Psychotherapy Research, Toronto, June 1989. I am grateful to the Social Sciences and Humanities Research Council of Canada and to the Faculty of Arts and the Faculty Association, York University, for supporting this work. I am also grateful to the clients and therapists who participated in the study, to Jeff Phillips and Charles Marino for assisting in interviewing the participants, and to Joanne Dolhanty, Gary Johnston, Jeanne Lowenstein-Watson, Jack Martin, Milan Pomichalek, and Malcolm Westcott for their comments on earlier drafts of the chapter.

in terms of the phenomena addressed and the method of analysis applied to them (see McLeod, 1990). I have adopted the approach of obtaining clients' tape-replay-assisted recollections of the experience of an entire hour of therapy that they have just experienced and then conducting a grounded theory (Glaser & Strauss, 1967) analysis of their reports. This work thus contrasts with that of other investigators who have gained access to the client's experience through questionnaires (Orlinsky & Howard, 1975; Strupp, Wallach, & Wogan, 1964), written reports (Rogers, 1951), or interviews about a course of therapy now finished (Mayer & Timms, 1973; Oldfield, 1983; Phillips, 1984, 1985). It also contrasts with the work of Elliott (1984, 1986; Elliott & Shaperio, this volume) in its focus on the client's experience of an entire hour of therapy and in its exclusive reliance on the grounded theory method.

The chapter is divided into two parts. It begins with an overview of the grounded theory approach and a description of how I have applied it to therapy process research. This section prepares the ground for the second half, which is an essay on clients' reflexivity, conceptualized to be the heart of numerous categories representing the client's experience of therapy. Supported by the taxonomy of categories it colligates and by illustrative reports by clients, I discuss the implications of clients' reflexivity for research and practice in therapy. This discussion in turn supports the argument that the indeterminacy arising from reflexivity cannot be ignored however much we might wish to reduce the therapeutic process to the level of mechanism in our attempts to achieve prediction and control.

Description of the Study

In the method of the study as it came to be finalized, clients come to the researcher with either a videotape or (as is more usually the case) an audiotape of a therapy session that they have just completed. Along lines pioneered by Kagan (1975), we replay the tape as a way of stimulating the client's recollection of what he or she experienced in the session. To get close to the client's recalled experience, a "free" recall procedure (cf. Elliott, 1986) is conducted. In this procedure, participants are asked to pay attention to anything of interest or significance that they recall experiencing in the session. It is suggested that they refrain from simply reexperiencing the session and that they instead assume an attitude of detachment wherein they appraise what happened. Within the constraints of this instruction, they are given "the lead" in controlling the stopping of the replay of the tape. I have found, however, that they will at times pass over without comment footage of tape that is of interest to me; during such moments, I may stop the tape and initiate the focus into the participant's internal experience. The ethical procedures entailed in this research are described elsewhere (Rennie, 1990).

This work began with colleagues interviewing two of my own clients, after which I have interviewed the clients of other colleagues. With the exception of two clients who were interviewed about each of two sessions, all of the other clients were interviewed about just one therapy session. The delay between the therapy session and the research interview about it was one week in the case of that first, pilot interview; all other research interviews were conducted immediately after the therapy session, although one of these inquiries was conducted in two 2-hour sessions, three days apart.

Up to the current time, the analysis has been applied to 16 reports given by 14 clients. Two clients were in the labor force and seeing a therapist in private practice; the other clients were seeing therapists at either the York University Counselling and Development Centre or the University of Waterloo Student Counselling Centre. All but one of the clients seen in the university centers were students. The group consisted of six men and eight women, ranging in age from the mid-twenties to the late forties. At the time of the research interview, they had been in therapy for a period ranging from six weeks to more than two years. Each client had developed a relationship with his or her therapist to the point that the latter could feel free to approach the client about the prospect of the research. It is also implicit that the therapists would only approach those clients whom they felt could "handle" such a sensitive research endeavor.

The last point means, of course, that the interviewees were volunteers from within each therapist's caseload. Furthermore, I have not been in a position to be especially selective about the kinds of therapy to which they were exposed. Nevertheless, the therapists proved to be reasonably diverse in their orientations. There were six men and five women (two of the therapists saw two clients each), all of whom had at least five years of experience. Seven were Ph.D.-level psychologists, two were graduate students in psychology, and two were social workers. In terms of orientation, five were person-centered, two had a Gestalt focus, one favored the rational-emotive approach, one combined the transactional-analytic and Gestalt approaches, one was a professed radical behaviorist who nevertheless practiced with a person-centered accent, and one drew heavily upon the therapeutic relationship and on self-disclosure.

The Method of Analysis

The research inquiries on the single therapy sessions lasted from 2 to 4 hours. When transcribed, each inquiry produced from 40 to 80 pages of material. How could one deal with such large volumes of data? In taking this approach to research, I realized at the outset that I was abandoning my earlier commitment to the quantitative paradigm in favor of the qualitative one (see Guba & Lincoln, 1989; Hoshmand, 1989; Smith & Heshusius, 1986), but the question of precisely which qualitative approach to adopt had to be resolved. We considered the approach developed by Bogdan (Bogdan & Bicklen, 1982; Bogdan & Taylor, 1975), and empirical phenomenology as developed by the group at Duquesne University (e.g., Giorgi, 1970; Keen, 1975), as well as grounded theory (Glaser & Strauss, 1967), and finally decided to use the latter.

The Grounded Theory Approach to Qualitative Research

The grounded theory approach to qualitative research was developed in the mid-1960s by two American sociologists in response to their concern that theorization in sociology was too removed from primary data. Working within the intellectual heritage of the University of Chicago school of symbolic interactionism (Mead, 1934), they systematized a method of developing theory that is "grounded" in the phenomenon under investigation. This method has been described by its originators in a series of monographs (Glaser, 1978; Glaser & Strauss, 1967; Strauss, 1987; Strauss & Corbin, 1990). It has been described by Rennie and Brewer (1987, pp. 11-12) as follows:

> Briefly, it is a research approach that emphasizes the theory-generative phase as opposed to the theory-verificational phase of induction. In the approach, a phenomenon of interest is identified. All elements (e.g., single lines, sentences, or complete thoughts in texts) of an initial set of data (e.g., archival information, interviewees' accounts) are compared and conceptualized in terms of commonalities. In the early stages of the analysis, these commonalities are lexically symbolized as descriptive categories that are closely tied to the language of the data. Each datum is

placed in as many categories as possible to preserve the conceptual richness of the phenomenon. Throughout the analysis, the analyst's hunches and theoretical ideas are recorded as memoranda that are kept separate from the documents on which the categories are recordèd. This recording of guiding assumptions is intended to reduce drift away from the grounding of the categories in the data. As the conceptual structure develops, new data sources are selected that promise to illuminate the nature of the structure. Eventually the new data add little to the development of new descriptive categories, at which point the categories are "saturated." The analyst increasingly draws upon the theoretical memoranda and begins to conceptualize more abstract categories that subsume the descriptive categories, yet are grounded in them. If possible, a "core" category is conceptualized that subsumes all other descriptive and conceptual categories. At this point, the conceptual structure is usually hierarchical, with lower-order conceptual categories serving as properties of the core category, and descriptive categories serving as properties of the lower-order conceptual categories. The final product is an elaboration of this conceptual structure of categories, including the relationships among them, and the relationships among the categories and the data.

The Nature of the Data in the Current Study

When qualitative data are reports given by participants to an interviewer, the method of interviewing influences the nature of those data. There are two schools of thought on the role of the interviewer in this type of inquiry. In support of his method of Brief Structured Recall, Robert Elliott (e.g., Elliott, 1984, 1986; Elliott & Shapiro, this volume) stresses that interviewers should keep their activity to a minimum, even to the point of resisting Rogerian-type reflections on the grounds that even they can "lead" the respondent (Elliott, personal communication, September 1988). Elliott thus inclines toward the position that a description of human interaction can be made objectively, independent of the contaminating influences of the researcher (see Packer & Addison, 1989).

The other position is that it is mythological to believe that human experience exists as objective monads independent of social interaction (Danziger, personal communication, October 20, 1988; Giorgi, 1989; Reason & Rowan, 1981; Spence, 1982). Applying this view to the situation of a research interview, it means that the respondent's account is constructed invariably in response to experienced demands of the situation.

I lean toward to the constructionist approach to inquiry. My interest is in the client's experience of an entire hour of therapy. The participant is given few guidelines when requested to focus on anything of interest or significance. Both the interviewer and the interviewee feel the importance of developing a comfortable relationship within the research interview to ease the participant's revelation of personal experience. Furthermore, the experience may be elusive and difficult to describe. In such a moment, the interviewer has to make a choice between letting the respondent struggle for expression and assisting in bringing that expression to the surface. In the first instance, important material could be missed. In the second, the material is co-constructed, and, even though the participant can be asked to ascertain the extent to which the interviewer has been leading the disclosure, the reassurance cannot be taken at face value because there is always the chance that the respondent has been deferring to the interviewer in the same way that he or she is inclined to defer to the therapist (Rennie, 1985, 1990).

In early interviews, I tended to take an active, co-constructing role in obtaining the client's representation of experience. Currently, my degree of involvement hinges on two main considerations. I am still as active as I feel is necessary to establish a comfortable relationship with the respondent. I am also inclined to be somewhat active with interviewees who have difficulty articulating their experience. During the last half of the research inquiries making up the body of the data in the study, however, I have been comparatively less active when interviewing articulate respondents who show little discomfort in the research situation. Here I have preferred the spontaneous over a mixture of the spontaneous and actively co-constructed material. I have learned in the light of the intensity of doing grounded analysis that, however limited they might appear to be in the heat of the inquiry, spontaneous reports generally prove to be rich in meaning when it comes time to analyze them. Also, it has become easier to lessen activity during the interview as categories developed during the course of the analysis have become increasingly saturated. Hence I have learned to feel best as a researcher when reining in the impulse to co-construct the client's experience. I still become actively engaged in the research inquiry if I sense it is warranted, however. A similar development in interviewing strategy is described by Dolhanty (1990).

Objectivism and the Grounded Analysis

The second aspect of the current approach in which objectivism is at issue is the analysis itself. There is a question of whether categories should be developed by the analyst working alone or in a team. As an empirical phenomenologist, Giorgi (1989) maintains that the single analyst becomes the expert on the phenomenon under investigation and is thus in the best position to understand and represent it. Among the grounded theory fraternity, Glaser and Strauss suggest that teamwork when categorizing is useful, but they do not insist upon it. On the other hand, when Elliott (see Elliott & Shapiro, this volume) uses the grounded theory approach to develop categories depicting experience of particular events in therapy, he prefers that a given category win the approval of as many as 12 analysts.

I have never seriously considered the possibility of engaging peers in developing categories in my project. I concur with the belief that the qualitative approach never can be objective and that its logic of justification entails consensus about constructed representations of reality (Giorgi, 1989; Smith & Heshusius, 1986). This agreement reflects a complex process. It is derived in part from the analyst's ability to demonstrate the grounding of the conceptualization in the data giving rise to it. It is also derived, however, from the extent to which the conceptualization makes sense to the reader in the light of his or her experience with the phenomenon in question. With respect to comprehensiveness, despite the laudability of this goal, the fact remains that every analysis is conducted within a particular framework. The same is true whether the analysis is done individually or in groups. It is sufficient that the aspect addressed by the conceptualization is grounded. Hence the use of a group to develop categories may enhance their groundedness and comprehensiveness. Group work, however, is neither necessary nor sufficient for the achievement of these criteria. They can be achieved by the analyst working alone; and whether or not they have been achieved hinges on the judgment of the larger collegium, just as it does in the case of a group effort.

The Structure of the Client's Experience of an Hour of Therapy

In the analysis of respondents' reports, each inquiry transcript was broken into "meaning units." These are passages of the transcript that "stand out" as conveying a main concept. Closer consideration of the unit, however, usually leads to the judgment that it contains other meanings as well. There is no standard determining the length of the unit; in the current

(Text continued on p. 221)

Table 9.1   Taxonomy of Categories Showing Number of Respondents (Rs) and Total Number of Meaning Units (MUs) Contributing to Each Category

CLIENTS' REFLEXIVITY (Core Category)	Rs	MUs

Main Category I: The Client's (C's) Relationship With Personal Meaning

(a) The pursuit of personal meaning

	Rs	MUs
C Scrutinizes Own Processes (C appraises or explains cognitive/ affective/volitional process)	16	302
Client's Track (C's train of thought/path/flow)	15	172
Insight (C's relationship with heightened awareness)	13	105
C's Contact With Feelings (questing/discovering/assimilating feeling)	12	92
Client's Narrative (telling a story/reviewing past events, with self-awareness)	11	89
Digestion (coming to terms, over time, with a new awareness)	10	47
Nonverbal Communication (description of processes beneath C's nonverbal communication/evaluation of C's/T's nonverbal communication)	10	27
Client's Attentiveness to Therapist (tearing away from self-focus to attend to T)	10	26
Discriminating Use of Therapist (controlling the influence of T)	7	23
Catharsis (expressing feeling/the importance of doing so)	6	20
Client's Metaphor (client's use of figurative language)	4	19
Confessions by Client (self-disclosing with embarrassment)	4	16
Root of Problem (getting/failing to get to the bottom of the problem)	6	13

(b) The avoidance of meaning

	Rs	MUs
Client's Defensiveness (defensiveness against self-awareness/cognitive-affective operation/ construed perception of C by T)	15	120
Client's Resistance (resisting T's response/strategy plan)	11	46
Playing for Effect (artifice to change perception of C by C and/or by T)	6	42
Willingness to Change (C's resistance to change/C's endorsement of change via intentions/implementation of change via actions	8	25

Table 9.1   Continued

CLIENTS' REFLEXIVITY (Core Category)	Rs	MUs
Lying to Therapist (lying to T/impact on C's internal processing)	5	17
Negative Preparatory Set (recalcitrant mood regarding willingness to work in the therapy session)	3	12·

Main Category II: The Client's Perception of the Relationship With the Therapist

(a) "Nonspecific" relationship factors

Relationship With the Therapist (+/– feelings about T; balance of power; caring for T's needs; stability of the relationship)	15	134
Client's Perception of the Therapeutic Task (C's perception/expectancies/evaluations of achievements/ roles/goals of both C and T)	14	102
Client's Dependence-Independence (C's concern about self-reliance vs. reliance on T)	12	78
Client's Perception of Therapist's Evaluation of C (conflict with/uncertainty about/influence on T's perception of C as a person)	12	71
Therapist's Manner (comfort/discomfort with T in response to T's expression and style)	12	52
Acceptance by the Therapist (C's perception of whether or not T accepts/judges/criticizes C)	7	49
Faith in Therapy (whether or not C has confidence in the therapy)	11	42
Trust in The Therapist (appraisal of whether or not C is in "good hands" in the person of T)	9	29
Therapist's Care (C's sense of whether or not T has C's interests at heart)	11	22

(b) Client's Deference

Concern About T's Approach (conflict with T regarding his/her responses/strategies/plans)	12	119
Fear of Criticizing T (expression/justification of fear of criticizing/challenging T)	10	91
C's Understanding of T's Frame of Reference (C's curiosity/concern about T's intentionality)	12	73

Continued

Table 9.1   Continued

CLIENTS' REFLEXIVITY (Core Category)	Rs	MUs

(b) Client's Deference (continued)

Meeting Perceived T's Expectations (pressure in C to
 comply with demands/expectancies of T) — 11 — 51

Acceptance of T's Limitations (C tolerates flaw in T's
 performance/personality/relationship) — 7 — 16

Client's Metacommunication (client's need for/experience
 of/C's communication about communication with T) — 4 — 14

Threatening T's Self-Esteem (C's diffidence about
 threatening/indirect challenge to T's self-esteem) — 4 — 14

Indebtedness to T (1-way nature of the relationship/
 subsidization of the therapy make(s) C feel indebted to T) — 5 — 11

**Main Category III: The Client's Experience of the
 Therapist's Operations**

(a) Operations bearing on the client-in-identity

Accuracy of T's Responding (extent to which T's
 responding captures C's felt meaning) — 13 — 86

T's Interpretation (T's implicit or explicit interpretation
 of C's experience) — 12 — 61

Questions (T's interrogation of C about C's experience) — 7 — 36

Reflections (T's mirroring of C's experience) — 5 — 21

T's Metaphor (T's use of figurative language) — 3 — 18

(b) Operations bearing on the client-as-agent

T's Use of Artifices in Directing C's Processing
 (1) Gestalt techniques — 6 — 89
 (2) Role playing — 3 — 17

Advice by T (T's admonition that C follow a particular
 line of conduct) — 8 — 66

T's Ordinary-Discourse Direction of C's Processing
 (C's experience of/need for direction entailing
 language/operations customarily used by C) — 11 — 61

Table 9.1 Continued

CLIENTS' REFLEXIVITY (Core Category)	Rs	MUs
(b) Operations bearing on the client-as-agent (continued)		
Homework (negotiation of C's conduct to be carried out in the back-home situation)	5	15
(c) Operations bearing on T in relation with C		
T's Active Support (T reassures C/reinforces/endorses something C has said or fails to when it was desired)	13	53
T's Self-Disclosure (T's act of revealing himself/herself to C)	6	35
T's Metacommunication (C's experience of/need for T's communication about the communication with C)	7	21
Main Category IV: The Client's Experience of Outcomes		
(a) Impact of the therapy (effectiveness of C/T operation(s)/relationship with T regarding thoughts/feelings/behavior regarding therapy moment/session/course)	14	146
(b) Impact of the inquiry (different/enriched view of the therapy session as a result of the IPR inquiry)	16	145
		3051

study, units varied from a line or two to more than a half page of text. Some examples of meaning units are presented following Table 9.1.

To date, the analysis has been performed on 1,118 meaning units. As shown in Table 9.1, 51 categories have been conceptualized and colligated under four main categories or clusters, and there have been 3,051 assignments of the 51 categories to the meaning units (see Rennie, Phillips, & Quartaro, 1988, for the details of the analysis).

It is not my intention in this chapter to dwell on the particular categories in this taxonomy. Instead, the focus will be on the core category. It will be recalled that, in the grounded theory approach, the core category is conceptualized to capture the meaning common to the other categories and to their interrelationships. It follows that this meaning should in the main be evident in the individual meaning units and in the relationships among them.

With this thought in mind, let us turn to three meaning units, each taken from the inquiry transcript of a different participant. We should note that at the end of each meaning unit are the categories assigned to it during the analysis. The categorization is included to provide a flavor of how the grounded approach works at this level of analysis and to tie the meaning units in with Table 9.1. Nevertheless, my main concern is to concentrate on the aspects in each unit that call for the core category.

Meaning unit 1: [It's] kind of like I'm feeding information through a—I don't like to say computer because I'm an inferring machine—Uh, I want to make sure that all the information is there, you know, before I start to get any feedback. That's all. But I'm also in a sense careful about what I'm saying 'cause, like, uh, I'm sort of a doctor to myself, you know? And it's not going to help me if the real doctor tells me what "my doctor" (laughs) doesn't agree with, you know? (Client's Track, Client Scrutinizes Own Processes, Client's Dependence-Independence)

Meaning unit 2: OK. I'm trying to think what—it's, well, OK: , I—It's because I understand that in a lot of cases she's [i.e., the therapist] not speaking to the actual situation, but feelings about situations and what one should do. It seems to me though that the indignation part comes from me thinking that, "That's all fine and dandy, and of course, I accept that but I'm an actual person in a context," that "If you could please explain to me how I'm supposed to get hold of my mother three thousand miles away," and "What the best method of approach is," and, you know, "Give me some pointers on how to deal with it." I mean, I am in touch with my feelings, and some of her feelings too. I want more practical help, I think. And I'm afraid to ask her for it because— that doesn't seem to be the way she is working. (Concern About the Therapist's Approach, Client's Perception of the Therapeutic Task, Fear of Criticizing the Therapist)

Meaning unit 3: This—I almost—I don't think I have to stop here. Am I stopping too often? (Interviewer: No. Definitely not). OK. This is so, uh, we are getting into the past. He [i.e., the therapist] knows that I hate this part, and I know that I hate this part, but (Interviewer: This part being what?)—When, when we start doing the two chairs, and I start acting out what I'm feeling and getting into emotions. I can't stand it. But I don't normally resist. A couple of times I will say, and I will stop it. But normally I hate it and he knows I hate it and I tell him I hate it but I do it anyway. I'm not really resisting. So that's what we're doing. It's just a bit of a joke that I really hate it. (Gestalt

Techniques, Meeting Perceived Therapist's Expectations, Client Scrutinizes
Own Processes, Client's Contact with Feelings, Resistance by Client)

What are the features of these reports? First, it is evident that in these
moments the participants were actively thinking and, as revealed by the
transcript of the therapy session that each report addresses, this thinking
was not expressed to the therapist. More fundamentally, there are a
number of features of this covert activity. They can be addressed on two
levels: on the formal level of processing irrespective of its content and
on the substantive level of the content of the activity.

Starting with the formal level, it is apparent that the participants were
self-aware and that this was an awareness of themselves in a context.
Second, within that self-awareness, they had a sense of what was right
for them. Third, within that sense of appropriateness, they monitored
alternative courses of action in the context of the situation of the
moment. Finally, in keeping with this monitoring, they elected and
implemented a particular course of action.

Turning to the substantive aspects, the context of the report constituting the first meaning unit was as follows. In his therapy session, this
male client in his twenties produced a lengthy narrative in which he
reviewed an event in which his girlfriend had spent an evening with one
of his male friends. The issue with which the client struggled was
whether or not she had been faithful to him. As he revealed in other
parts of the inquiry, it was important that he convince both himself and
his therapist that his girlfriend had indeed remained true to him despite
the advances of the male friend. In this particular excerpt, he reported
that he characteristically monitored and controlled what he said to the
therapist. The client did this because he was his "own doctor" and was
thereby forming his own conclusions about what was best for him. It
was important that he frame his experience in such a way as to foster
agreement between his therapist's and his own point of view; his view
was primary, and the therapist would be helpful only if he agreed with
the client's view.

The context of the second meaning unit, provided by a woman in her
twenties, was a feeling that she was misunderstood by her therapist. Her
therapist seemed to want to view the client's difficulties with her mother
as being derivative of the client's difficulties with experiencing and preferred to work with the client's personality while the client wanted practical suggestions about how to deal with her troublesome mother. In this
particular excerpt, the client reviewed the reasons for her indignation over

her therapist's approach to the therapy. In this review, she thought of some criticisms and prescriptions but chose not to voice these with the therapist.

Finally, the third meaning unit came from the inquiry transcript of an interview with a professional woman in her midthirties who was in a good working relationship with a Gestalt therapist. The therapy session upon which the inquiry was based was midway in the full course of the therapy and by this time the client had become "seasoned" to Gestalt interventions. As revealed in the meaning unit, however, despite this acclimatization, she still typically had a negative reaction to having to respond to the interventions because they forced her into experiencing her emotions, which she did not want to do. This resistance was at only one level of her experience, however. At another level, she realized that it was important for her get to get into her feelings. She also realized that her therapist realized that she operated on these two levels. Hence her "resistance" was really a game because she had decided earlier on that she must not in fact resist.

The substantive aspects of these meaning units are illustrative of what was found in the reports of all 14 participants in the study. Generalizing from all of these reports, it is evident that clients take a hand in controlling what goes on in the therapy. They control it by forming a plan for the given session and by devising one or more strategies for achieving the plan. They control it by changing a given plan or strategy depending on the exigencies of the particular moment. They control it by attending to and working with the therapist's responses experienced as relevant and by either ignoring or giving lip service to responses experienced as irrelevant. They control it by evaluating the therapist's appraisal of them and by offering to the therapist material that is construed as being acceptable to the therapist. They control it by deciding whether they should challenge the therapist about an aspect of their relationship or about an error in the therapist's activity and/or judgment. And they control it by electing to give control to the therapist (Rennie, 1990).

The Core Category

What name can we give to this quality of self-awareness and self-control that is revealed in the respondents' reports and that colligates the categories conceptualized in the grounded analysis of them? Throughout the history of philosophy and psychology, the quality has been described as *consciousness, will, thinking, reason, judgment, reflection, agency, self-monitoring, recursion, metacognition,* and reflexivity, among others. In earlier papers (see Rennie, 1990), I chose *agency* but more recently have decided that this notion is too limiting. Lately, I have preferred the term *reflexivity.* Lawson (1985) defines *reflexivity* as "a turning back on the self." As a concept, reflexivity is broad enough to encompass both self-awareness and agency. Accordingly, I am now calling the core category *clients' reflexivity.*

In the remainder of the chapter, I examine the influence of the method of the study on the salience of clients' reflexivity as the core experience of the therapy hour. Following this examination, I discuss the implications of clients' reflexivity for research and practice in therapy.

The Influence of Method on the Centrality of Reflexivity

In the current study, the participants' reports of their experience of an hour of therapy are permeated with what appears to be evidence of reflexivity. There are aspects of reflexivity itself, and of the method of inquiry into the client's experience of therapy, however, that may falsely illuminate reflexivity at the expense of nonreflexive consciousness.

As the negative of reflexivity, *nonreflexivity* is the state of acting (including thinking) without awareness of the action. As Searle (1983) puts it, the individual is not aware of doing but instead is "just doing." Subjectively, the experience is one of being "lost" in the action. In psychotherapy parlance, it is "pure" processing. It is conceivable that the reflexive state is more salient and hence more memorable than the nonreflexive state by virtue of the self-awareness intrinsic to the former. Support for this possibility comes from the debate on the validity of self-reports (see Ericsson & Simon, 1980; Nisbett & Wilson, 1977). To the extent that reflexive moments are generally more salient than nonreflexive ones, the "free" recall method of the current study potentiated a focus by the participant on moments of reflexivity.

Another problem is that the research task itself requires participants to be reflexive. In providing evidence of reflexivity in the moment in therapy, they must recall being reflexive, and not project onto the moment in therapy reflexivity experienced during the inquiry. It is not always easy in the inquiry to determine whether participants are recalling or constructing experience, especially when they use present-tense language in describing past experience, as they often do. The task is made easier, however, if they are asked to make the discrimination. I have found that, when this is done, they can usually distinguish between when they are recalling and when they are constructing in the light of the inquiry. I have further found that some participants quickly incorporate the distinction and spontaneously comment when they are unsure about whether they are recalling or constructing. (It hardly needs to be mentioned in this context, of course, that even their recollections invariably are constructed to a certain extent—see Spence, 1982; I am talking about a matter of degree and not of kind.) I have also found, however, that other participants get "caught up" in the inquiry and seem to "lose distance" to a certain extent. Such respondents need to be reminded from time to time of the distinction and to be probed as to which activity is at play in a given representation. At the same time, such probing should not be overdone, to safeguard the flow of the interview.

Hence the method used in the inquiry meant that, at times, there was a possibility that reflexivity within the therapy session was conflated with reflexivity in the inquiry. To a considerable extent, this conflation was controlled by inviting the participant to make the distinction. This control procedure was not applied consistently, however. We must thus conclude that clients' reflexivity in the therapy session was not quite as pervasive as would appear to be the case. Nevertheless, even when this caveat is taken into account, reflexivity is still the most central quality of the client's experience of therapy, in my view.

Clients' Reflexivity and Therapy Process Research

Two things stand out as implications of clients' reflexivity for therapy process research. First, reflexivity creates a world of the covert and thus imposes a limit on the extent to which psychotherapy can be understood on the basis of the analysis of dialogue alone. Second, reflexivity surely must play a role in therapeutic change, and the nature of that role should be examined more fully. Each of these implications will be discussed in turn.

Reflexivity and the Covert

The difference between the deliberation about and the enactment of action has profound implications for the expression of experience in therapy. When in a state of high comfort both in self-experiencing and in the relationship with the therapist, it is conceivable that clients say uninhibitedly whatever they are thinking. Any disjunctions in self-experiencing and in the experience of the therapeutic relationship, however, create choice points for clients in which they must decide whether or not to express everything that is being thought in the moment. Furthermore, when in the heat of the pursuit of meaning in which they are flooded with images, memories, and associations (Angus & Rennie, 1989), they may elect not to attempt to express all that is being experienced because to do so would be to slow down the processing (Rennie, 1990).

Another consideration is that, even in the case of verbal expression, it is often difficult in the analysis of dialogue to apprehend the intentionality guiding the expression. We have found in a related study that the client and therapist can carry on a dialogue in which each believes that he or she knows what the other means, yet, when each is interviewed about his or her understanding of the dialogue, it is evident that each was on an entirely different "wave length" (Angus & Rennie, 1988). If such misunderstandings can occur between the participants in therapy, *a fortiori* they must befall external appraisers of that participation.

Hence, in the state of reflexivity, the person creates the unspoken, and the intentionality behind the spoken. Unless research strategies are used that access this reflexivity, the researcher's understanding of clients' processing will be either incomplete or misguided. Although it has limitations, as we have seen, the technique of securing participants' reports of their covert experience of therapy is a considerable advance over the more conventional approach of simply analyzing discourse and/or its paralinguistic features.

Reflexivity and Change

Given that reflexivity is the fount of intentionality, how does this translate into change? It is in the reflexive moment that intentions are formed, but forming an intention is not the same as carrying it out. The enactment requires a "follow through" of the intention into action. The reflexive moment is a "safety zone": It is there that a course of action can be contemplated. It is also the form of consciousness in which a decision may be reached about a contemplated action and in which the decision may be converted to action. The operative word, however, is *may*: It is in the indeterminacy of reflexivity that the individual has choices, and hence the possibility of control over change.

Is there any evidence supporting this proposition? The reports of the participants in the current study primarily addressed the experience of therapy in general rather than the experience of change within it. Nevertheless, there were instances wherein respondents did in fact indicate that they had achieved a new understanding and that they would now have to decide what to do about it, and when. These instances were colligated into the categories titled Insight, Digestion, Willingness to Change, and Impact of the Therapy (see Table 9.1).

There should be further research into this question of the role of reflexivity in change. In this work, the focus needs to be on the experience of change in particular as opposed to that of therapy in general. One approach might be to have the respondent isolate significant events in therapy. To allow for evidence of the role of reflexivity, however, the inquiry should exceed a focus on what it is about the event that is experienced as significant. More fundamentally, the inquiry should be directed to what the participant intends to do in light of the event, and to what he or she then does. For example, it is conceivable that he or she might achieve an insight that is associated with the realization that a new line of behavior is now to be preferred over that which had gone on before. As I have indicated, however, there is a difference between being aware of such a preference and intending to enact it. There is also a difference between intending to enact it and actually enacting it. I am suggesting that, in keeping with the formulation of Frankfurt (1971), it may not be the first level of desire but the second or an even higher order of desire that is most germane to the actual course of action. Hence it may not be sufficient simply to want to change; it may be necessary to *desire* to want to change. Understanding the role played by such higher-order processing would necessitate a longitudinal tracking of how the individual deals with the event, as an extension of the work by Martin and Stelmaczonek (1988) on the long-term memory of significant events in counseling.

If we think of "positive" action as action that is taken after deliberation about it, and "negative" action as action that is not taken after deliberation, it can be anticipated that this research strategy would uncover instances of such positive and negative intentionality and action. A careful analysis of the positive and negative instances would expand our understanding of the ways in which clients' reflexivity contributes to change. It would also arbitrate the question of whether or not constructors of models of therapeutic change can afford to ignore reflexivity as a component of the change process.

Clients' Reflexivity and the Practice of Therapy

As we have seen, when clients are given the opportunity to report on what they were experiencing from moment to moment in therapy, we get a picture of an inner world of decision and action, often accompanied by a higher-order decision to keep such decision and action silent. How are we to interpret such reports? What bearing do they have on the supposition that the reason that clients are in therapy in the first place is that their abilities to assume conscious control over their lives has failed them and that they consequently need the assistance of an external agent?

Clearly, the reports are valueless with respect to the existence and influence of unconscious processes (except, of course, for the "manifest content" of such processes, such as reports on dreams). The reports do, however, give us an insight into the dimensions of conscious experiencing. Here, the main thing we can learn is that what the client says in therapy does not necessarily reflect what he or she is thinking. Applied to ordinary conversation, such a statement is a truism. Nevertheless, perhaps extending from the dictate that full disclosure is required in free association in psychoanalysis, it is easy to fall under the spell that psychotherapeutic conversation is different than ordinary conversation. Spence (1982) has dispelled this notion regarding free association itself, and the current study dispels it more generally. As indicated above, under certain conditions, the client's discourse may be at one with his or her thinking; however, it appears to be more generally the case that a host of things are going on that are not expressed.

In terms of the practice of therapy, the implications of the client's decision not to reveal aspects of experience vary depending on the nature of the experience. If the unspoken pertains to what the client considers to be good work, then the fact that the therapist is left in the dark is of little importance; the presence of the therapist is the occasion for the productive covert activity. The therapist's assistance becomes important, however, when the unspoken refers to a disturbance in self-experiencing with which the client feels either unwilling or unable to deal. When the client is at ease with the therapist and the therapy, the matter is relatively straightforward. The therapist draws upon clinical skills to detect the disjunction; it is either implicitly understood or explicitly agreed upon that the therapeutic task is to resolve it; and the therapist supports the client's processing of it during the bid for resolution (e.g., Greenberg, 1984, this volume; Rice, this volume; Rice & Saperia, 1984; Toukmanian, 1986, this volume).

The matter is more complicated when there is a disjunction in the relationship with the therapist and/or in the experience of the therapist's performances. Such disjunctions typically lead to negative appraisals. More important, clients may make second-order appraisals of the first appraisals. The reports of the interviewees in this study suggest that it is the second-order appraisals that determine the client's sense of the working alliance (Bordin, 1979; Horvath & Greenberg, 1986). Thus clients may feel uncomfortable about the therapist's conduct of the therapy but decide that it is good for them and that it is in their best interests to persevere with it. Such resolutions with respect to discomforting therapist operations appear quite common, and they reduce the necessity of probing into the discomfort.

Alternatively, clients may feel uncomfortable about the conduct of the therapy and conclude that their discomfort is justified. In this regard, one of the stronger findings of the current study is that clients are very reluctant to voice their discontent about their therapy. Instead, for a variety of reasons, they mutely defer to the therapist (Rennie, 1985, 1990). In the context of a poor working alliance, failure on the part of the therapist to address the discomfort can serve only to weaken the alliance. There is an indication from the current study, however, that the therapist's attempt to probe into discomfort about an intervention in such circumstances is not a panacea. Occasionally, participants reported that, even when the therapist invited them to metacommunicate (Kiesler, 1982) about a troublesome intervention, they *still* deferred! The endurance of the deference despite the probe suggests that, in the situation of a tenuous alliance, the issue of trust in the therapist must be dealt with before issues around particular interventions can be addressed.

In conclusion, it is tempting for therapists and researchers to view clients as patients. After all, in coming to therapy in the first place, clients signal that their own agency has been inadequate and they are appealing to the agency of the therapist. Furthermore, there are grounds for the view that therapy is an intervention into aspects of the clients' experiencing over which they lack awareness and/or control. Nevertheless, the centrality of clients' reflexivity in their inner experience of therapy reminds us that, *within* that encounter, clients are agents as well as patients. The challenge of therapy is to control sensitively what clients cannot control and to work productively with the ways in which they assume control.

References

Angus, L. E., & Rennie, D. L. (1988). Therapist participation in metaphor generation: Collaborative and noncollaborative styles. *Psychotherapy, 25,* 552-560.

Angus, L. E., & Rennie, D. L. (1989). Envisioning the representational world: The client's experience of metaphoric expressiveness in psychotherapy. *Psychotherapy, 26,* 373-379.

Bogdan, R., & Bicklen, S. K. (1982). *Qualitative research for education: An introduction to theory and methods.* Boston: Allyn & Bacon.

Bogdan, R., & Taylor, S. J. (1975). *Introduction to qualitative research methods: A phenomenological approach to the social sciences.* New York: John Wiley.

Bordin, E. (1979). The generalizability of the psychoanalytic concept of the working alliance. *Psychotherapy: Theory, Research and Practice, 16,* 252-260.

Dolhanty, J. (1990). *The urge to overeat: A qualitative analysis of personal accounts.* Unpublished master's thesis, York University, North York, Ontario.

Elliott, R. (1984). A discovery-oriented approach to significant events in psychotherapy: Interpersonal Process Recall and Comprehensive Process Analysis. In L. Rice & L. Greenberg (Eds.), *Patterns of change: Intensive analysis of psychotherapy process: A research handbook* (pp. 249-286). New York: Guilford.

Elliott, R. (1986). Interpersonal Process Recall (IPR) as a process research method. In L. Greenberg & W. Pinsof (Eds.), *The psychotherapeutic process: A research handbook* (pp. 503-528). New York: Guilford.

Ericsson, K. A., & Simon, H. A. (1980). Verbal reports as data. *Psychological Review, 87,* 215-251.

Frankfurt, H. G. (1971). The freedom of the will and the concept of a person. *The Journal of Philosophy, 68,* 5-20.

Giorgi, A. (1970). *Psychology as a human science: A phenomenologically based approach.* New York: Harper & Row.

Giorgi, A. (1989, August). *The status of qualitative research from a phenomenological perspective.* Paper presented at the Eighth Annual Human Science Research Conference, Aarhus, Denmark.

Glaser, B. G. (1978). *Theoretical sensitivity: Advances in the methodology of grounded theory.* Mill Valley, CA: Sociology Press.

Glaser, B. G., & Strauss, A. (1967). *The discovery of grounded theory: Strategies for qualitative research.* Chicago: Aldine.

Greenberg, L. (1984). A task analysis of intrapersonal conflict resolution. In L. Rice & L. Greenberg (Eds.), *Patterns of change: Intensive analysis of psychotherapeutic process* (pp. 67-123). New York: Guilford.

Guba, E. G., & Lincoln, Y. S. (1989). *Fourth generation evaluation.* Newbury Park, CA: Sage.

Horvath, A. O., & Greenberg, L. (1986). The development of the Working Alliance Inventory. In L. Greenberg & W. Pinsof (Eds.), *The psychotherapeutic process: A research handbook* (pp. 529-556). New York: Guilford.

Hoshmand, L. (1989). Alternate research paradigms: A review and teaching proposal. *The Counseling Psychologist, 17,* 3-79.

Kagan, N. (1975). *Interpersonal Process Recall: A method for influencing human action.* Educational Psychology Department, (Available from N. Kagan, Educational Psychology Department, University of Houston, University Park, Houston, TX, 77004)

Keen, E. (1975). *A primer in phenomenological psychology.* New York: Holt, Rinehart & Winston.

Kiesler, D. J. (1982). Confronting the client-therapist relationship in psychotherapy. In J. C. Anchin & D. J. Kiesler (Eds.), *Handbook of interpersonal psychotherapy* (pp. 274-295). Toronto: Pergamon.

Lawson, H. (1985). *Reflexivity: A post-modern predicament.* La Salle, IL: Open Court.

Martin, J., & Stelmaczonek, K. (1988). Participant identification and recall of important events in counseling. *Journal of Counseling Psychology, 35,* 385-390.

Mayer, J., & Timms, N. (1970). *The client speaks: Working-class impressions of casework.* London: Routledge & Kegan Paul.

McLeod, J. (1990). The client's experience of counselling and psychotherapy: A review of the research literature. In D. Mearns & W. Dryden (Eds.), *Experiences of counselling in action* (pp. 1-19). London: Sage.

Mead, G. H. (1934). *Mind, self, and society.* Chicago: University of Chicago Press.

Nisbett, R. E., & Wilson, T. D. (1977). Telling more than we know: Verbal reports on mental processes. *Psychological Review, 84,* 231-259.

Oldfield, S. (1983). *The counselling relationship: A study of the client's experience.* London: Routledge & Kegan Paul.

Orlinsky, D. E., & Howard, K. I. (1975). *Varieties of psychotherapeutic experience: Multivariate analyses of patients' and therapists' reports.* New York: Teacher's College Press.

Packer, M. J., & Addison, R. B. (1989). Overview. In M. Packer & R. Addison (Eds.), *Entering the circle: Hermeneutic investigation in psychology* (pp. 1-12). Albany: SUNY Press.

Phillips, J. R. (1984). Influences on personal growth as viewed by former psychotherapy patients. *Dissertation Abstracts International, 46,* 2820B.

Phillips, J. R. (1985, May). The influence of personal growth as viewed by former psychotherapy patients. In D. Rennie (Chair), *The phenomenological experience of psychological treatment.* Symposium conducted at the annual meeting of the International Human Science Research Conference, Edmonton, Alberta.

Reason, P., & Rowan, J. (Eds.). (1981). *Human inquiry: A sourcebook of new paradigm research.* New York: John Wiley.

Rennie, D. L. (1985, June). Client deference in the psychotherapy relationship. In D. Rennie (Chair), *The client's phenomenological experience of psychotherapy.* Symposium conducted at the annual meeting of the Society for Psychotherapy Research, Evanston, IL.

Rennie, D. L. (1990). Toward a representation of the client's experience of the psychotherapy hour. In G. Lietaer, J. Rombauts, & R. Van Balen (Eds.), *Client-centered and experiential therapy in the nineties* (pp. 155-172). Leuven, Belgium: Leuven University Press.

Rennie, D. L., & Brewer, L. (1987). A grounded theory of thesis blocking. *Teaching of Psychology, 14,* 10-16.

Rennie, D. L., Brewster, L., & Toukmanian, S. G. (1985). The trainee as client: Client process measures as predictors of counselling skill acquisition. *Canadian Journal of Behavioural Science, 17,* 16-28.

Rennie, D. L., Phillips, J. R., & Quartaro, G. K. (1988). Grounded theory: A promising approach to conceptualization in psychology? *Canadian Psychology, 29,* 139-150.

Rice, L. N., & Saperia, E. P. (1984). Task analysis of the resolution of problematic reactions. In L. Rice & L. Greenberg (Eds.), *Patterns of change: Intensive analysis of psychotherapeutic process* (pp. 29-66). New York: Guilford.

Rogers, C. R. (1951). *Client-centered therapy: Its current practice, implications and theory.* Boston: Houghton Mifflin.

Searle, J. (1983). *Intentionality: An essay in the philosophy of mind.* Cambridge: Cambridge University Press.

Smith, J., & Heshusius, L. (1986). Closing down the conversation: The end of the quantitative-qualitative debate among educational inquirers. *Educational Researcher, 15,* 4-12.

Spence, D. P. (1982). *Narrative truth and historical truth: Meaning and interpretation in psychoanalysis.* New York: Norton.

Strauss, A. (1987). *Qualitative analysis for social scientists.* New York: Cambridge University Press.

Strauss, A., & Corbin, J. (1990). *Basics of qualitative research: Grounded theory procedures and techniques.* Newbury Park, CA: Sage.

Strupp, H., Wallach, M., & Wogan, M. (1964). Psychotherapy experience in retrospect: Questionnaire survey of former patients and their therapists. *Psychological Monographs: General and Applied, 78*(11, Whole No. 588).

Toukmanian, S. G. (1986). A measure of client perceptual processing. In L. Greenberg & W. Pinsof (Eds.), *The psychotherapeutic process: A research handbook* (pp. 107-130). New York: Guilford.

Toukmanian, S. G., & Rennie, D. L. (1975). Microcounseling and human relations training: Relative effectiveness with undergraduate trainees. *Journal of Counseling Psychology, 22,* 345-352.

10

Explanation in Psychotherapy Process Research

DAVID L. RENNIE
SHAKÉ G. TOUKMANIAN

A major theme of this volume is that in human science there are two fundamental approaches to explanation and both are currently represented in psychotherapy process research. These are what Bruner (1986) has described as the "paradigmatic" approach and the "narrative" approach. Paradigmatic explanation is logico-scientific (see also Polkinghorne, 1988); demonstrative reasoning gives rise to hypotheses about the causes of relations among phenomena, and verification of the hypotheses is taken as evidence of general laws. Although challenged by quantum physics and by constructionists (e.g., Gergen, 1982; Rorty, 1979), practitioners of paradigmatic explanation generally adhere to a realist philosophical attitude. It is assumed that there is a world external to the observer that can be understood objectively. Accordingly, the logic of justification mounted in support of paradigmatic explanation stresses quantification, interobserver agreement on indices of cause and effect, and procedures that control for threats to the cause-effect relationship(s) being claimed.

There are regularities in human behavior, if only in terms of probabilities (see Martin, this volume). Despite occasional behavioristic attacks (e.g., Ryle, 1949; Wittgenstein, 1968), however, philosophical and psychological views of personhood have upheld the notion that action is more than an expression of regularities; it is also an expression of intentionality. People have reasons for their actions, and these reasons are contextualized and particularized (Bruner, 1986). Thus, while paradigmatic explanation is deductive, demonstrative, and quantitative, narrative explanation is inductive, hermeneutical, and qualitative. Reasons for actions are not only particular, they are the products of agents' interpretation of their experience. Furthermore, when communicated to another person, they are the products of the representations of those interpretations. Yet, again, when the second person attempts to explain the first person's behavior, then the representations are in turn interpreted and the explanation is a representation of that interpretation. Thus narrative explanation is constructive rather than objective and is more in keeping with an idealist than a realist philosophical orientation.

In the history of psychotherapy process research and of psychology generally, the paradigmatic approach has prevailed; the use of the narrative approach is relatively new and comparatively untried. Yet its major appeal is that it inherently addresses meaning and is thus in principle more suitable as a way of understanding the psychotherapeutic process at what we refer to below as the first level of reduction in explaining human behavior—the level of the person.

The integration of the paradigmatic and narrative approaches is problematic. Currently under debate is whether or not the two approaches are compatible. As discussed cogently by Smith and Heshusius (1986), some methodologists (e.g., Guba, 1981; Guba & Lincoln, 1982; Miles & Huberman, 1984) maintain that in principle the same standards of reliability and validity can be applied to qualitative research (i.e., narrative explanation) as to quantitative research (i.e., paradigmatic explanation) and that all that is necessary is to develop procedures within narrative research that meet these standards.[1] Alternatively, others (Bruner, 1986; Polkinghorne, 1988; Smith & Heshusius, 1986) advocate that narrative explanation is based on a different logic of justification than that used in paradigmatic explanation and that the differing logics make the two approaches fundamentally incompatible.

According to this view, the objectivism, demonstrative reasoning, and quantification constituting the logic of justification in paradigmatic explanation does not apply to narrative explanation. Instead, the credibility of a given explanation is a matter of the extent to which the hermeneutic researcher can win the consensus of the consumers of the explanation. This consensus is derived from (a) the extent to which the researcher can convince consumers that he or she has been evenhanded in the hermeneutic investigation (Giorgi, 1989; Smith, 1989) and (b) the extent to which the explanation is judged by consumers to make sense in the light of their own understanding of the phenomenon in question (Polkinghorne, 1988; Rennie, this volume; Rorty, 1979; Smith & Heshusius, 1986).

In addition to the broad issue of the preferred approach to explanation in psychotherapy process research, there are dimensions that character-ize the structure of the research, and there are issues pertaining to each of these dimensions. Addressing these dimensions has currency be-cause, in most instances, they cut across both approaches to explana-tion. Thus, through the examination of the dimensions of research practice, the issues raised by the two approaches to explanation are given form. We shall return to the basic question of the compatibility of the two approaches to explanation once we have considered the dimensions of therapy process research as we understand them.

The Dimensions of Psychotherapy Process Research

What are these dimensions? Having examined the contributions to this volume in the context of the psychotherapy process research liter-ature as a whole, we have isolated five dimensions that we believe characterize the structure of research practice in the field—object of the research, level of reduction, vantage point, mode of inquiry, and unit of inquiry (cf. Elliott, 1991). Each of these dimensions is discussed in turn. Illustrating the discussion is Table 10.1, which portrays our judgment of how each of the contributions to this volume is expressed in terms of each of these dimensions.

The Object of the Research

There appear to be two main objects of psychotherapy process research. The one is the study of the process of therapeutic change while the other is the study of participants' experience of therapy. Researchers studying change are interested in describing, analyzing, and understanding what is being changed, and how, in service of the improvement of psychotherapy as an intervention. Alternatively, the second purpose is to understand the therapy participants' experience of therapy regardless of the nature of that experience.

The first objective walks hand in hand with the paradigmatic approach to explanation. It is assumed that there are regularities in psychotherapy,

Table 10.1 Five Dimensions of Psychotherapy Process Research Reflected in the Contributions to This Volume

Dimensions Contributors	Object of Research	Level of Reduction	Vantage Point	Mode of Inquiry	Unit of Inquiry
Rice	Client's change	Client's in-therapy performance	Observer	Self-reports and coding systems	Therapy event
Greenberg	Client's change	Client's in-therapy performance	Observer	Self-reports and coding systems	Therapy event
Wiseman	Client's change	Client's in-therapy performance	Client and observer	Self-reports* and coding systems	Therapy event
Toukmanian	Client's change	Client's in-therapy cognitive process	Observer	Self-reports and coding systems	Therapy event and session(s)
Martin	Client's change and experience	Client's in-therapy cognitive process and the person	Client, therapist, and observer	Self-reports* and coding systems	Therapy event and session(s)
Lietaer	Client's and therapist's experience	The person	Client and therapist	Self-reports	Therapy session(s)
Elliott and Shapiro	Client's and therapist's experience	The person	Client, therapist, and observer	Self-reports* and coding systems	Therapy event
Angus	Client's and therapist's experience	The person and client's in-therapy cognitive process	Client, therapist, and observer	Self-reports* and coding systems	Therapy event
Rennie	Client's experience	The person	Client	Self-reports**	Therapy session

*Includes use of tape-assisted recall.
**Exclusive use of tape-assisted recall.

that they can be conceptualized through a combination of empiricism and rationalism, and that the end result will be a lexicon of change "episodes." Each episode is viewed as being constituted of a particular therapeutic goal that can be met by particular client and therapist performances. The parameters of each change episode may be manualized, which in turn offers the promise of systematizing therapy at the levels of both practice and training.

Research in expression of the second objective is broader. Its primary focus is on the meaning of the experience of therapy for its participants, and this approach thus has kinship with the narrative approach to explanation. The meaning may be in terms of various facets of the experience ranging from internal processing to the relationship with the other member of the therapy dyad. The breadth offered by the approach provides the opportunity to discover aspects of therapy that could be overlooked by researchers operating within the change-process perspective. On the other hand, it can be argued that the scope offered by the second approach is its greatest weakness in that it makes therapy process research too inductive, unfocused, and impractical.

Level of Reduction

Three levels of reduction of human functioning are represented in the contributions to this volume: the person, performances, and cognitive processes and structures. The level of reduction influences the constructs used in explaining psychotherapy.

At the level of the person, behavior is seen as an expression of agency in the form of intentionality and will. Within the phenomenology of agency, it is as if the person not only is *constituted of* beliefs, values, needs, and desires but *has* them as well (see A. Rorty, 1976). Thus the person may act not only in terms of them but also upon them. In acting in terms of them, the person is determined by them; in acting upon them, the person is determining them. It can be maintained that neurosis may be seen as a state of being in which the individual is determined by beliefs and values and incapable of intervention into them (see Macmurray, 1957). This type of argument can be used by psychotherapy process researchers to support the view that the client's agency has little currency in the psychotherapeutic process and can be dismissed. It can also be argued, however, that, even if clients in therapy may be required to enter it because of such determination, the extent of it is never total. Conse-

quently, conceptualizing at the level of the person introduces an element
of indeterminacy into the process of therapy.

Conceptualizing at the second level of reduction—the level of performances—offers the promise of the discovery of regularities in response to environmental impacts, thus providing grounds for the claim
of the existence of determinism in the therapy process. To the extent
that determinism is valued, there may be a constraint against recognizing the role of agency in that process even though this awareness may
be implicit. Alternatively, although the potential utility of conceptualizing
at the third and lowest level of reduction may be recognized, there may be
a reluctance to attempt seriously to forge the integration of the second and
third levels because of the challenges it imposes.

Finally, theorizing at the third level of reduction—that of cognitive
processes and structures—holds forth the appeal of grounding psychotherapeutic theory in the basic concepts and findings of cognitive science
(Goldfried, 1991; Shohan-Shalomon, 1991; Smith & Sechrest, 1991). It
can be maintained, however, that to do so runs the risk of getting bogged
down in the intricacies of cognitive processing and thereby of losing sight
of the therapeutic forest for the trees. Furthermore, because it is difficult
to impute agency to schematic structures and cognitive processes, at this
level of reduction, agency can be acknowledged only implicitly.

Vantage Point

In psychotherapy process research, three vantage points can be used
in the attempt to understand the phenomena in question: the perspective
of the external observer, client, or therapist.

By the term *external observer,* we mean third-party involvement at all
levels of the research, extending from conceptualization to data generation,
analysis, and interpretation. This vantage point promises objectivity and
the freedom to work outside of the framework of the phenomenology
of the participants. These advantages are especially pertinent if it is
believed that there are processes/structures/mechanisms outside the
individual's awareness that influence/determine experience and behavior. Furthermore, the third-party perspective provides the opportunity
to establish interobserver agreement. This vantage point is distant from
the phenomenon under study, however. Regardless of how well the
theoretician-researcher is informed about the therapy process, the fact
remains that the conceptualization of it comes from the framework of

an external observer. Thus important aspects of the phenomenon may be overlooked.

The second vantage point is the one provided by clients. Therapy can be seen as a service, and clients as the consumers of it. It may be assumed that clients are capable of offering authoritative opinions on the nature of the service. Such opinions come from their value systems and experience. A corollary of this advantage is that clients are generally less versed in psychotherapeutic lore and their views may provide a fresh perspective. The assumption that clients may be seen as authorities presupposes, however, that they (a) know what they are experiencing, (b) are able to verbalize what they know, and (c) are willing to be truthful in reporting what they know. With respect to point a, there is debate about whether or not people are capable of knowing why they act as they do (e.g., Ericsson & Simon, 1980; Nisbett & Wilson, 1977). Regarding b, the experience of therapy may at times be so ineffable as to preclude the possibility of the client's representation of it. Nevertheless, such ineffable processes may still be powerful. The ineffability may especially pertain to "lower-level" cognitive-affective processes such as shifts in schematic structuring. Finally, in terms of c, even though clients may be requested to report honestly and to report on how honest they have been, the fact remains that clients have the option of being dishonest in a research inquiry.

The third vantage point is that of the therapist. In the main, the phenomenology of the therapist's experience is somewhat different than the client's in that the former's intentionality is directed more toward the client than to the self. Moreover, the therapist's perspective is between that of the client and the third-party observer. The therapist is subjectively involved in the client's subjectivity. Yet the therapist is operating within a theoretical orientation drawn from the perspective of the external observer. To the extent that the therapist's perspective is an expression of his or her subjectivity, however, the three difficulties associated with verbal report indicated above in reference to the client's perspective apply equally well to the therapist, as is illustrated by the work of Lietaer (this volume).

Mode of Inquiry

The mode of inquiry in psychotherapy process research is an expression of the approach to explanation subscribed to by the researcher. In the paradigmatic approach, it is assumed that objectivity and the apprehension of causation are threatened by the dual subjectivities of (a) the object of investigation or inquiry (which in psychotherapy research means the therapy participants) and (b) the subjectivity of the researcher and of his or her research team. The first subjectivity can be reduced by assigning to the researcher the role of theorizing about the phenomenon under study. The subjectivity also can be diminished through the use of stimuli that control the participant's attention. The second subjectivity is always present but is open to public scrutiny in a variety of ways. The soundness of rationally derived conceptualizations is the product of debate among research team members and is recursively informed by appeals to the data. The conceptualizations are standardized and procedures are manualized. Multiple judges are informed by the manualization and requirements can be set regarding intersubjective consistency. The construct validity of the conceptualizations may be tested as a further check against drift into the researcher's subjectivity.

As we have seen, in the narrative approach to explanation, the implicit guiding assumptions are that in human science there is no objective reality awaiting discovery and that human affairs are to be understood in terms of reasons rather than causes. Hence, in this approach, subjectivity is the subject matter rather than a source of error interfering with the subject matter. Within this framework, reality is the co-constructed product of the interaction between persons in whatever social contexts they find themselves. Hence the subjectivity of the person serving as the object of inquiry and the subjectivity of the researcher are intertwined.

In terms of procedure, the mode of inquiry is expressed as either the application of coding systems or the use of various forms of verbal report. These two main categories will be addressed now. It will become apparent that the application of coding systems is an expression of the paradigmatic approach, whereas the use of verbal report expresses either the paradigmatic or the narrative approach depending upon the particular method of obtaining and interpreting such reports.

Coding systems. The term *coding system* refers to measures or instruments devised to assess particular constructs that can be apprehended from a third-party perspective. Hence the constructs pertain to phenomena that are "out there" in the world external of the observer. In psychotherapy process research, such constructs address any conceivable aspect of the process of psychotherapy, such as the working alliance, attributes of linguistic style, voice quality, modes of cognitive processing, and so on. There are a number of advantages to using coding systems. First, a fundamental presupposition underlying their use is that a third-party perspective may be necessary to understand the process of psychotherapy. The rationale supporting this presupposition is that the participants in therapy may be only partially aware of the full range of processes, as was discussed above in the context of levels of reduction. Accordingly, the third-party perspective in potential holds forth the promise of giving rise to a more penetrating explanation than is possible through a reliance on verbal report. Second, coding systems allow the researcher to focus exclusively on whatever psychotherapeutic process is of interest and thus provide for precision in conceptualization. Third, such systems give researchers a common or standard language and an "objective" way of representing what is observed and described. A number of coders or raters can use the same system, and interjudge reliability can be established. In addition, coding systems can be subjected to validation procedures to test the adequacy of the researcher's understanding and conceptualization of the various dimensions of the phenomenon. Finally, the application of coding systems is systematic in the sense that they are invariant. Any coder or rater can be trained in their use, given well-specified instructions in how to apply them, and the scores or evaluations obtained from them are derived and interpreted in a prescribed manner.

The use of coding systems involves several problems, however. First, the third-party perspective involves the researcher-theoretician's subjectivity. It may be constrained by the rational-empirical method underpinning the development of coding systems. Nevertheless, the fact remains that the development and use of coding systems are influenced by the researcher-theoretician's unique way of understanding the phenomenon under inquiry. Accordingly, the third-party perspective may be limited or distorted according to the particular phenomenology of the persons holding that perspective.

Second, coding systems may achieve precision at the expense of comprehensiveness. They typically present a view of therapy process microscopically and in depth but may obscure the larger picture of therapy. Even an ambitious attempt to use several coding systems in the same study does not mitigate the difficulty. Finally, coding systems share with other psychometric approaches problems pertaining to the adequacy of measurement. The production of coding systems that are both valid and reliable usually requires an enormous amount of work. There are some coding systems in therapy process research that meet this requirement. There is, however, a temptation in this field to produce coding systems that are tailor-made for specific purposes and that are not subjected to the same rigor. To the extent that coding systems have not been subjected to the required developmental work, the adequacy of the representations of therapy resulting from such work may be called into question.

Self-report. In the current context, the term *self-report* refers to therapy participants' representation of their experience of therapy. Self-report involves a variety of forms of representation such as choices among numerical alternatives on rating scales, selection among prepared items in inventories, endorsement of items on checklists, written responses to either structured or unstructured questions, and oral responses during either structured or unstructured interviews. It is pertinent to both the paradigmatic mode and the narrative mode of explanation, depending on how self-report is used.

It is logical that, if an investigator wishes to learn about the nature of therapy, he or she should turn to the participants as authorities because, after all, it is their experience that is being investigated. Self-reports, then, provide the researcher with an opportunity to get "inside" therapy, in contrast to opting to stay "outside" of it when using coding systems. The use of participants' self-reports is a check against the reification of constructs emerging from the external perspective. To a certain extent, of course, there is no "pure" guard against reification. When the self-reports of therapists are used as data, those reports will be influenced by the therapists' immersion in the same theoretical perspectives that have given rise to the reification in the first place. And, to a lesser extent, the same is true of clients' reports because few clients are completely uninformed about psychotherapy theory. Nevertheless, if we are prepared to talk in terms of degree rather than kind, there is some basis for the argument that the participants in therapy are in a position to provide a closer look at therapy than is possible with researchers/theoreticians working with coding systems.

Within this framework, a distinction must be made between experience per se and the content of that experience, and this distinction in turn is an expression of the various methods of obtaining self-reports. Self-report in response to various structured inquiries such as rating scales, inventories, and structured interviews secures the respondents' experience within the frame of reference of the researcher. Alternatively, when unstructured inquiries are done, both the experience and the content of the experience are primarily within the frame of reference of the participant. Controlling the content is in keeping with a deductive, theory-driven research strategy, while giving the participant control over the content is consonant with an inductive, theory-generative strategy.

The use of self-reports as data introduces a whole range of problems intrinsic to introspection. The broad outline of the difficulties has been presented above under the dimension of the vantage point taken in the research endeavor. Beyond these difficulties, there are drawbacks specific to each method of securing self-reports. For example, the use of rating scales and inventories calls upon the respondent to give a presentation of self in a particular social context. The respondent is thus subject to the demands of the situation. In addition, the meaning of any element in the instrument being used may be different for the scale constructor and the respondent. The use of unstructured interviews raises similar problems. Regardless of how much the interviewer may wish not to influence the course of such an interview, the fact remains that it is co-constructed by the interviewer and interviewee. Accordingly, different interviewers will vary in the ways in which they engage in this co-constructive activity, the consequence of which is a lack of standardization among interviews.

Unit of Inquiry

A chronic problem in therapy process research is the determination of the appropriate unit of analysis. As described elsewhere (Greenberg, 1986; Kiesler, 1973), the choice of unit has ranged from a fragment of a speaking turn taken by either the client or therapist to an entire course of therapy. Recently, as we have seen, one school of thought holds that the study of the therapeutic "episode" or "event" (Greenberg, 1986; Rice & Greenberg, 1984) is a promising approach. The rationale of this strategy is that it may eventually be established that there is a circumscribed number of important types of occurrences in therapy, each with its own parameters and ideal performances. Some examples are events such as the resolution of problematic reactions and conflicts, client-identified most-significant moments, and moments of metaphoric expressiveness. The event as a type of unit is seen as being broad enough to capture the main themes of therapy yet narrow enough to enable an in-depth study of the therapy process. In this focus, multiple perspectives can be brought to bear on the event, as can multiple levels of reduction (at least in principle).

The tenability of the "events paradigm" hinges on the assumption that the resolving power of the event is "resident" in it, as it were. But the question may be asked, "How do we define an event?" Is it a monad bounded by the framework of time within which it occurs and that impacts on the client within that framework? Or is it a particular experience that becomes a focus of ongoing awareness, deliberation, and action, the course of which may extend over the therapy hour or indeed over the entire course of therapy and beyond? It can be argued that a therapeutic event is not monadic and is instead an occasion for two main forms of activity. The first form is reflexive (see Rennie, this volume). The client is aware of the event, deliberates on its significance, and decides what to do about it, if anything, and when and how. The second form of activity is more nonreflexive. The event in therapy may be thought of as being experienced as a "step"—a shift in the direction of experiencing things differently. In terms of the third level of reduction, the process of the development of elaborated schematic networks is now in place, however rudimentary (Toukmanian, this volume). From that point onward, the client encounters the self and the world within the framework of the new step, assimilates new information to it, and furthers the evolution of the new construction. This evolution may occur in the context of the client's relationship with the self, the therapist, and/or the world.

The same argument can be applied to other units of analysis. The processes entailed in an hour of therapy are contextualized within the overall treatment, just as it in turn is contextualized within the client's life experiences before and after the therapy. Given the constraints imposed by the pragmatics of therapy research, the three main units of analysis—the event, session, and course of therapy—thus entail a tension between detail and scope. A focus on the events may disguise critical factors occurring in the therapy hour. Similarly, concentrating on the therapy hour may obscure factors that can only become apparent through a study of the entire course of therapy.

New Directions for Psychotherapy Process Research

When we take stock of the paradigmatic and narrative approaches to explanation, we can see that each has special contributions to make to psychotherapy process research. The paradigmatic approach is suited to the study of performances that can be observed and assessed from the third-party perspective. It is also the best of the two approaches for explaining cognitive processes and structures that function and exist out of awareness. On the other hand, the narrative approach is suited to explaining the role of the person in the therapy process. Persons have reasons for doing what they do, and it is the narrative approach that works with verbal reports as data representing those reasons.

A gulf, however, separates these two approaches to explanation in human science, including psychotherapy process research. As indicated, advocates of the paradigmatic mode are guided by the belief that science is defined by a search for laws representing predictable relationships between antecedents and consequents and pay little or no attention to human reflexivity and will. As Westcott (in press) remarks delightfully, the notion of human freedom throws the proponents of this approach into shallow breathing. On the other hand, practitioners of the narrative approach to explanation are guided by the belief that human behavior is an expression of intentionality and that such intentionality may not be reducible to lower levels of explanation.

Yet, when we look at our five dimensions of therapy process research, only the dimension of unit of analysis is independent of the two fundamental approaches to explanation. Regardless of whether the therapy process researcher wishes to focus on an utterance, event, therapy hour, or entire course of therapy, this focus can be pursued in terms of either the paradigmatic or the narrative approach to explanation, or both. All of the other dimensions are in the main constituted by contrasts between the two explanatory approaches. Hence the purpose of research is to understand either change (paradigmatic) or experience (narrative); the level of reduction may be the person (narrative), performance (paradigmatic), or cognitive process/structure (paradigmatic); the vantage point may be the external observer (paradigmatic), the client (narrative/paradigmatic), or the therapist (narrative/paradigmatic); the mode of inquiry may be the use of coding systems (paradigmatic) or of verbal reports (narrative).

There appears to be a need for methodological pluralism and/or epistemological synthesis. By *methodological pluralism*, we mean the combination, in the same study, of procedures expressive of both the narrative and the paradigmatic approaches to explanation. *Epistemological synthesis* refers to the incorporation, into theorizing done within the one approach to explanation, of information derived from the alternative approach to explanation.

To be useful, methodological pluralism requires its practitioners not to violate the strengths of each approach to explanation. We are inclined to concur with the view that each of the two approaches to explanation entails a different logic of justification and that attempts to bring both approaches under one roof could result in a weakening of each of them. Alternatively, if both logics of justification are kept intact, then attempts at methodological pluralism could introduce a number of conflicts in research procedure. For example, the emphasis on constructionism and on consensus as the arbiter of its soundness allows investigators working with the narrative approach to study small numbers of people who are not sampled randomly, not to worry about control group designs, and to make observations that are not necessarily supported by indices of interobserver agreement—procedures that are not acceptable within the paradigmatic approach. Conversely, attempts by narrative researchers to meet the canons of paradigmatic research would severely impede the kind of intensive analysis that is the strength of the narrative approach. Hence meeting the challenge of methodological pluralism is not easy.

This approach to method is being attempted to a varying extent in the programs of some of the contributors to this volume. Angus is shifting between the use of narratology in theory generation and of the paradigmatic approach in theory verification; Elliott (see Elliott & Shapiro, this volume) is increasingly incorporating into his Comprehensive Process Analysis the application of the qualitative research strategy; Lietaer is essentially doing a hermeneutic analysis of verbal reports in the creation of categories of helping and hindering processes in therapy that have been subjected to the standards of objectification held forth by the paradigmatic approach; Wiseman has used clients' verbal reports as a way of validating Rice's model of the resolution of problematic reactions; and Martin has practiced narratology when using verbal reports to gain access to therapy participants' intentionality and the paradigmatic approach when using third-party observations that are tested for their reliability and analyzed quantitatively.

Among the members of this group, Elliott, Angus, and Martin are making the most concerted effort to use the two approaches to explanation. That these initiatives entail strain can be inferred in the case of Elliott and Angus and has been commented on explicitly by Martin. Up to the current time, Elliott has been practicing narratology with a paradigmatic accent. Angus is using the paradigmatic approach as a way of verifying hypotheses derived from narratology, but it can be argued that, from the vantage point of constructionism, this strategy amounts to subsuming the logic of justification of narrative explanation under a "higher" logic of paradigmatic explanation and as such is "old hat" (Smith, 1989). Martin (personal communication, August 21, 1991) has remarked that, in looking back on his research program, he can see where he has used both approaches to explanation, but never in the same project.

In these programs, the primary investigator (supported by his or her research group) is assuming the responsibility of integrating the two types of explanation. Another strategy is to practice methodological pluralism as a research team. The potential advantage of this strategy is that each member of the team is called upon to be expert in just one of the two modes of explanation. Hence their integration is a matter for negotiation among the members of the team, which conceivably is less stressful than attempting to integrate them individually. An example of a team approach was a collaboration by Greenberg, Rennie, and Toukmanian (1988) on the most important event in a therapy session involving Greenberg and one of his clients. While Greenberg kept his own counsel on his judgment of the most important event, Rennie interviewed the client to learn what she considered it to be and then proceeded to conduct a tape-replay-assisted inquiry into her experience of the event that she nominated. Meanwhile, Toukmanian worked independently with the transcript of the therapy session, located what she considered to be the most important event, and rated it for levels of perceptual processing using her taxonomy (see Toukmanian, this volume). It turned out that the therapist, client, and external observer all nominated the same event as being the most important. The three team members withheld their respective views on the event until a conference proceeding, at which time they and the members of the audience co-constructed an explanation of the event, taking the information from the three perspectives into consideration. At the time, this effort was considered simply to be an exercise, and no attempt was made to formalize the returns from it. Nevertheless, it was the beginning of current efforts by our group to resolve the issues involved in a pluralistic approach to method.

Apart from methodological pluralism, theorizing about the therapy process could be furthered through epistemological synthesis. This initiative would also demand an attitude of equanimity toward the two approaches to explanation, but not to the extent that the researcher-theorist need feel required to adopt the research procedures of the alternative approach. Accordingly, researcher-theorists working within the paradigmatic approach to explanation would take at face value the information coming in from the alternative approach and enter it into the conceptualization of theory. To illustrate, an investigator working within the paradigmatic mode might prefer to do verificational studies at the level of performances and/or of cognitive processes and structures. At this level of reduction, it is easy to lose sight of the person. Yet, if the alternative epistemology is appealed to, then the researcher-theorist is confronted squarely with the indeterminacy of intentionality and is challenged to incorporate it into his or her model/theory. Martin (this volume) recognizes this aspect when, while attempting to identify and document regularities in the psychotherapeutic process, he acknowledges that they are probablistic because people are agential. He has thus in effect made agency a boundary condition constraining the regularities that he has identified. On the other side of the coin, it is easy for theorists preferring the narrative approach to explanation to get wrapped up in sequelae of human reflexivity and to lose sight of the influences on behavior that operate out of awareness, whether in the form of habits, cognitive processes/structures, or unconscious motivation. Attention to such factors could be incorporated into theory as boundary conditions constraining the role of reflexivity in behavior.

Ultimately, methodological pluralism and epistemological synthesis depend on values (see Conway, 1992). To be entered jointly into research practice and/or theorizing, each approach to explanation and the information arising from it must be seen to be credible. It is only when credibility is granted that relevance can be entertained. Idealist versus realist approaches to understanding what it is to be human have marked the history of philosophy. The past century of thought in psychology has been dominated by realism and hence objectivism. There is, however, currently under way a reawakening of idealism in the form of constructionism. Although the legitimacy of the narrative approach to explanation is gaining ground in psychology and related disciplines through the contributions of thinkers such as Bakan (1967), Danziger (1990), Gergen (1982), Giorgi (1970, 1989), Howard (1984), Patton (1984), Polkinghorne (1984, 1988), Rychlak (1988), and Westcott (1988, in press), we are still a long way from achieving the kind of transcendental attitude that is required for full-blooded methodological pluralism and epistemological synthesis. Nevertheless, judging from the work of the contributors to this volume, movement toward this end is under way.

Note

1. More recently, Guba and Lincoln have changed their thinking on the matter and now favor the position advocated by Smith and Heshusius (see Guba & Lincoln, 1989).

References

Bakan, D. (1967). *On method: Toward a reconstruction of psychological investigation.* San Francisco: Jossey-Bass.
Bruner, J. (1986). *Actual minds, possible worlds.* Cambridge, MA: Harvard University Press.
Conway, J. (1992). A world of differences among psychologists. *Canadian Psychology, 33.*1-22.
Danziger, K. (1990). *Constructing the subject: Historical origins of psychological research.* Cambridge, UK: Cambridge University Press.
Elliott, R. (1991). Five dimensions of therapy process. Psychotherapy *Research, 1,* 92-103.
Ericsson, K. A., & Simon, H. A. (1980). Verbal reports as data. *Psychological Review, 87,* 215-251.
Gergen, K. J. (1982). *Toward a transformation of social knowledge.* New York: Springer-Verlag.
Giorgi, A. (1970). *Psychology as a human science: A phenomenologically based approach.* New York: Harper & Row.
Giorgi, A. (1989, August). *The status of qualitative research from a phenomenological perspective.* Paper presented at the Eighth Annual Human Science Research Conference, Aarhus, Denmark.
Goldfried, M. (1991). Research issues in psychotherapy integration. *Journal of Psychotherapy Integration, 1,* 5-25.
Greenberg, L. S. (1986). Change process research. *Journal of Consulting and Clinical Psychology, 54,* 4-15.
Greenberg, L. S., Rennie, D. L., & Toukmanian, S. G. (1988, June). *Change processes in experientially oriented psychotherapy.* Workshop presented at the annual meeting of the Canadian Psychological Association, Montreal.
Guba, E. (1981). Criteria for assessing the trustworthiness of naturalistic inquiry. *Educational Communication and Technology Journal, 29,* 79-92.
Guba, E., & Lincoln, Y. (1982). Epistemological and methodological bases of naturalistic inquiry. *Educational and Communication Technology Journal, 30,* 233-252.
Guba, E., & Lincoln, Y. (1989). *Fourth generation evaluation.* Newbury Park, CA: Sage.
Howard, G. S. (1984). A modest proposal for a revision of strategies for counseling research. *Journal of Counseling Psychology, 31,* 430-441.
Kiesler, D. J. (1973). *The process of psychotherapy: Empirical foundations and systems of analysis.* Chicago: Aldine.
Macmurray, J. (1957). *The self as agent.* New York: Harper.
Miles, M., & Huberman, M. (1984). *Qualitative data analysis.* Beverly Hills, CA: Sage.
Nisbett, R. E., & Wilson, T. D. (1977). Telling more than we know: Verbal reports on mental processes. *Psychological Review, 84,* 231-259.

Patton, M. J. (1984). Managing social interaction in counseling: A contribution from the philosophy of science. *Journal of Counseling Psychology, 31,* 442-456.

Polkinghorne, D. E. (1984). Further extensions of methodological diversity for counseling psychology. *Journal of Counseling Psychology, 31,* 416-429.

Polkinghorne, D. E. (1988). *Narrative knowing and the human sciences.* Albany: SUNY Press.

Rice, L. N., & Greenberg, L. S. (1984). The new research paradigm. In L. Rice & L. Greenberg (Eds.), *Patterns of change: Intensive analysis of psychotherapeutic process* (pp. 7-26). New York: Guilford.

Rorty, A. O. (1976). Introduction. In A. Rorty (Ed.), *The identities of reasons* (pp. 1-15). Berkely: University of California Press.

Rorty, R. (1979). *Philosophy and the mirror of nature.* Princeton, NJ: Princeton University Press.

Rychlak, J. F. (1988). *The psychology of rigorous humanism* (2nd ed.). New York: New York University Press.

Ryle, G. (1949). *The concept of mind.* New York: Penguin.

Shohan-Shalomon, V. (1991). Studying therapeutic modules precedes the integration of models. *Journal of Psychotherapy Integration, 1,* 35-41.

Smith, B., & Sechrest, L. (1991). Treatment of aptitude × treatment interactions. *Journal of Consulting and Clinical Psychology, 59,* 233-244.

Smith, J. K. (1989, March). *Alternative research paradigms and the problem of criteria.* Paper presented at the International Conference on Alternative Paradigms for Inquiry, San Francisco.

Smith, J. K., & Heshusius, L. (1986). Closing down the conversation: The end of the quantitative-qualitative debate among educational inquirers. *Educational Researcher, 15,* 4-12.

Westcott, M. (1988). *The psychology of human freedom: A human science perspective and critique.* New York: Springer-Verlag.

Westcott, M. (in press). The discursive construction of human freedom. *Human Behavioral Scientist.*

Wittgenstein, L. (1968). *Philosophical investigations* (G. E. M. Anscombe, Trans., 3rd ed.). New York: Macmillan.

Index

therapeutic target and, 25
Markov chain analyses, 15
Martin, J., 108-131, 234, 248, 249
Martin, W., 115, 117, 118, 123, 131
Mastery, 147
Mathieu, P. L., 12, 27-28, 58, 158
Mathieu-Coughlan, P. L., 58, 206
Meaning:
  metaphor and, 188
  paradigmatic explanation and, 235
  perceptual-processing model and, 79
Meaning bridge, 49, 58, 60, 64-68
Meaning conjunction, 196
Meaning disjunction, 196
Meaning units, 217, 221, 222-224
Measurement theory, traditional, 165
Memory:
  changes to structures, 110
  dual coding, 122, 192-194
  grounded theory approach and, 71
  long-term, 121-122
  thematically linked, 190-191
Metacommunication, 230
Metaphor(s), 187-208, 244
  Associated Meaning Context and, 189-196
  defined, 188
  Levels of Client Perceptual Processing and, 96-98
  long-term therapy effects and, 122
  qualitative analysis of, 187-189
  referential activity and, 192-196
  visual images and, 199-200
Metaphor Communication Interaction, 189, 200-206
Metaphoric event, 96-98
Metaphoric language, 193-194
Methodological pluralism, 246-248, 249
Meyer, M., 118, 123
Microtheories of change events, 51-73
Misunderstandings. value of, 183
Model building, 28-31, 53
Mood ratings, 53, 60, 64, 72
Mood Rating Scale, 53-54, 72

Nadler, U. P., 122, 164

Narrative explanation, 204, 234-236, 241, 243, 246, 247, 249
Narrative Sequences Coding Manual, 206
Naturalistic observation, 1-19
Neirinck, M., 135, 136, 137, 139, 140
Necessary and sufficient conditions, 12
Neisser, U., 78, 80, 81
Neo-Piagetian approach, 16
Networking strategies, 83, 96
Neuroses, 137, 238
Nonaffiliative focus, 41
Nonspecific sessions, 16

Observer, external, 239
O'Grady, K. E., 53, 117, 118
Open-ended questions, 135
Open-ended reflections, 58
Openness to Experience Scale, 195
Options, reevaluating, 43
Orlinsky, D. E., 165, 166, 212
Outcome:
  client vocal quality and, 5, 8
  comparative studies of, 14
  immediate, 158
  Levels of Client Perceptual Processing and, 102
  predictors of, 11
  task analysis and, 31-32
  therapist's style and, 7
  therapist versus client view of, 5

Painful interventions, 158
Paivio, A., 188, 192
Paivio, S. C., 116, 117, 127
Paradigmatic explanation, 234-238, 240-241, 245-246
Pascual-Leone, J., 16, 23, 24
Perception(s), 109
  awareness of one's own, 55
  discrepancies between client and therapist, 172-181
  habitual, 82
  integrative function, 78
  internalization and, 110
  perceptual-processing model and, 79

About the Contributors

Lynne E. Angus is Assistant Professor of Psychology at York University in Toronto, Canada. Her current research interests include the exploration of the role of narrative and metaphor in psychotherapeutic discourse. She has published in *Psychotherapy,* the *American Journal of Psychiatry,* and *Social Behavior and Personality.*

Robert Elliott is Professor of Psychology at the University of Toledo. He received his Ph.D. from the University of California, Los Angeles, and was a Visiting Researcher at the University of Sheffield during the 1984-1985 academic year. He has served as President of the North American Chapter of the Society for Psychotherapy Research. His psychotherapy process research has centered on the study of client experiences and significant events in therapy. His current interests are in the application of qualitative-phenomenological research methods in the exploration of change processes in experiential therapy.

Leslie S. Greenberg is Professor of Psychology at York University in Toronto, Canada. He is the coauthor of a number of books on psychotherapy including *Emotion in Psychotherapy* with J. Safran and the coeditor of a number of books on psychotherapy process research

263

including *The Psychotherapeutic Process: A Research Handbook*, with W. Pinsof. He is a past President of the Society for Psychotherapy Research and the current Director of the Psychotherapy Research Centre at York University.

Germain Lietaer is Professor of Clinical Psychology at the Catholic University of Leuven, Belgium. He is the Director of the Centrum voor Client-centered Psychotherapie en Counselling, where he is responsible for the part-time postgraduate training program in client-centered/experiential psychotherapy.

Jack Martin is Professor of Counselling and Educational Psychology at Simon Fraser University in Burnaby, British Columbia, Canada. He received his Ph.D. from the University of Alberta and has held academic positions at the University of Alberta, the University of Western Ontario, the University of Iowa, and Simon Fraser University. His work examines the role of cognitive mediation and episodic memory in human learning and change, especially in therapeutic and educational contexts.

David L. Rennie received his Ph.D. from the University of Missouri at Columbia and joined the Department of Psychology at York University, where he is currently Associate Professor and member of the Psychotherapy Research Centre. His current research interest is in the use of the qualitative research approach as a way of accessing and representing the client's subjective experience of psychotherapy.

Laura N. Rice is Professor Emeritus of Psychology at York University in Toronto, Canada, and is a member of the York University Psychotherapy Research Centre. She is the coeditor of *Innovations in Client-Centered Therapy* with D. A. Wexler and *Patterns of Change: Intensive Analysis of Psychotherapy Process* with L. S. Greenberg.

David A. Shapiro was trained as a clinical psychologist at the Institute of Psychiatry (Maudsley Hospital) in London, England. Currently, he is Professor of Psychology at the University of Sheffield, United Kingdom, where he heads a research team, which is concerned mainly with the study of the process and outcome of contrasting psychotherapies for depression, within the Social and Applied Psychology Unit. He has served as Editor of the *British*

Journal of Clinical Psychology and is the current Managing Editor of *Psychotherapy Research.*

Shaké G. Toukmanian is Associate Professor of Psychology and the current Director of Clinical Training at York University in Toronto, Canada. She received her Ph.D. from the University of Utah in Salt Lake City and has held academic positions at Bishop's and McGill Universities in Quebec, Canada. A member of the York University Psychotherapy Research Centre, her current research interest is in the application of relevant concepts and research findings in the cognitive sciences to the study of change processes in experiential psychotherapies.

Hadas Wiseman is Lecturer in School Counseling at the Department of Education of the University of Haifa and a registered clinical psychologist in private practice. Her work in the area of psychotherapy research has been published in the *Journal of Consulting and Clinical Psychology; Psychotherapy: Theory, Research and Practice;* and *Sihot-Dialogue: Israel Journal of Psychotherapy.*